In the Name of
the Boss Upstairs

The Father Ray Brennan Story

Jerry   Hopkins

This is an authorized biography of Father Raymond A. Brennan, authorized by the Brennan Family and the Father Ray Foundation. The proceeds from the sale of this book are for the benefit of the Thomas J. Vincent Trust established in Thailand and administered by the Fr. Ray Foundation to provide for the higher education of the children under their care.

IN THE NAME OF THE BOSS UPSTAIRS:
    THE FATHER RAY BRENNAN STORY

Copyright © 2004 by The Thomas J. Vincent Foundation

Published by The Thomas J. Vincent Foundation, Inc., Honolulu, Hawaii

ISBN 0-9759284-0-6

First edition: October 2004

Design and layout: Surachit Kamchaitaworn

Printed in Thailand by
Thai Watana Panich Press Co., Ltd.

All the characters in this book are real people, although the names of some of the children have been changed.

Chapter 1

It is no secret that the United States is a nation founded and formed by upstart immigrants, most of them seeking freedom from oppression and escape from poverty. What is not given proper recognition, perhaps, is how many of them during the period of greatest migration were Irish. Blame the potato.

By the early 1800s, over one-third of the Irish had been reduced to surviving on nothing but potatoes, one of the consequences of some 600 years as an English colony. In some places in Ireland, the potato had replaced hard currency. Then, in 1845, when the peasants dug up their crop, they found it had turned into putridity by blight, a previously unknown disease. The famine that followed killed more than a million people, most from starvation or cholera. Another million left their homeland, many of them on crowded ships where disease killed thousands more. By the end of the century, Ireland's population had been cut in half.

Between 1820 and 1920, about fifty million people emigrated from Europe and of these, thirty-five million came to the United States…and of these, nearly one out of four came from Ireland.

Raymond Alan Brennan's grandparents were among them. Donald Eugene Brennan and Sharron Gail Mary Brennan Purtell, Father Ray's siblings---Don six years older, Sharron twelve years younger---said they didn't know why, specifically, their families came to the United States, but surely Don didn't expect an argument when he said they were attracted by the "opportunities available."

Both families came to America's second-largest city's South Side, Chicago's first slum, called in its early days Hardscrabble, a name that surely fit. Many of the area's earliest settlers, arriving in the 1830s and 1840s, were the Irish "shovel men," who built the nearby Illinois & Michigan Canal, working for whiskey and a dollar a day, and living in slapped-together shanties along the Chicago River.

From the 1850s, when the slaughterhouses were moved out of the city center, this neighborhood became the center of a meat-packing industry that served not just the American Midwest but also much of the East and West coasts. In a 1906 novel called *The Jungle*, Upton Sinclair shocked America with a description of the horrific conditions in which much of the nation's protein was butchered and packaged, and made clear the size of the industry. There were, Sinclair wrote, "so many cattle no one had ever dreamed existed in the world. The sound of them here was as of all the barnyards of the universe; and as for counting them---it would have taken all day simply to count the pens."

Father Ray's paternal grandfather, Thomas Brennan, was from County Mayo, where, as Father Ray recalled years later in a letter to a friend, he married a girl with the same surname, but unrelated. "She died after only a few months of marriage," he said. "My grandfather then emigrated to the United States and worked at the Morton Salt Company. First, he dug salt from under the city of Detroit, but was moved up at a later date to be a driver of a horse carriage. Finally, he became the driver (again of a horse carriage) of Mr. Morton himself."

Morton was headquartered then, as now, in Chicago, so there is some doubt about the Detroit connection. (Father Ray's siblings could not confirm it.) Father Ray further recalled, with great pleasure, that when his grandfather married again, it was to another woman named Brennan---once more, he claimed, no kin. Her name was Mary and together they had eight children; Father Ray's father, Walter Joseph Brennan, born in 1899, was the third.

Ray's maternal grandparents, Maurice O'Connell and Mary Doherty, were from County Kerry and went directly to Chicago, where Maurice found a job in the Union Stock Yards. Maurice and his wife had ten children, Norrine and her twin sister, Betty, being the eighth and ninth. Norrine became Ray's mother. They also took in twelve cousins who were orphaned by two different sets of aunts and uncles, so the couple, according to Ray's sister Sharron, "raised twenty-two children on one salary."

Walter Brennan and Norrine O'Connell were married in 1923 and their first son, Donald Eugene, was born four years later. Raymond Alan followed on December 7, 1932, and for the next four years the family lived in what Don remembered as a series of "upper middle-class apartments, spacious, very nice neighborhoods, safe, [with] friendly people." Their father, who had dropped out of high school to help his parents, later attended night school and now worked in the accounting department of the Western Electric Company, an employer to whom he remained loyal for forty-two years.

The Chicago of Al Capone was gone by the time Father Ray was born---the gangster retired to Florida in 1929, same year as Chicago's St. Valentine's Day Massacre and the year the stock market crashed. Capone was convicted and jailed in 1931 for failing to pay his federal income tax. Gambling resorts, brothels, and speakeasies---the latter word an Irish contribution to the language---once crowded Chicago's suburbs, and now one of the most infamous, Cicero, was where the Western Electric Company had its offices. Although the ethnic composition of the South Side was changing as more blacks moved into the neighborhood--- in 1928 it sent a black congressman to Washington and reelected him twice---the Irish still ruled the political roost.

The Irish had adapted to their new country more rapidly and comfortably than many other immigrant groups, if for no other reason than that most spoke English---unlike the Germans, the Poles, the Italians, the Czechs, and the Russian Jews---and from the time of their arrival they fitted themselves into existing Catholic communities and political organizations in major cities with comparative ease. In Chicago, they helped shape a tough Democratic political machine known for its corruption and cronyism that elected three Irish-Catholic mayors in a row, all from the South Side. From the time Edward Kelly was elected in 1933, through the administration of Martin Kennelly and the long, iron-fisted domination of Richard Daley---that is, for all of Ray Brennan's residence in the Chicago area---an Irish Democrat from his old neighborhood ruled City Hall.

For Ray, it all nearly ended at the age of three, in 1935, when following a tonsillectomy, he suffered near fatal complications. "He was released from hospital," his brother Don recalled, "and at home I remember waking up during the night and seeing his bed and bathtub filled with blood. He was a bleeder"---his sister Sharron described it as a mild form of hemophilia---"and was rushed back to hospital where he was in critical condition for a few days."

Sharron continued the story: "My mother told me she was in the hospital chapel praying when our dear family friend, Father Leo McNamara, or Mac, as we all called him, tapped her on the shoulder and said she had to give Ray to God. She cried and said she just couldn't, but after a long time there, she finally said okay: 'You win, Ray is Yours.' With that, a nurse tapped my mom on the shoulder and said a little color had returned to Ray's cheeks. He continued to recover and apparently God took my mother at her word and kept Ray for His work."

Two years later, the family left Chicago, moving into a small Georgian-style house in Riverside, a community along the Des Plaines River nine miles west of Chicago that was designed in the 1860s by two now-famous landscape architects, Frederick Law Olmsted and Calvert Vaux. Its character was unlike other suburbs at the time. Olmsted, who with Vaux, also designed New York City's Central Park, prescribed well-built, well-drained roads with gracefully curved roads and generous plantings. The idea was to create an attractive town that, with the avoidance of right angles, created more public space. He also decided that the space between public streets and houses was private land with a public function: it was the transitional area between public and private.

Don remembered, "upper-class homes, winding streets, beautiful lawns and gardens, and public parks...a great place to raise kids. We grew up in the Depression, but my father had a good job and while so many thousands were without jobs and family living was very difficult, we always were well off, and to our minds we had the best of everything."

Chapter 2

"Our parents sent us to military school in those days," recalls Don Brennan, "because only the better-off kids could go to such schools. Those days saw military schools as offering the best education to children. In a way, it was a mark of prestige to see your children in a military school. It was sort of an elitist thing."

First Don and then Ray were enrolled at Bishop Quarter, a grade school run by the Dominican Sisters in Oak Park, an upper middle-class Chicago suburb ten miles from Riverside that soon would become famous for being the hometown of Ernest Hemingway. Here, Don said, there was not only an excellent educational system, but also "better than normal discipline," no great surprise when you consider what the merging of military and Catholic lifestyles might portend.

If Ray's survival as a three-year-old "bleeder" was a story often told at family gatherings---and it was, to be retold and retold years later after he became a priest and a missionary---to this was added in his pre-teen years another tale with religious overtones. "My mother told the story of overhearing Ray saying his prayers one night," his sister Sharron recalled. "She had an overnight friend from New York and they heard him saying the 'Our Father' and when he got to the part about 'Thy will be done,' he said, 'Tonight it's going to be different. Tonight it is my will be done, and I want a puppy and a baby sister.' The next day, mom's friend brought Ray a puppy and nine months later, I was born. My parents had been married twenty-three years when I came along. I'm sure I was a surprise to them. The way I was told the story, he wanted a sister to make fudge for him."

The Brennans were good Irish Catholics, the Church and its ritual and belief system forming a demanding yet comforting core for all aspects of family life. While shifting from apartment to apartment in Chicago's South Side, they slipped easily into each new parish community, from St. Paul's---where Ray was born---to Little Flower, then to St. Adrian's. In Riverside, it was St. Mary's. (In Chicago, it was possible to find three Catholic churches in three successful blocks, one Irish, one Polish, and one Italian.) Each was a small Irish-Catholic village-within-a-village of a size where the parish priests could know personally every man, woman, and child in it, and the annual parish fair, which featured gambling games, a booth selling oyster stew, and a Hibernian band playing in the corner, was almost a family gathering. Don said the Brennans counted many priests among their close friends---Father Mac (who comforted the family during Ray's early illness), Father Conlin, Father Lawrence, and Bishop Sheild among them. "They were frequently invited to family dinners."

Sharron said, "Mom was a great joiner of clubs. She was always involved as long as I can remember. She was very active in an organization called Big Sisters. They supported young women. The clubs were all charity based. She was a very good fund-raiser and thoroughly enjoyed the social aspect of the charities." Indeed she did...and for a time, Ray later told friends, she had slot machines installed in the basement of their home and, following dinners and parties, invited guests to play, turning over all profits to the church or the St. Theresa Society or one of her other charities.

"I remember Mom always said, 'You only keep what you give away,'" Sharron said. "She was a very generous person. She would meet someone in the grocery store who was having trouble and the next thing I knew, I was carrying dinner to their house. Mom also told me that a lady never left the house without her gloves. She believed in a sense of decorum. I never had a pair of blue jeans. She stressed always being a lady. She also had nicknames for all of us. Don was her 'pride and joy,' Ray was her 'secret passion' and I was her 'precious stuff.' "

Don said, "Mom was the disciplinarian. We listened to her---or else. Dad was always encouraging us, but Mom gave the orders. Mom had a very strong and outgoing personality, while Dad was rather quiet and unassuming. Mom belonged to a number of clubs and organizations, while Dad was a homebody."

Mr. Brennan was blind in one eye and never learned to drive, so he commuted to and from work by bus, a journey of about forty-five minutes each way. He had what Sharron called "a typical Irish complexion, fair skin [that would] get red in the heat. Mom was more dark Irish and would tan. Both were heavy-set. Dad never wore anything other than a white starched-collar shirt. When he retired, Don gave him two blue, long-sleeved shirts that we had to beg him to wear."

While in grade school at Bishop Quarter, a boarding school, Don Brennan said he met a number of Augustinian priests and "hung around" in Riverside during the holidays with some seminarians who attended Augustinian Prep High School on Staten Island, New York. "And they were always telling me of the good times and wonderful experiences. I thought it would be 'cool' for me to go to high school in New York, from Chicago." He was enrolled in 1941, when Ray was nine, three years before their sister was born. He remained in the seminary for the next thirteen years. During that time, Don was permitted to visit his family for only forty-eight hours every two years, and following ordination in 1953, he went on to his church assignments, so he missed most of his siblings' growing up.

Three children born over a period of eighteen years was unusual by anyone's standards and the boarding schools and seminaries that followed for the two boys took even more away from what some might call a normal family life. When Sharron was born, in 1944, both her brothers were gone and remained absent for all her childhood. It would not be until they were adults that she said they actually got to know each other. As Don himself recalled, "Life at home was almost nonexistent."

Ray left Bishop Quarter soon after Sharron's birth, at first going on, briefly, to a diocesan seminary in Indiana. He told her years later that he didn't like it and that, apparently, was when he went to his older brother for advice. "Ray told me he was interested in becoming a priest and wanted to join the Augustinians," Don said. "In conversation, I told him that after ordination we would be involved in teaching. He replied, 'No way!' He didn't want to be a teacher and that was the end of seeking to be an 'Augie.' " Father Pat Morrissy, a friend many years later in Thailand, said Ray told him that it was after he attended a sermon preached by a well-known Redemptorist, Father Liguori Nugent that he "felt that God was calling him to service as a Redemptorist."

Along the way, Ray's personality took shape; strong characteristics developing that would remain prominent throughout his life...as a scavenger and pack rat, as a mischievous practical joker and something of a con man...as an ambitious and resourceful entrepreneur...and in social settings, as the center of attention.

Unlike his brother Don, he had no interest in participating in athletics, but later said that for a time he followed the local professional hockey team. "When I was a boy," he wrote when he was no longer young, "I used to collect broken hockey sticks. I would race down from the stands and ask for the broken stick. Then I would ask the hockey star to sign it for me." Also unlike Don, Ray was loath to tidy his room and often it had the look of an ill-kept nest, inspiring his mother to move in with a broom and a container for what she considered trash. One day, Ray reported, she threw all of his hockey sticks out. "I was furious!" he said. Another portent of things to come, whenever anyone attempted to clean up after him.

Ray also read voraciously, everything from *Aesop's Fables* to *The Book of Knowledge*. He devoured dozens of magazines every week and, like a housewife clipping coupons that earned discounts when buying groceries and household goods, he tore out all the advertisements that offered free samples. He didn't care what was offered; even if he had no use for it, it was worth a stamp. "I loved to get all that mail with the strange free samples different companies would send," he wrote in a letter to a friend many years later. "I used to get large cards filled with wool samples, paint color cards, and even something called Lydia Pinkham's

Vegetable Compound. Needless to say, my mother got a little worried about this last one...since it is something for pregnant women."

His prankish nature also emerged early. "I remember when I had measles as a child my mom used to bring me buttered toast and sweet tea," he wrote in another letter. 'In those days, they put a quarantine sign on the front door of our home. I don't think they do that any more. Anyway, when I got well again, I saved the sign. There was a butcher in our area who was always shouting at us kids. My buddies and I decided to put the sign on his door, over an advertisement that was already there. That way, he could not see it from inside the shop. We did exactly that…and then hid behind a billboard to see what would happen. We just about burst a gut watching people come up to the butcher shop, read the quarantine sign and walk away. It took the poor butcher several hours to find out why his customers were retreating from his door. My parents eventually found out about the prank and I received a new shade of color on my backside. I was real mad, because the other kids got off scot-free. However, true to the criminal code of honor, I did not divulge their names."

Another plot produced the same result, but that didn't stop Ray recalling it years later with pleasure: "When I was a boy, my mother used to make me write thank-you letters when I received a birthday gift or the like. It was usually to my aunts and uncles. I hated it. I would write with big letters to help fill up the page. However, I noticed one very important thing. Whenever I did write a 'good' letter, my uncles and aunts would always thank me for it when they saw me next. Besides that, they would usually squeeze a half-dollar into my hand for being an appreciative nephew!

"It was a great way to get movie and ice-cream money. So then I decided that maybe if I wrote another letter thanking them for the half dollar, they would give me another half dollar when they saw me again. So I turned out a pile of letters to all my uncles and aunts with the expectation of becoming the richest kid on the block. My mother figured something was strange about me suddenly becoming a great letter writer, so she used parental privilege and intercepted them. I got a good scolding and never did become the richest kid on the block. Apparently, she did tell the story to my uncles and aunts, though, because even to this very day they joke with me about it."

Other stunts were actually enjoyed by the family. His brother Don said that by the age of eleven or twelve, Ray showed an interest in photography and by the time he was in high school he owned several cameras, including one of those big press cameras that used four-by-five-inch negatives and flash bulbs the size of ping-pong balls. Ray had this camera when he, his parents and young sister visited Don at an Augustinian summer retreat near Atlantic City the same week that the beach community hosted the annual Miss America beauty pageant.

They arrived at the Atlantic City airport just before a plane transporting several of the contestants landed. Ray watched several photographers follow a rolling staircase as it was being pushed up to the airplane's door. As he approached, police said only professional photographers were permitted to pass. He held up his big camera and smiled graciously; spending the next several minutes snapping pictures as the young women struck poses and smiled. He was practically roaring with laughter when he rejoined his family. There was no film in the camera, he told them.

Later, he took his photography more seriously. Like the letter-writing of his youth aimed at squeezing coins from relatives, this scheme, too, was contrived to make him not just the richest kid on the block, he boasted to friends, but a millionaire. During summer vacation and other holidays when he was home from seminary, every day he read the society pages of the Chicago Tribune, noting upcoming social events in his calendar. Wedding anniversaries of the rich and famous, engagement and birthday parties of their pampered offspring, debutante balls, and charity fund-raisers held at private clubs.

On the day or evening of the function, he bathed and shaved and pomaded his hair and put on his tuxedo and crashed the party. Full of confidence. New jokes committed to memory. Camera in hand, his pockets packed with flash bulbs and film. Quickly, he moved through the glamorous crowd, taking pictures. Then he rushed home to develop them in a small darkroom he'd built in the basement, taking them back to the party as soon as he could, finding the subjects of his photography and offering the pictures for sale.

"Ray had a very outgoing and exuberant personality," his brother recalled. "He always had friends and was as fully alive with adults as with his peers. He could make adults laugh and at times take over being the center of attention. His personality was attractive to all and enjoyed by all. He was not unruly or spoiled, but had a way of drawing others to him in the best possible way."

Chapter 3

It wasn't easy to become a Catholic priest. It wasn't like going off to college and majoring in accounting and then going to work for PriceWaterhouse, or studying teaching or computer programming or journalism or a hundred other subjects that prepared you, or didn't prepare you, for the work that would come, or not come, after collecting a diploma.

There were numerous significant differences. It was more like going for a PhD or an MD or an LLD, at least in the time allotted for the study's completion, and it was a great deal more complex than that. After six years in what was called a "minor seminary," encompassing junior (or intermediate) and senior high school, there came fourteen months in a "novitiate," or spiritual retreat, and that was followed by six more years in a "major seminary" before ordination.

Holidays at home were infrequent, discipline was sternly introduced and rigidly enforced, the course of study was intense, and at every step the worthiness of candidates was thoroughly examined. It was a life shared only with other boys and men. Halfway through their time in major seminary, the students were required to take temporary vows of obedience, poverty, and chastity (three years later, Perpetual vows were taken). Once the men were ordained, these vows would become permanent, irrevocable. Perhaps it was not surprising that only fifteen percent of those who started along this path made it all the way through.

When Ray decided against becoming an Augustinian and chose the Redemptorists, an Order founded by St. Alphonsus Liguori, the son of a Neapolitan naval officer, it was to dedicate himself to what Liguori called "the care of the most neglected," those who were untouched by ordinary pastoral care, the poorest of the poor. Liguori was born in Marianella near Naples, Italy, in 1696. Trained as a lawyer but later disgusted by the corruption he found in the courts, he abandoned his promising legal career to study theology, establishing the Congregation of the Most Holy Savior. He changed the name to Most Holy Redeemer in 1749, the year given as the official start of the Redemptorist Order.

He was beatified by Pius VII in 1816, canonized by Gregory XVI in 1839, and in 1871 declared Doctor of the Church by Pius IX. Finally, in 1950, when Ray Brennan was a student in minor seminary, Pius XII declared St. Alphonsus the Patron of confessors and moralists. By then, the Redemptorists were well established worldwide, working in seventy-seven countries on five continents.

Instruction during the first four years at the minor seminary, in Kirkwood, Missouri, a suburb of St. Louis, was much like that at any boarding school during what, in the United States, are called the high school years. Dormitory living with common toilets and showers and cafeteria dining together. Mass every morning. Evening prayers. Study hall. Thursdays and Sundays free for sports and hobbies. And, unlike brother Don, Ray was home for the summers, when he resumed his photography and coupon-clipping for free samples. One summer he took his first job, going to work in an ice-cream factory owned by a man who lived next door. His love of ice cream continued through adulthood and he talked about this early job frequently, as if to hint that he at least sensed the subtleties of this frozen dessert made with cream or milk, sweeteners, and flavoring in the same fashion a restaurant sommelier knew his wine.

The next two years at minor seminary, the emphasis shifted. Now, students and their classes were devoted to the classics. For two hours a day, five days a week---plus homework---they studied Latin until they were fluent and could read and write in the ancient language of the Church. They also studied Greek, Hebrew and French and, some of them, German and Spanish as well, so that they could read not only the Scriptures in their original languages, but also the many religious texts, commentaries and interpretations written in other European languages and never translated into English. The Latin was simpler than that of Horace and Cicero---call it Church Latin---and it was Koine Greek that was taught, the ancient Greek of the texts, so that what the aspiring priests learned was of no value if they ever should find themselves in Greece and wanted to order a meal or find their way to the train station.

A secondary educational emphasis was on history---mainly Church history---and there were classes in beginning philosophy, biology, physics, first-year algebra, and geometry, but nothing advanced like trigonometry or calculus. "Every year you were graded and judged by your superiors," said Father Joe Maier, who followed Ray at Kirkwood seven years later and thus missed him by a year, though they would become close friends in Thailand. "The superiors were from the faculty, plus the *socius* (priest disciplinarian), the counselors in the dorms, the other priests in the seminary. The evaluation was not just academic, but also behavioral."

Regarding the latter, the young man who regularly boasted that he was from Chicago's tough South Side, although his family had left the neighborhood before he was school age, was regarded by his superiors as among the most "rambunctious." There was, for example, the time he came upon a manikin on the second floor of one of the seminary buildings, dressed it in clothing from his own wardrobe, and with a loud scream, threw it out the window, terrifying the people passing by below as they scattered to avoid getting hit by the falling "body." In years to come, such stories were passed up and down the line about the more colorful candidates and Ray clearly was one of them. They were not, however, held against him, but, rather, ascribed to his high energy, a trait much desired if it could be channeled properly.

Following minor seminary came a period of fourteen months that, in the words of Father Patrick Morrissy, "separated the goats from the sheep." Father Morrissy was from Detroit and older than Ray and knew him only slightly during the seminary period, but years later in Thailand they worked together for many years and became close friends. Father Morrissy said they reminisced often about the spiritual training in DeSoto, Missouri, in the foothills of the Ozark Mountains.

"We both remembered it as the best year of our life," said Father Morrissy, tall and strongly built and as much interested in sports as the young priest-in-training from Chicago was not. "It was our real introduction to religious life, to learning about spirituality, what religious life was all about, with no outside activities or distractions. We couldn't even listen to the radio. It was peaceful, centered on God, and we were considering our future life. It was a holy time. We even had lessons in politeness and when the next class came along, overlapping ours by six months, we thought they were wild men, we'd changed that much."

Another older friend in Thailand, Father Francis "Frank" Gautreaux, confirmed Ray's feelings about his time in DeSoto. "He didn't say why, but I think it was because of the library. He was a rabid seeker of information and he devoured it."

Father Joe Maier compared the novitiate experience to "religious life in the Middle Ages: up at five, prayers, meditation, Mass with a short sermon, followed by another thirty minutes of meditation, breakfast in silence, after which we had 'conferences' on the lives of the saints, church history, things like that. Then at 10:30, spiritual exercises: learning the rosary, singing practice, chanting.

"Five minutes before noon, there were prayers again or we were instructed to examine how we had spent the morning, and that was followed by a silent lunch, during which we'd listened as a spiritual book was read to us. After eating, we had a half hour, maybe forty-five minutes to walk and talk and after that, we took a short nap.

"From 3:30 or so, we were free for sports or to work on a nearby farm. Then we showered, ate supper at six, prayed again, and read or enjoyed quiet time until 9 o'clock when we went to bed, starting what we called the Big Silence, lasting until after breakfast the next morning. When we started the routine again."

However controlled and strict this routine, Ray found outlets for his ebullience. Silence was required while bathing and Father Gautreaux said it was well known that Ray enjoyed singing in the shower. "Father Joe Powers, his novice master, who remained a lifelong friend, was hard on Ray. He knocked at the shower door and hollered over the sound of the water, 'You're breaking the rules! Get down on your knees and say three Hail Marys!' "

It wasn't hard to imagine an army drill instructor telling a recruit to drop and 'give me fifty (pushups)!' It is more difficult to imagine, without laughing, the young novice on his knees, the water pounding atop his bowed head, waiting for his master to leave so he could resume his interrupted song.

Ray also was known for his relentless baiting of a classmate and friend, John Hacker, fondly called "Jack the Hack."

"Hacker was sort of precise and meticulous," said Father Joe Maier. "Everything had to be just so and Ray delighted in taking advantage of that, he enjoyed taunting and teasing him. Hacker would return to his room and find a picture of Esther Williams in a bathing suit when he opened the door and he just went nuts, fearing he'd be caught with it, and not quite knowing how to get rid of it. Needless to say, pin-ups were not permitted in seminary rooms. Forty years later, Hacker is still talking about how Ray pulled his leg all the time."

Following novitiate came six years in the major seminary in Oconomowoc, Wisconsin, a small farming community founded in 1837 whose Indian name meant "waters meet" or "river of lakes." If what was taught at minor seminary resembled a Western high school curriculum in some ways, with heavy, classical overtones, and what was espoused during novitiate instruction was more contemplative, at major seminary the lessons were focused on philosophy, ethics, and theology. This was when the students were trained to be Redemptorist priests.

During the first two years, the tall, lean young man with a full head of dark, wavy hair cropped short was instructed in logic, ethics, and the principles of Western philosophy. This last emphasized the teachings of Aristotle, the fourth-century B.C. student of Plato, and St. Thomas á Kempis, the German priest whose *Imitation of Christ* (1418) has been translated into more languages than any other book save the Bible.

During the next four years, Ray studied theology and was exposed to everything there was to know about the system of the Roman Catholic Church. Most of the texts were in Latin and Mass was said in Latin. Little did anyone know at the time that in just a few years, Latin would be virtually swept away, ordered abandoned by the Vatican.

There were courses in the Philosophy of Inanimate Nature, Animate Nature, Man, Being, Knowledge, and God. There were classes in Material Logic and Formal Logic, and in Dogmatic and Moral Theology, along with a Survey of Early Christian Authors and a class called General Ethical Norms. Other instruction was more practical, providing guidance in Vocal Techniques, Reading Interpretation, Fundamentals of Speech, and Church Music and Chant. It was then, friends said, that Ray gained partial control over a slight stammer that had bothered him since childhood; henceforth, the hesitation would continue to appear informally, but never when he spoke publicly.

Now, separation from his family in Riverside was nearly complete. "He didn't come home at all during the six years in Oconomowoc," his sister recalled, "and we were allowed to visit him three days, three times a year, at Christmas and Easter, and once during the summer. The times were very strict for the young seminarians."

Thus, Ray lived from 1953 to 1959, apart from family, both insulated and isolated from the outside world. Physically, he was in Wisconsin, but one of the U.S. senators from that state, Joseph McCarthy, and his ego-driven anti-Communist crusade and subsequent Senate condemnation were events on another plane. Racial segregation in the public schools was ruled unconstitutional by the U.S. Supreme Court during this period, and Rosa Parks refused to give her seat to a white man on a bus in Alabama. The United States put its first satellite into orbit and exploded the first H-bomb. Khrushchev and DeGaulle became top chiefs in the Soviet Union and France, respectively, and Castro threw Batista out of Cuba. In 1955, a year after the Vietnamese defeated the French, the U.S. agreed to help train the South Vietnamese army. Ray was not unaware of such events, but for him what was important, besides his studies, was to avoid physical discomfort and physical activity.

Seminarians were encouraged to participate in baseball, football, soccer, canoeing and sailing and, in the icy Wisconsin winters, ice hockey, ice boating, and ice skating. Ray had no interest in any of it.

Summers, they camped out on farm land about five miles from the seminary, sleeping in six-man tents. "For the rest of us, it was a wonderful part of the year," said Father Morrissy, "but Ray hated it. Sports were still of no interest to him and he asked what was so great about sleeping under a mosquito net."

Of course, Ray found an escape. When the camp truck went to town each morning following morning prayers and breakfast to pick up the next day's food and other supplies, he wrangled permission to leave on it, so long as he returned in time for supper and evening prayers. The consensus is that he was on the truck nearly every day, spending his days working his way through the seminary library.

Father Ray was ordained in Oconomowoc on July 2, 1959. His family was present when in his white vestment, he knelt before the bishop. By now, the new priest had been told he was going to Thailand and his brother Don recalled that at the ordination luncheon afterwards, one of the priests who spoke said in jest, "In two years, Ray will own Thailand."

The next year passed quickly in St. Louis, Missouri, for a final period of instruction, called Second Novitiate (pastoral training). "That was when we prepared for our mission," said Father Pat Morrissy, who would go to Thailand four years ahead of Ray.

And then it was time to go. It could honestly be said that probably was the second greatest step of his young adult life. The first was when he wed Christ and left home; now he was leaving the United States.

Chapter 4

Father Ray was told a year before his ordination that he would be sent to Thailand. Years later, he said he didn't much like the idea. The more likely alternatives were Brazil, where the Redemptorists also had several missions, or an assignment in the United States.

"To be honest, I had no desire to go to Thailand," he told a periodical called *Bible Alive*. "I felt paralyzed. The World Series was coming up and I wanted to stay home. I tried everything to get out of it---limping, pleading illness."

Maybe. Although Chicago won the American League pennant in 1959 (losing the series to Los Angeles), Father Ray had never shown any particular interest in baseball and, according to his brother Don, "from all I know, he said it was fine with him and he was anxious to go."

For the same magazine, Father Ray also recalled his father's reaction to the assignment. "When we were young," he said, "Dad would have a 'sacred hour' in which he had a Pilsner beer and read the right-wing Herald Tribune and we weren't allowed to interrupt. On the day I told him I was being posted to Thailand, he put down the paper for the first time ever and said, 'What the hell are you going there for?'

"My mother somehow wasn't surprised," he went on. "It's funny how mothers can tell. I expected tears, but she just shook her head and said, 'I knew God had a reason and now I know---of all my children, you are the one who likes to eat rice!' "

In dozens of media reports and television documentaries that would follow the priest's career, even in his obituary, this story of his reluctance to go and his love of rice was told again and again, joining the growing collection of what were becoming called "Father Ray stories," most of them perpetuated, over time, by Father Ray himself. However accurate the stories may or may not be, Father Joe Maier was one of several who came to believe that some of the tales bordered on fiction, and even his sister Sharron, who said she practically hero-worshipped her brother, admitted that he tended to exaggerate, but "usually to make a point."

The United States had begun an exciting new chapter of its own when the slim and handsome new missionary started out on his great adventure. The same year, in November, another young Irish Catholic, John Fitzgerald Kennedy, was elected President and in January he exclaimed in his inaugural speech, "Ask not what your country can do for you, but what you can do for your country." By March, the new president created by executive order the Peace Corps, a program that would send thousands of idealistic Americans---most of them young---to Thailand and elsewhere in the world to work in poor rural areas. They taught English and farming skills, dug wells, and set up agricultural co-ops. This also was a time when the plight of the disenfranchised African-American (then called Negro) minority in the American South inspired voter registration drives and Freedom Rides and sit-ins and marches led by still another young man of the cloth, Rev. Martin Luther King, Jr. Father Ray Brennan didn't attract the same attention as he set forth in 1961 for a country that most people in the United States probably couldn't find on a map, but it would not be inappropriate to think he was a part of the same movement and spirit.

No such mood existed that year in Thailand, then regarded as one of the poorest countries in the so-called Third World. In 1957, a general named Sarit Thanarat overthrew a long-serving general-cum-prime minister. But Sarit destroyed all pretenses of democracy---abolishing the constitution, dissolving parliament, banning all political parties, jailing even minor critics, and remaining in power until his death by cirrhosis in 1963. Two more generals, Sarit's protégés, ruled

Thailand all the way to 1973. All these generals were diehard anti-communists, greatly afraid of China and Vietnam, and allies of the United States in its war in Vietnam. They were also recipients of millions of dollars of U.S. military and economic aid every year. Father Ray was entering what was, quite simply, a military dictatorship.

The first European missionaries who came to Siam were Dominican Friars who arrived in Ayutthaya in 1567, followed by Franciscans and Jesuits in the seventeenth century. Most of the early missionaries were French priests who believed they could convert the entire country to Christianity. It was not to be. "Today," said Father Francisco Kriengsak of the Assumption Cathedral, Thailand's center of Catholicism, "the Catholic population of Thailand is 250,000 people, which is very small, after four hundred years of evangelization and considering the country's total population is sixty million."

In this historical context, when the first four Redemptorist priests came in 1948---a mission planned to begin a decade earlier but delayed by World War Two---surely little notice was given them.

At first, there were hints of comedy. The Redemptorists thought, mistakenly, that missionaries with French surnames would be most acceptable to the Siamese. But the Siamese had borne a grudge against the French since the late nineteenth century, when the French had successfully claimed a large chunk of the western bank of the Mekong as part of its new colony of Laos. The Siamese believed it was rightfully theirs. So, in fact, French surnames were not going to offer advantage to the Church. Nonetheless, the names of Duhart, Godbout, LaRiviere and Kane, and soon afterward Cotant and Gautreaux, were among the earliest sent. The Redemptorist missionaries also were taught the Thai dialect common in Bangkok and central Thailand---what was regarded as "proper" Thai---but they were then invariably sent off to the Northeast to start new parishes and tend old ones, and to comfort the lepers and the poorest of the poor. And in the Northeast, known as Isaan, most people spoke a very different dialect that more closely resembled Lao than the central Thai dialect.

In addition, there was a sort of eccentricity common to some of the priests. Upon arriving, they rented a house not far from the present Holy Redeemer Church in Bangkok, converting one end of the building designed for cars into a chapel and naming it "Our Lady of the Garage." The Soviet Embassy was nearby and in those Cold War days it was forbidding, its gates always locked. One day when the gates were open, Father Godbout pedaled into the atheist enclave on his bicycle and said he was doing a census of his parish and wondered if there were any Catholics in residence. He was quickly shown the way out. Bishop Claude Bayet was another character---a giant of a man with a booming voice and in the words of Father Morrissy, in a history of the Redemptorists inThailand, "a beard almost long as himself." In fact, in Father Morrissy's history, *Golden Jubilee of the Redemptorists in Thailand*, there was a photograph in which not one but two priests had beards that fell almost to their waists, while others were shown in various amusing poses: pedaling a bicycle in ankle-length robes through a rural village, and while garbed in the same garment wearing a pith helmet.

"We thought of Thailand as being at the end of the earth," said Father Charlie Cotant, thirty-three years of age when he was in the second Redemptorist group of missionaries in 1949. "It was better than we thought, but it was extremely primitive. Bangkok at that time had one good restaurant and two hotels, the Tropicana and the Oriental, and what is now Sukhumvit, where later we built Holy Redeemer Church, well, that was all rice paddies. There were more water buffalo than people."

Bangkok had developed minimally when Father Ray passed through a dozen years later on his way to his first posting in Sri Racha, a small fishing village about two hours from Bangkok on the Gulf of Thailand. Here, the Redemptorists had two cottages and a large house by the water's edge and worshipped in a small chapel erected in the garden of a wealthy Catholic businessman. Where it was customary for missionaries to learn the new language in a school, a course that usually lasted up to a year, Father Ray studied for six months with a native speaker whose name seems to be forgotten.

The way Father Ray told the story later, his teacher spoke to him only in Thai and spoke no English, so far as he knew. Thus, the young priest said, he would vent his considerable frustration by calling the Thai father a variety of impolite names. "And I'm from Chicago," he told friends, "so I know some real bad names."

Then, at the end of their time together, to his great mortification, his teacher bade him farewell in perfect English.

The young missionary next journeyed to Isaan, the vast, flat northeastern part of the country that was, along with the newly-independent country of Laos, the territory designated for his mission. Isaan was characterized then, as now, by Thailand's harshest weather, greatest population density, and lowest per capita income. Because of their dark skin and Lao dialect, most Isaan people were instantly pegged by other Thais as being from the peasant class. It was a region where the land was plowed with wood implements and water buffalo, where rice was planted and harvested by hand, and the diet included insects and reptiles. Residents of Bangkok and the wealthier central part of the country regarded these "Lao" as suitable for domestic labor and factory work and very little else.

It was this community of some of Thailand's poorest of the poor that the Redemptorists came to serve, setting up two bases---called "houses" because they occupied former private residences. One was in Khon Kaen, a rural province about 450 kilometers north of Bangkok where farming and textiles were the primary occupations. The other was in Nong Khai, a long, narrow province with 300 kilometers of its length running along the Mekong River where it formed the border between Thailand and Laos. In these houses, the priests met approximately for four or five days once a month, spending the rest of their time in rural villages where they preached in small churches, started rural schools, and established clinics to aid the sick. With virtually nonexistent medical supplies, the priests, according to Father Joe Maier, were left to diagnose illness by consulting a Merck Manual, a book published by the pharmaceutical house that offered description of symptoms and treatment. "And," said Father Joe, "us guessing."

"There was no medicine and death was quick," said Father Frank Gautreaux, who shared a tiny house for three months with Father Ray in Phonsung, a small village near the provincial capital of Udon Thani.

Father Gautreaux was born in 1925, the last of twelve children raised in the "Irish Channel" section of New Orleans, one of seven from his grammar school who went to the Redemptorist seminary in Kirkwood, Missouri. Like many men who are small physically, he had the personality of a firecracker, making up for his lack of size with explosive energy, and like Father Ray, who was eight years his junior, he spoke frankly. He recalled that he wanted to be sent to Brazil rather than Thailand because the South American country had "God's alphabet and Thailand had squiggles." He also remembered that his fellow priest didn't like his middle name, Alan, so he always called him "Father Ray Alan." In return, Father Ray called him "Gogs."

It was while serving with Father Gautreaux that Father Ray struggled to learn the Lao dialect and once he was familiar enough to get by, he was given his own parish in a village in Loei, a mountainous and sparsely populated province to the west that was one of Thailand's most scenic and unspoiled. The geography was mountainous and the temperature seasonally ping-ponged between hotter and colder than almost anywhere else; this was the only province in Thailand where temperatures occasionally dropped to 0 degrees Celsius, freezing on the Fahrenheit scale.

Father Ray's village was partly populated by the Hmong, a hill tribe known for its independence and whose language was incomprehensible to both Laotians and Thais. The village was also quite distant from any semblance of civilization. Father Ray recalled years later that there was no electricity and illumination after dark was by Coleman lamp, a kerosene-fueled lantern that used a silk bag as a wick. "When I worked up north, everyone had one in their homes. I had two in my rectory. They give brilliant white light and last for weeks before you had to change the silk bag." The "rectory" initially was quite primitive, no more than a open-sided platform on stilts with a thatched roof.

Father Ray also remembered "when we walked through mud and had to pull all the blood suckers off our legs each time we got out of water."

Villagers mainly traveled by foot, or possibly in a cart pulled by cattle or water buffalo. So the priest's choice of transportation was quite amazing to them. "He had a Land Rover that he used to visit the villages," said Father Robert Martin, who arrived with Father Gautreaux in 1952. "At the time, he was working with the farmers, setting up a rice bank, trying to help them develop silkworm farms, and he insisted on the big car because he wanted it to be a dramatic event when he arrived. Not for personal reasons, but because 'The Priest' was there, as a Representative of the Church."

Father Martin, who was from Wichita, Kansas, said Father Ray was a "great leg-puller. He always had a joke or a story. He told us that in Chicago they had a movie theater when you saw flowers on the screen, you could smell them throughout the theater."

There was another story Father Ray told in subsequent years that was only slightly more believable. He was washing his clothes in the Mekong River, he said, when he noticed a woman on the opposite bank with a child. To his horror, he realized that she was drowning it. So, he said, he dove into the water and swam like the championship swimmer he said he was back in military school. Still, he was too late to save the child. This was a bizarre tale, almost humorous when trying to imagine Father Ray ever participating in any physical activity let alone becoming a champion at it, but also shocking to consider the desperate act and its outcome. His sister Sharron said she never heard the story. Perhaps the incident itself was true and his effort to cross the river was merely tacked on. But why?

The apocryphal stories piled up. Often told in the years to come was another that concerned the time his poor village parishioners obliged him to pray for rain, when against his will, he prayed the rain began.

Father Ray had been in Thailand less than four years and was more than a year short of getting his first "home leave" when he was visited by his mother in Loei in 1965. Soon after she arrived, another priest from Khon Kaen appeared at Father Ray's small church unexpectedly. Father Ray looked at him and said, "You've come to tell me that my father died."

He had guessed it---his father had died January 30 of a cerebral hemorrhage ---and he accompanied his mother back to Chicago. "He was allowed to stay for eight months and during this time John [Purtell] and I decided to marry," Sharron recalled. "Ray, Don, and Father Mac said our wedding Mass. Ray stuttered during the 'Our Father' and said, 'lead us into temptation.' I asked him about it later and he said he had performed many marriages, but when he looked down and it was his baby sister, it just got to him.

"It was during this trip that he gained weight," Sharron added. His sister said he especially loved White Castle hamburgers sold by a national chain with that name. Measuring about two inches in diameter, the little burgers were served with onions on a white bun. "The first trip Don and I made to Asia, he asked me to bring White Castles," Sharron recalled. "I bought him a dozen and packed them in many layers of plastic in my suitcase. We met in Manila and he immediately had us stop at a little restaurant and had them heat the hamburgers. He ate every one. My suitcase and clothes smelled of onions for the duration of the trip."

And so it was that his eating habits apparently changed, in Chicago when his father died. "He had always been thin before," his sister said, "but so enjoyed feasting on all the foods he had missed that [in eight weeks] he gained fifty pounds."

Chapter 5

In the United States, the heat and ardor of 1967 was called the Summer of Love. It was a time when the young proclaimed, "Make Love, Not War," a season when thousands of young Americans migrated to San Francisco with flowers in their hair and psychotropic drugs in their bloodstream. Both the very public war in Vietnam and the "Secret War" in Laos were escalating, as was an increasingly visible and vociferous protest at home in the U.S. Not in a hundred years, since the American Civil War, had the nation been so divided.

Yet in Thailand, the "conflict" in Vietnam was welcomed in numerous ways. Not only was the United States building an infrastructure of ports and airfields and highways that would help move the Third World kingdom closer to "developed" status, it was providing a welcome security force. Only two dozen years earlier, Thailand had been an ally of Japan's in World War Two, but now it was America's new best friend. Thailand had no love for Vietnam, an old enemy, and its government subscribed to the so-called Domino Theory, espoused by the United States. According to this theory, if South Vietnam fell to the Communists, and Laos and Cambodia followed, Thailand could be next, so it made very good sense to welcome the heavily-armed foreigners with the smiles for which the Thais were known.

By now, Thailand was the United States' most important staging area for the war. This was where the U.S. had more than twenty military installations. Many of the most remote were linked by hundreds of miles of new roads constructed by Army engineers so that bombs carried across the Pacific by ship could be transported by truck to airfields near the Lao and Cambodian borders; from there, planes bombed much of the Ho Chi Minh Trail, part of which ran through eastern Laos, and tried to bomb areas of Vietnam and Laos held by North Vietnamese forces "back to the Stone Age." Meanwhile, on the ground there was a policy aimed---Washington said---at winning the Vietnamese "hearts and minds." Years later, the policy would seem as tragic as it was misinformed, but at the time Presidents Johnson and Nixon were not to be deflected from their own mission.

Through much of the 1960s, America pumped countless millions of dollars into the Thai economy in numerous large and small ways. Not the least of these was the money spent by individuals either based in Thailand or visiting it on "rest and recuperation" (called R&R), providing impetus for the numerous new hotels and restaurants and shops and bars to accommodate their growing numbers, and in driving a real estate boom by the need for offices and residences. Some said that at any given time in the late 1960s, there were at least ten thousand American servicemen in Thailand. All thirsty and hungry and looking for respite and relief, with wallets fat with cash.

For a period of about three years, starting in 1968, Father Ray and Father Joe Maier were told to try to win the hearts and minds---and in the effort, try to control the libidos---of many of these men. It may have been the young Redemptorists' greatest challenge. Surely, it was one of the most unusual and, according to Father Joe, one of the most interesting and, in a way, most pleasurable.

Ray and Joe were a good match. Both were one of three children and they had come from the Midwest---Joe spending his childhood in North Dakota---and they shared an Irish-Catholic heritage (Joe was half-Irish, half-German). They both were non-athletic, scholarly, and not opposed to enjoying what Joe called "a jar" or two of alcohol at the end of the day. Even their dissimilarities meshed in the way that opposites sometimes attract. Where Ray always tried to please and kept his opinions and thoughts to himself, Joe was an outspoken rebel and didn't much care how people reacted; in seminary, he lobbied to get some of the rules changed (for instance, he wanted to smoke cigarettes openly, something Father Ray now applauded) and he protested against the war in Vietnam.

They weren't like Batman and Robin. More like Superman and the Silver Surfer. With a little of Laurel and Hardy added in.

"Ray-Ray---I always called him that---and I were asked to give retreats for the military," said Father Joe. "We did this all over Thailand. The retreats would last the weekend and always were held in the base chapel. Attendance was optional, so we'd arrive two or three days ahead of time so we could do some promotion on the military radio station and move around, meet some of the men."

First, they went to the Non-Commissioned Officers' Club and drank with the NCOs, and then to the Officers' Club for more of the same, matching their new friends and potential retreat attendees jar for jar. Both priests had silver tongues and because of their different personalities, they appealed to numerous types. Base chapel, they always reminded the men...this weekend, and the preaching will be over before the bars closed. That was a promise.

"Ray-Ray was always the organizer," said Father Joe, "the guy who planned everything, the life of the party. He had a great ability never to get anybody upset, and he spoke plainly. He told the men, 'We're gonna talk about God and you won't be bored, so get your asses over there.' "

Father Robert Martin, who had been director of the Khon Kaen house when Father Ray was in Loei, and was serving as an auxiliary chaplain to the U.S. Army, confirmed the younger priest's salty language. "He didn't pull any punches," he said, "and he had a good imagination."

"It was pure macho," said Father Joe. "The military was paying for this and we said that if we didn't increase attendance by twenty men each of the three nights of a retreat, they could have their money back. We did this for three years and we were well known, I say that in all modesty."

In addition to saying Mass and hearing confession for the Catholic servicemen, the two young priests made themselves available for counseling and because of their reputation as regular guys, not far removed from the backgrounds and ages of the men, and ready to match them joke for joke and drink for drink, sometimes there'd be fifteen or twenty lined up to talk.

"It was straight-from-the-shoulder spirituality," said Father Joe. "We said, 'Be faithful to your wife...don't gamble away all the money...and don't forget that there's life after Thailand and Vietnam.'

"We also talked to men who wanted to marry Thai women they'd met in the bars. Dozens, maybe hundreds of them.

"We'd tell them it was really dumb."

The assistance flowed both ways. Father Joe eventually served along the northern Thai border, too, and then crossed into Laos to minister to the Hmong hill tribe. Thousands of Hmong men and boys soon joined the CIA-run "secret war" against the Vietnamese, fighting alongside Royal Lao Army and Thai troops. Father Ray remained in Loei, trying, vainly more often than not, to improve the economical and physical if not the spiritual health of some of the same hill tribes, early refugees from the war. Eventually, they would number in the tens of thousands. Known to the U.S. military because of his and Father Joe's retreats, Father Ray frequently was sent food and medical supplies.

On his own, while serving in a village, numbering between three hundred to four hundred people in Loei, the young priest introduced several programs aimed at improving his parishioners' self-sufficiency. Some ended in disaster, both comically and tragically.

One of the indigenous products for which northeastern Thailand was famed was silk and Father Ray figured if he could encourage the Hmong to grow silkworms instead of their traditional revenue source, the opium poppy, he'd help eliminate drugs while delivering a livelihood with less risk. Father Gautreaux, who was the Loei parish priest before Father Ray arrived, said that when the young priest introduced a silk "center" in the village, the provincial governor didn't attend opening ceremonies. Next day, the older priest said, Father Ray "drove to the governor's house, parked his jeep outside and with the motor left running, he confronted the local politician and made it very clear how disappointed he was. The governor apologized."

That was not the only disappointment. After the naturally yellow thread that forms the cocoons was unwound, it was bleached and then dyed a variety of colors, according to the weaver's wish. Father Ray figured if he injected dye directly into the live caterpillar with a syringe, he could hasten production while getting around the high cost of chemicals used to color the thread.

Of course, all the caterpillars died instead of dyed.

His attempt to introduce egg farming was more hazardous---for him, not the chickens. Father Joe said that eggs in the region were wildly overpriced because the market was controlled by "merchants" who shipped eggs from Bangkok. This prompted Father Ray to start a chicken farm and market the eggs at one-third the current extortionist price. The merchants were not amused and, mysteriously, all of Father Ray's chickens died. While the priest was warned that it might not be a good idea to try again, if he wanted to hear another confession or say another Mass or hear a rooster's crow.

In one effort, however, Father Ray was not only resourceful but also immensely successful. That was when he grew weary of the boasts of a priest in another village that his soccer team could beat the team in Father Ray's village. Father Ray took the challenge and quietly hired all the best footballers in the provincial capital as ringers.

"They beat the poop out of the other team," said Father Joe, "and it was five years before the other priest found out."

In 1969, there was more bad news from home. His mother had died January 15, four years to the month after the death of his father, also of a cerebral hemorrhage. Her death was not expected, but she often had said, following her husband's demise, that she was guaranteed a place in Heaven because she had entrance through her sons to both the front and rear doors. Father Ray was not given permission to go home for the funeral.

Chapter 6

After ten years in Thailand's Northeast, Father Ray was assigned to replace a parish priest in Pattaya, on Thailand's eastern seaboard. About 150 kilometers (90 miles) from Bangkok, Pattaya once was a fishing community, usually described as sleepy. By 1971 when Father Ray arrived, the proximity of a large American army base at Sattahip and a massive airfield at U-tapao, just forty-five minutes away from Pattaya, had turned the town into a favorite R&R destination for U.S. soldiers.

The Redemptorists had arrived in Chon Buri, the province in which Pattaya was the second largest town, in 1959 when they opened a minor seminary in Sri Racha, another small coastal town. About the same time, Father Patrick Morrissy, who in the years ahead would become one of Father Ray's closest friends, was offering Mass at the seaside cottage of Dr. Lert Srichantra in nearby Bang Lamung.

The first step taken toward building a parish church in the area for the growing Catholic community was taken by another Catholic layman who had a vacation home in Pattaya. This was Walter Meyer, a Swiss expatriate who had lived in Thailand since 1941. He was 25 when he joined the German News Agency in Shanghai in 1940 and was sent to Bangkok to open a branch of the agency shortly before World War Two began and Thailand was occupied by the Japanese. The young journalist continued in his post until Germany surrendered in 1945 and the British military took over all German assets in the country. Walter then joined the Berli Jucker Company Ltd., one of the Kingdom of Siam's earliest trading companies, a firm that dated back to 1882 when its interests were in rice milling, mining, timber, shipping, imports and other businesses that supported a pre-industrial economy.

Walter joined the firm as an "assistant" when it began to diversify into manufacturing, packaging, and distribution. By 1948, he was an Assistant Managing Partner, rising to Managing Partner in 1957. He and his family spent many weekends in his Pattaya house. As an alternative to praying in Sri Racha or driving to the Holy Redeemer Church for Sunday Mass in Bangkok, in 1961 he constructed a pavilion and offered services on his forty-meter-long beachfront property. Six years later, as the war in Vietnam escalated, bringing hundreds of American Catholic military men to the area, he added a small chapel.

Walter had a special devotion to St. Nikolaus De Flue, a fifteenth century hermit and mystic who became the patron saint of Switzerland, revered across denominational barriers for his spirit of reconciliation and agreement, credited with influencing Swiss politics for centuries to come. The chapel was dedicated to him as its patron and was under the direction of a Redemptorist missionary, Father Roger Godbout, who previously had founded the Holy Redeemer parish in Bangkok and once was described by Cardinal Spellman as the "best-known priest from Hawaii to Rome." (Father Godbout is the priest who had entered the compound of the Soviet embassy in Bangkok on his bicycle, claiming he was taking a census of Catholics, and then quickly was escorted to the gate.)

The Meyer family and others wished to establish a cemetery in Pattaya and this led to the founding of the Pattaya Cemetery Association and the acquisition of nearly two and a half acres of vacant land on the Sukhumvit Highway, a four-lane avenue that more or less tracked the coastline a few miles inland from the gulf, stretching from Bangkok to the Cambodian border. The land had been owned by Walter's wife and money realized from the sale of burial plots provided the sum of US$8,000 for the construction of a parish church that was to be named for Walter's revered Swiss saint.

Construction was accomplished with the assistance of the American military---which provided material, engineers and labor---as Father Godbout continued to conduct services in the chapel on the Meyers' property. The chapel accommodated fewer than one hundred worshippers and, in Walter's words, had "become too small." Initially, there was no assigned priest.

Father Godbout was the first permanent pastor appointed to Pattaya, taking this position in 1967 and remaining until 1969, when he had a "nervous breakdown" and was succeeded by Father Ray. About half of the congregation came from the U.S. military bases at nearby U-tapao and Sattahip, others from the growing area population and holiday weekenders from Bangkok.

At Mrs. Meyer's suggestion, the St. Nikolaus Church was constructed in the Thai style, taking the appearance of a sala, or open pavilion with only one wall, backing the pulpit. There were no solid walls at the rear or two sides. Thus the church was open to breezes at daily services, along with the fragrance of the nearby frangipani trees. The church was entered from the back, farthest from the highway, and the cemetery was behind it. The new church was dedicated and blessed on November 26, 1967.

Years later, Father Ray was asked what he recalled about his early days in Pattaya. He said, "There were dolphins in the bay and the water was crystal clear. I'd go fishing with a piece of white cloth as bait, that's all you needed to catch fish. In the evening, you could see phosphorus glisten atop the waves. I used to just sit there and enjoy the view with a bottle of beer. The road down the coast was made up of dirt tracks and narrow wooden bridges."

While a small rectory was being built on the parish property, between the church and the highway, Father Ray was a guest of the Meyer family, staying in a bungalow one block from the beach for more than a year. By all reports, their relationship was one of great mutual affection and respect. Walter called his friend "Father Brennan," the more formal or traditional address; it was never "Father Ray."

Walter said the congregation loved its new parish priest. His sermons were short, many of them starting with Father Ray saying, "When I was a little boy…" And then he told a story. Walter smiled and added something that may have added to Father Ray's popularity: "He didn't condemn people who went to him for confession." The Hail Marys were assigned, but parishioners said that there was a kind of forgiveness that seemed Thai rather than Western in style, that delivered a sense of mai pen rai, a phrase that defined an important part of the Thai character, translating "never mind…it's okay."

Father Ray also was candid about his own history, or at least seemed to be, if, as his sister said, he thought it would carry a message. John Francis Moriarty, a lay Jesuit missionary from the United States then teaching Sunday School in Bangkok, planned a weekend-long retreat in Pattaya and asked Father Ray to say Mass and deliver the homily, a brief sermon about being a Christian in the modern world.

"The retreat was mainly for American kids going to international schools," John said. "The kids were pretty messed up, drugs and all that, and their parents were U.S. Embassy people who were much the same, not paying much attention to their marital vows or spending much time with their kids. So it was a group dynamics thing, with a lot of free discussion led by facilitators. Father Ray was our chaplain and coordinator and when he talked to them, he told them interesting adventures of the time when he was a boy. The American kids really liked that. They thought Father Ray was cool."

When Father Ray's new home on the parish grounds was completed, it had two rooms, the downstairs one for meeting parishioners and greeting guests, the upstairs for sleep at the end of the day. This was about as luxurious as it ever would get for him. Until he died, his living accommodations were seldom more than monastic, by choice.

"When he moved into the parish house," Walter recalled, "my wife visited him. She said it was a mess. Said he was a poor housekeeper. He told her to get away."

Years later, when Father Ray was running his orphanage, a representative from the Vatican came to Pattaya to see it and to meet Father Ray. Father Ray took him to his rooms and left him to rest, telling him there was food in the kitchen and to help himself if he got hungry. When the priest returned, the man said he'd eaten the stew he found in the refrigerator. Father Ray knew he had no stew, and then remembered that he had a container into which he'd dumped leftovers for several days and added worm pills for the dog that lived on the church grounds. The visitor did not get sick and Father Ray said nothing.

The priest's housekeeping might fairly be said to epitomize the way he ran much of his life: haphazardly, almost carelessly at times, taking what came his way almost matter-of-factly. He had a two-pack-a-day cigarette habit, leaving a haze of smoke and overflowing ashtrays behind him, and when not wearing his clerical robes he didn't seem to worry much about his wardrobe.

Unplanned, too, was what happened about a year after he started saying Mass at St. Nikolaus. The way he told it, one day at the end of services, a woman approached him with a baby in her arms: "She told me that the father, her husband, had run away, and that she had since found a new husband, the problem being that he refused to have anything to do with offspring from her previous marriage." In time, other versions of the same story emerged as well, the most frequently told involving a mother who was a bar worker, the father an unidentified American soldier.

Whatever the truth, Father Ray told the young Thai woman that he would take the child, not having a clue what he would do with it. He then gave the baby to a local woman named Lamom who, with her own young children, was paid to clean the church and prepare his meals.

In the three years that followed, more infants were left in his care, until there were seven, and in time, the first adoptions were arranged. The childless couple that adopted the first child, a boy, Father Ray said, were Indians living in Bangkok. Other children came directly from the hospital where they were born when the mothers pled extreme poverty. Some were---without doubt---the offspring of Thai bargirls and American servicemen. Several babies came when a small orphanage run by the Salesian Sisters at St. Mary's School in Udon Thani was closed. A few were found abandoned on the beach or in dustbins.

News of the priest's kindness spread. At first, he placed the infants in the temporary custody of local families, providing an allowance to pay for their care. Then, in 1974, someone came to him and gave him some money, saying, "This is for your orphanage."

"But I don't have an orphanage," he said.

"Oh, yes, you do," the man replied.

In April 1975, two years after the Americans signed a cease-fire agreement with Vietnam, as Uncle Ho's troops swept south toward Saigon, hundreds of thousands of South Vietnamese fled the country. Some humanitarian groups working with orphans in Vietnam were planning their own evacuation when U.S. President Gerald Ford announced a program called Operation Babylift. This was designed to fly several thousand children from Vietnamese orphanages to the United States.

Tragedy struck the first flight when just twelve minutes after an Air Force C-5 cargo plane, the largest plane in the skies at that time, took off, its rear cargo doors blowing off. Many passengers were sucked out of the plane, yet the pilot was able to turn the crippled craft and head back toward Saigon. The plane touched down in an open field two miles short of the runway at about double the normal speed for landing. The huge aircraft bounced into the air and over the Saigon River before hitting an irrigation ditch and breaking into four parts. Almost half the estimated three hundred adults and children aboard were killed and following religious services the ashes of a number of the children were flown to U-tapao, Thailand. (Reports vary as to the number of children involved, but with reasonable certainty it was more than seventy).

Soon after that, the U.S. chaplain and the base commander at U-tapao together asked Father Ray if the ashes of the children could be buried at St. Nikolaus. Father Ray gave his permission and today there is a gravesite in the small cemetery where a stone reads, "Rest in Peace/Gentle Little Souls/For God Loves You." Beside it is a small statue of a Thai child holding a younger child on his back. It reminds some visitors of an American movie from the 1930s in which

Spencer Tracy played an Irish Catholic priest and Mickey Rooney went down in cinema history when he arrived at Boys Town (a home for juvenile delinquents and the name of the film) with a boy on his back and he said, "He ain't heavy, he's my brother."

This statue would become the symbol of Father Ray's soon-to-be orphanage.

Chapter 7

Father Ray served as parish priest at St. Nikolaus for seven years, but from 1974, when the Pattaya Children Supporting Foundation was formed, the direction of his life changed. The man who would often tell people that he became a Redemptorist, rather than follow his older brother into the Augustinian order, because he didn't want anything to do with children or teaching now became a "father" to what soon would become the largest family not only in Pattaya, but in all of Thailand.

As would prove in later years to be his style---if that's the correct term---Father Ray committed himself to a project before he had the funding and the knowledge to make it work. In this fashion, the first building on the sprawling, flat-as-a-table but heavily treed property was still under construction when he ran out of money.

The diocese of Chantaburi owned an eighteen-rai (seven-acre) parcel of vacant land on Sukhumvit Highway, about one kilometer from St. Nikolaus Church, and Bishop Sanguan granted permission to Father Ray to build an orphanage. Even so, the early years were not easy.

Providentially, Walter Meyer told him that the manager of the Hong Kong and Shanghai Banking Corporation would be attending Mass with him the next Sunday, so Father Ray devoted his sermon to needy orphans. After the service, the priest was introduced to the banker. How much money did Father Ray need? One million baht, he said, then the equivalent of about US$40,000, at the time a princely sum in Thailand. The banker said his bank could help, but he told Walter that he would have to guarantee the loan.

"So I became his financial advisor," Walter recalled.

Once again, much of the actual construction, along with much of the material, was provided by the U.S. Army Corps of Engineers. The officer who saw that Father Ray got whatever he wanted if it was in any way possible wanted no credit, then or now. The inspiration for his generosity was no secret, however. He and his men built hundreds of kilometers of roads in Thailand, creating a highway system that helped modernize the country, but during the war in Vietnam was used to move hundreds of thousands of tons of bombs from ships docking near Pattaya to American air bases stretching from U-tapao to locations in the Northeast near the Laos and Cambodian borders, where Father Ray had once preached. In a word, the officer felt guilty and he wished in some way to atone.

The building was still under construction in 1974 when Corinna Davidson arrived. She had stopped in Thailand on her way from Burma to Australia. After meeting Father Ray at St. Nikolaus after Mass one Sunday, she decided to stay, going to work for him as a secretary. "At that time," she remembered, "there was an American volunteer, a resident of Pattaya named Gene Farley, a retired U.S. Army colonel, who was helping at the Orphanage, and on the weekends there were groups of GIs who came to help out in whatever needed doing. This went on for several months. Finally, the interior of the upstairs left wing and right wing of the building were completed, while the downstairs was partially completed. So the children's quarters were temporarily located upstairs with a milk room and an infirmary.

"In September, while Father Ray was away on leave in the United States, the Orphanage officially opened with five children in residence and Gene Farley at the helm. The paid staff comprised a cook, two caregivers, a cleaner, a laundry person, a groundskeeper, and myself. Some months later, two religious Sisters from the Order of St. Paul arrived to care for the orphans. The downstairs was completed, so the children were moved downstairs and the Sisters lived upstairs. From there on, the children kept arriving. Some of the children were from Thai-GI parents---need I say more? Many came from villages in the north and Isaan.

"Father Ray returned before Christmas and in early 1975 Gene Farley left," Corinna continued. "There was a nursery school set up for the children, with the wife of an American soldier volunteering as a teacher and some parents helping out. There were many military families living in Pattaya then and some sent their children to the school. Then some of the hoteliers sent their kids and then some of the expats who owned bars. The school fees were a source of income.

"That was the biggest problem. M-O-N-E-Y! Initially, Rotary and Rotary International were big contributors. So were international companies and some local ones in Bangkok, along with the hotels in Pattaya. There were lots of fund-raising events held periodically. The U.S. military continued to help. We also had some individual sponsors and contributors locally and overseas. But I remember there were times when payday came around, there wasn't enough to pay wages. So off I went on my rounds, to all the hotels, banks, and restaurants where we had our donation boxes placed. I would empty the boxes with a little prayer to the bloke upstairs that there would be enough to see us through."

As the war in Vietnam was winding down and both the troops and military bases in the area were being reduced in size, a U.S. Air Force supply sergeant at U-tapao got drunk with some of his mates. A trailer about eight meters (twenty-five feet) long and maybe two meters wide that looked like a shipping container on wheels was to be sold at auction and the sergeant decided that Father Ray could use it, so he and his buddies hooked it to a "borrowed" military vehicle and towed it to Pattaya in the middle of the night. For several years, the priest occupied one end of it, Corinna the other, with a bathroom in the middle.

The trailer had been unused for years and when it arrived it contained piles of dust-covered cartons of what appeared at first to be junk. Several contained military letterheads and envelopes that were stuck closed by time and humidity. Betty Roy, the wife of an executive at the Esso refinery at Sri Racha, joined Corinna in 1977 and would help Father Ray with his correspondence for most of the next fifteen years. Betty remembered opening the envelopes with pens and sealing them again with cello tape when sending mail. They also used Polaroid film they found, surprised that it was still serviceable five years past its expiry date.

"When I arrived, Father Brennan had a manual typewriter, but had kept no copies of his letters. He also had no files, no address books. He didn't even have a mailing list. There were only thirty kids at the time and he knew everyone who'd ever given him a dollar. He kept it all in his head," Betty said.

Betty became a full-time volunteer and remained with Father Ray for three years. She then accompanied her husband Joe to Japan, returned in 1980 when Joe was transferred back to the Esso Sri Racha refinery, and remained for another thirteen years. Father Ray was a dedicated letter writer and when he composed a few paragraphs in reply to an inquiry, she would expand upon them, and tell him when he was repeating himself, as he sometimes did after he started sending out newsletters in 1978. Although Betty won't take credit for conceiving the idea of the newsletter, she was instrumental in its distribution, thus freeing the priest for his continuing duties at St. Nikolaus Church and the constant hustling required to keep the Orphanage afloat. With a severely limited budget and an unpredictable revenue flow, the dedication to the thrift and self-sufficiency devised when preaching in the rural villages of Isaan became necessary again, as he continued to live close to the land, dependent on do-it-yourself, recycling, and scavenging.

He planted a garden with vegetables and fruit trees at the end of the property nearest Sukhumvit Road, the main artery leading to and from Bangkok. At the other end, there were pens and shelters for chickens, ducks, and pigs.

Betty Roy said the pig farm started the same way the Orphanage did. One New Year's Eve, Father Ray was at the Pattaya Holiday Inn, where part of the festivities involved a waiter's traveling through the dining room carrying a live baby pig. "I think it was part of a good luck ceremony," Betty said, "and when the waiter came to the table Father Brennan was sharing with the hotel's manager and asked his boss what he wanted him to do with the pig, the manager said, 'Give it to Father Brennan.' "

More pigs were soon added and to discourage flies and control the smell, eucalyptus trees were planted all around the pens, the strong, menthol-like scent of the leaves making Orphanage visitors marvel at the cleanliness. In time, Betty said, her boss also became well-known among pig farmers throughout the area, who paid him a fee to use one of his biggest boars for stud service---a source of funds that inspired many ribald comments, both on the Orphanage grounds and off.

"We slaughter about two pigs a month for food, plus chickens and ducks," he wrote in one of the first newsletters. "Last month we got over one-thousand eggs from the chickens and ducks. What is more surprising is that we consumed most of them!!! Of course, we saved a few hundred to hatch in our incubator. We keep up with the consumption of poultry by hatching about two-hundred chicks and ducklings per month."

In a year, the number of children at the Orphanage doubled, so that by 1978 there were fifty-eight, most of them less than two years of age, sleeping in cribs placed in rows, frequently two to a crib. "Believe it or not," the priest wrote in another newsletter, "we serve over four-hundred and fifty bottles of baby formula a day!" And for all the diapers…he converted a portable concrete mixer into a washing machine for them.

Most inventive of all, or at least most unusual, was the methane generator constructed to produce cooking gas for the kitchen. Many assumed that the manure used in it came from the chickens and pigs. No. At that time, there was an elephant show staged nearby for the growing tourist trade and once a day, Father Ray dispatched the Orphanage van to transport the football-sized droppings.

"Once," recalled Betty Roy, "I asked to have the van take me to Sri Racha and Father Brennan told me to wait. A little later, I spoke to him again, and again he asked me to wait. I didn't know that the van was being used as part of the methane operation and he was stalling me until it could be hosed down and washed."

"Our expenses here at the Orphanage are getting higher, just like yours," Father Ray wrote in 1979. "The electric bill will be raised fifty percent all over Thailand. I am making a new information sheet and am amazed at how prices have soared."

Somehow, he managed, and as the number of children increased, so too did the number of donors. Contributions were often small, but always found immediate use; if someone gave Father Ray $100, he went out and bought some rice. There was a woman in the United States, Betty Roy recalled, who faithfully sent four quarters (one U.S. dollar) taped to a three-by-five-inch card every month …although the postage to send it cost nearly as much as her donation.

One day, a man visiting Thailand showed up and after being taken for a tour of the baby room, the garden, and the livestock pens, he was introduced to Father Ray and for a while they sat in his cluttered office and talked. Back in his hotel, after giving the American priest and his work some thought, the visitor called the Orphanage and said he wanted to make a contribution that would pay for something that the priest could only dream about.

"He didn't want to buy rice or pay for paint or anything ordinary," Betty said. "So Father Brennan made a wish list of items that were not crucial, but highly desired nonetheless. It included the paving of what was then a dirt driveway so the kids could have a wide, flat space where they could ride their bicycles. He told the man what it would cost and the man said the sum seemed small. Father Brennan said it was for a driveway from the highway to the Orphanage building, a distance of about fifty meters. The man asked if there were other areas he wanted paved. Father Brennan said yes and after getting a bid to pave parking lots and driveways that circumnavigated the large property, he called the man again. This time, Father Ray thought the total was pretty big, and although the man didn't seem to care, he said he wanted to see construction under way before he left Thailand to go home."

Now, Betty said, Father Brennan was presented with a conundrum. The man wrote a check that appeared to be in order, but he was planning to leave Thailand before it would clear the bank. If he contracted the paving company and they started work in order to satisfy the heretofore unknown donor, and then the check bounced, he'd be stuck with a big bill. And if work did not begin right away, presumably the man could stop payment on the check. What to do?

Father Ray did what he always did---he trusted his instincts and prayed. Betty recalled, "I don't know how many times I heard him say, 'If the Boss Upstairs screws me, he screws the kids, and I don't think He'd do that."

The concrete was poured and the check cleared the bank.

Chapter 8

In the 1970s, Thailand was considered a Third World country, a phrase used to describe "undeveloped" nations in corners of the earth whose history usually included exploitation and abuse by the First World. The First World was mainly in what was called the West---Europe, North America, Australia, New Zealand--- and Japan. Second World countries included the industrialized nations of the Eastern Bloc (Russia, Poland, etc.) and, as of the late 1970s and 1980s, Asia's Newly Emerging Countries---Singapore, South Korea, Taiwan, and the British colony of Hong Kong.

Thailand was emerging, too, of course, and in a decade it would become the world's fastest growing economy, but in the middle to late 1970s, at least seventy percent of the population remained anchored to the soil, where incomes ranged from subsistence to survival. At the same time, after three years of chaotic democracy, a military crackdown in 1976 ushered in Thailand's most repressive period. Freedom of speech, the press and association were curtailed and a strict curfew was enforced in Bangkok. By the early 1980s, more moderate generals were in charge and they granted amnesties to Communists, former students and others in hiding and exile. Still, virtually every level of bureaucracy and government was corrupt.

Nonetheless, it was far worse in Thailand's neighboring countries, as the Communists grabbed Laos and Vietnam, the Khmer Rouge (who called themselves Communists, but were a bloodier shade of red) introduced the concept of holocaust to modern Southeast Asia in Cambodia.

In Burma, Thailand's western neighbor, xenophobic General Ne Win had since 1962 been driving the resource-rich country down with "The Burmese Way to Socialism," a highway that led to a wrecked economy, and long little wars against a Communist army and an array of ethnic insurgencies. In 1970, the Mon and Karen insurgent armies close to the Thai border joined forces with a new anti-Ne Win party and army led by a group of prominent leaders from the independence fight and the democratic era of the 1950s.

Then came 1974. First oil workers, then workers at railways and dockyards in Rangoon went on strike to protest food shortages and rising prices. Soldiers, sent in by Ne Win, fired on them indiscriminately. In November, U.N. Secretary-General U Thant died in New York. He was Burma's best-known and most respected statesman. He was also a long-time antagonist of Ne Win. When the body arrived in Rangoon, therefore, the government authorities did not meet the coffin at the airport and planned a burial in an obscure cemetery. Students were outraged. During the funeral procession, they seized the coffin and took it to the University of Rangoon. Buddhist monks joined them to conduct rites and bury the body at a revered site.

Ne Win sent in troops again, retrieved the body, and arrested hundreds of students and monks. More violence followed. Hundreds fled to join the insurgent armies along the Thai border, while others fled across it. There, some heard a rumor: if they could find their way to Pattaya and to the always open door of an American priest called Father Ray, possibly he could help.

Father Ray clearly had a soft spot in his heart for the Burmese. Perhaps it was because the parents of his first secretary, Corinna Davidson, were part Burmese and she shared some of her personal experiences. Or maybe it was because refugees from Laos, Cambodia, and Vietnam were regarded as political refugees and, thus, welcome, and word came down from on high that the Burmese were "economic" exiles, though obviously that was far from the truth.

Father Joe Maier, who worked with Father Ray with refugees, along with an Anglican chaplain at Bangkok's Christ Church, John Taylor, thought his interest came simply because no one else was doing anything to help the Burmese and the Pattaya priest believed that when you saw people who'd fallen through the bureaucratic, social, economic, or political cracks, you did whatever you could.

Always ready to go against the grain, not caring what was "official" and what was not, in the years that followed, Father Ray embraced scores of young Burmese rebels and, after being helped to obtain documentation that would permit them to leave Thailand more or less legally, many went on to become European and U.S. residents and, in some cases, citizens.

How did he do it? It was easy, thanks to something called a World Passport. This was a document that was recognized by only a handful of countries, Australia and some Eastern European nations among them. When Father Ray heard from a friend about someone who could make such documents available for a reasonable price, introductions were made and passports were ordered from Berne, Switzerland.

The World Passport was not just a scam, but a concept, defined by its administrators as "more than merely a political strategy. It 'verticalizes' the individual, raising him or her above the 'left' or 'right' of nationalistic politics, to meet and make functional the perennial value systems that heretofore have been only the subject of religious credence. Thus it complements and fulfills all religious prophecies and integrates at the same time the synergistic worlds of instantaneous communications.

"The 'Promised Land' of the Hebrews, the 'Peace on Earth' and 'Thy will be done on earth...' of the Christians, the benevolent social order of the Moslems, the world fraternal order of the Sikhs, the 'Middle Way' of the Buddhists, the 'universal world order' of the Bah'a'is, all are contained in and can grow out of the multi-dimensional, human, spiritual/political dispensation of universal world citizenship."

The rhetoric epitomized idealism and innocence---and it is easy to see how it might have appealed to Father Ray---but the truth was that the World Passport was invented by an American who owed taxes back in the United States, so he renounced his U.S. citizenship and moved to Berne, where he declared himself a "citizen of the world."

Send him a name and a photo and a "country of residence" (no country of birth was asked) and a couple of hundred dollars, and he'd reply with an impressive little book that looked little different from a legal passport issued by a country you could find on a map.

"Ignorance is what legitimized it," said the middleman in Bangkok who put Father Ray in touch with the self-imposed exile in Switzerland. "Some countries just didn't know and when someone showed up with a World Passport, the immigration people said, sure, why not? That was what made it so cool."

It was believed that a Burmese name might cause troubles at immigration checkpoints on departure, so each runaway was given a Western name, many of them concocted by the priest himself. Some stayed on for a while at the Orphanage. One, who took Brennan as his new surname, worked for Father Ray as a sort of handyman for a few years. Betty Roy said Father Ray usually forgot the new names, adding genuine confusion to the fact that, for obvious reasons, no records were kept. Even those who were involved or witnessed the arrivals from the north and their subsequent departures kept no notes, not even an accurate count. Betty remembered it as being in the "hundreds."

"There may have been as many as fifty," said someone who was one of the few involved in the operation, "but probably the number was closer to twenty. I don't think anyone really knows.

"The way it worked," he said, "was that they went to one of the countries that accepted the World Passport and got a legal entry stamp. Once you had the first stamp, the second one was easier. And so on. Until finally you got to where you wanted to be, with a new name and a passport that looked pretty good and had several legitimate country stamps. The idea was that maybe, in time, it could be exchanged for an American or a European one."

It was risky harboring what were, after all, illegal aliens, but here, too, Father Ray was given support, in this instance by the Pattaya police. They raided the

Orphanage occasionally, ostensibly to search for illegal aliens who were rumored to be staying there, but always telephoned Father Ray a day ahead to say they were coming. Next day, they'd find the one old Burmese man; the police would fine the priest five hundred baht (US$20) and tell him never to do it again. And leave the Burmese man in residence.

More help for moving the refugees came from the chaos of the times and the legal movement of thousands of refugees through Thailand by the U.N. High Commissioner for Refugees (UNHCR), a chair then filled by Sadruddin Aga Khan. "I understand that in the period between June and September 1975 more than 3,500 persons have been referred to your Committee by my Representative," he wrote in a letter to Canon Taylor, who chaired the committee on which Fathers Joe and Ray served. "Despite the limited administrative and other personnel resources at the disposal of the Committee, it has risen to the challenge in a splendid manner, providing material support and advice to the needy, humanely and effectively. In this connection, I should like to place on record my deep appreciation of the devoted efforts of the large number of volunteers whom your Committee has been able to mobilize in the service of these unfortunate persons."

Father Ray's refugee programs continued for more than ten years and at times, there were as many as two hundred staying at the Orphanage, as happened in 1979 when busloads of Cambodian children, refugees fleeing the Vietnamese occupation of their homeland, arrived from the border just a few hours away from Pattaya. "These kids were very critical when they arrived in Thailand and were sent to a hospital in Bangkok by the U.N.," Father Ray wrote in his newsletter. "They are all suffering from malnutrition, malaria, parasites, skin diseases of various types, tuberculosis, anemia, etc.

They are here for recovery and they have already begun to gain weight. Our present problem is no one here speaks Cambodian. However, having worked with children for a long time, we are very adept at hand language. In the meantime, we are learning some Cambodian words and they are learning Thai words."

They also were learning a new diet. Years later, Father Ray remembered that "all of them needed a great amount of 'iron' in their diet. The doctor suggested the best and fastest way to give it to them was by using congealed blood. Sister went to the slaughterhouse each day and got a bucket of pig's blood. She solidified it like jelly and a small square was given to each Cambodian orphan at every meal. They hated it and tried all kind of means to get rid of it without eating it. One put a plastic bag in his pocket and when no one was looking, put the jelly-like square of blood into the bag and disposed of it later. But there was one little guy who we knew was not eating his ration of iron and we could not figure out how he was getting rid of it. Finally, we caught him dissolving it in his tea … we [had] only checked the plates and the pockets of the kids."

The priest wrote in a Christmas newsletter after they had gone: "Last year at this time, we had several groups of Cambodian refugee children living with us, trying to regain their health. I am delighted to tell you they did! Some even got chubby! When Christmas came, we had a fantastic time with parties, fireworks, gifts, love and fun. For those refugee children who had seen the horrors of war and famine, it was a new world.

They will never forget it. Some of those children have gone to a third country. Others, unfortunately, have been sent back to refugee camps. Thanks to you and us, we made life happy for them, as it should be, at least for a while."

Chapter 9

Never has it been easy for the handicapped, whether they are physically handicapped---sidelined by birth defects, disease, accidents, or other misfortune---or mentally deficient.   For thousands of years, such people have been overly protected at best and at worst, ignored and hidden away at home, teased by their peers, abused by their elders, locked up in asylums and sometimes killed at birth.

Heartwarming images of handicapped individuals pepper history, literature, popular entertainment and politics, and surely every part of life. From the deaf Beethoven and deaf and blind Helen Keller to paraplegics like Stephen Hawking (Stephen Hawking has amyotrophic lateral sclerosis) and Christopher Reeve, from the kid on crutches in A Christmas Carol and Dustin Hoffman playing an autistic Rain Man to the one-armed U.S. Senator Daniel Inouye and the numerous handicapped who have climbed Mt. Everest and run marathons, many have won great respect. Yet, up until the 1950s, when the tide slowly began to turn, even in an advanced country like the United States, "moron" jokes were shared with glee and people with physical deformities and abnormalities were called freaks and displayed in circus and carnival side shows. Even today, despite all the progress, when confronted by someone who is disabled, most people either stare or look away. And in most of the developing world, little has changed since feudal times. Like race and religion and class and ethnic origin, a handicap is still accompanied by prejudice, social exile and exploitation, thereby heaping handicap upon handicap.

In some parts of the world, including rural Thailand, the handicapped are still victims of superstition. In a magazine interview Father Ray once described how "with a crippled kid, the family or village may feel he is cursed and brings bad luck. Maybe the rice harvest has been bad or no rains have come since the child was born."

In Buddhist countries, the plight of the handicapped and disadvantaged was further compounded by the widespread belief that a person was so burdened because of his or her actions in a previous life. Many Thais believe that the blind, the deaf, and those who are missing limbs or suffering from other disfigurement, mental or physical, are the embodiment of karmic consequence, getting---in the very harshest terms---what they themselves had caused. Adding shame to the already overpowering sense of helplessness and hopelessness.

Many Thai families are embarrassed when their children are born with defects or family members and friends become incapacitated following grievous illness or injury. Parents frequently keep such offspring at home, sometimes merely to protect them, and thus deprive them of an education or normal contact with the outside world. Others cynically regard them as an asset, putting them on the streets to beg. In Bangkok and other metropolitan areas, people missing arms and legs and victims of Hansen's disease (leprosy) are commonly seen begging on the sidewalks. The best many of the deaf and blind can hope for is a job selling government lottery tickets or hawking counterfeit designer clothing at a street stall, communicating with their customers with a digital calculator, and with each other in sign language. It is also common that these vendors are paid less by their stall owners than hearing vendors.

So perhaps it was inevitable that Father Ray would want to do something and as was true of so much of his effort, his commitment to the disabled young people was somewhat haphazardly planned, starting in 1981 when he began planning a school for deaf children. At the time, there were more than half a million hearing-impaired people in Thailand and only ten government-operated schools for them nationwide. None was in the eastern seaboard, where population growth and commercial development were booming.

As is still true today, most deaf Thais did not go to school and even today, only half of the deaf in Thailand can sign. Most of those who don't learn the international language that includes both an alphabet and signs for words and phrases, all "spelled" out in finger and hand movement, live in rural Thailand. They sometimes find work as field workers or in construction, taking jobs that don't require much verbal communication, only physical strength. They, too, are paid less than their hearing peers; after all, doesn't deaf also mean "dumb"? Or at the least, unable to follow instructions?

Many Thai families fall apart when a child is born deaf and this adds more difficulty. The parents are embarrassed, ashamed, or depressed. Many no longer want the child. And even when the family remains intact, when parents take the children with them in public, the children are told to remain silent and not try to communicate with the adult in the manner used at home, usually by making physical contact or "loudly" waving arms and hands, or using a sort of code comprised of grunts and cries. Even if the child and parent know how to sign, in public this is considered by many parents to be unacceptable, as it calls attention to the handicap and causes both parent and child to lose face.

In remote rural areas there may not be another deaf person. Only in metropolitan areas is there an opportunity to find a small community of others similarly impaired. So most deaf Thais remain alone in their silent world. Mostly, the girls remain at home, never marrying. While the males, young and adult, often are ignored or teased.

In the beginning, in the small school on the Orphanage grounds, there were six teachers and eighteen students, aged five to eight, ten boys and eight girls. Several came from Bangkok, others from as far away as Udon Thani and Buri Ram in Isaan. Those living nearby went home on the weekends; all boarded at the school, on the Orphanage grounds, during the week.

Although deafness can be caused by ear infections, severe head injury, prolonged exposure to loud noises or meningitis, most causes are congenital---the result of genetic or inherited abnormalities, malformation of the ear canal or middle or inner ear, and, most often in poor countries, when the mother has had German measles (rubella) during pregnancy. So it was, and would be, at this new school. Most of the moms had had German measles, by now rare in the developed world, but not so uncommon elsewhere.

The small children were taught sign, mathematics, and Thai. Some of the children had learned a sort of hand language at home, used within the family, and this had to be unlearned and replaced.

Yet, progress was quick. It took just two months to learn enough sign to cover the most common functions and activities in daily life, such as eating, sleeping, bathing, playing, working, and counting. Along with the most common expressions, the letters for I and L and Y were combined by making a fist and then extending the thumb, first and small fingers: "I Love You!" Then came colors and food and the environment (sky, tree, birds, stars) and objects (ball, pencil, paper, television set). In six months, the eighteen youngsters were waggling their fingers constantly, delighted to have found a way out of their soundlessness.

"One of the most beautiful things that happened this year was the opening of our newly built school for poor children who are deaf," Father Ray wrote in his annual Christmas letter in 1982. "The children never had the experience of being with other deaf children before. When the first day of school came and they all came together, it was a very moving thing to see them come to the realization that all the other kids were deaf, too. It was a new experience for them. They were used to normal children laughing at them, and they probably expected the same here. When they came to the realization that they were all the same, they became happy. On that day, I watched from my window…and I am not ashamed to say my eyes filled with water."

As was true for the children given to the Orphanage for care, there was no charge made to the families of the deaf children, and only the poor were enrolled. The school was then and now a preparatory one, designed to give children---most of whom, even at age ten or twelve, have never gone to any school---the lessons that will allow them to enter one of the state-operated institutions that teach the higher grades. In the meantime, they were encouraged to teach parents and siblings and friends how to sign.

The School for Deaf Children was the country's first private school for the deaf and many thought it quickly became the best.

When new children began classes, Father Ray wrote in a newsletter in 1984, they "were not too anxious to be in such a strange place. They were also rather suspicious their mom and dad intended to leave them here alone. The faces of the parents showed fear as much as the children. I am sure most of them never thought they would parent a deaf child. But here they are with their deaf child, bringing him or her to the first day of school. They looked at the charts on the wall showing the Thai alphabet in sign language. They saw the older kids, who were happy to be with other deaf children again, delightfully conversing away in 'sign' about their experiences during vacation. It was plain to see the parents were more frightened than their children. They were brave and tried to hide it. But twenty-five years as a priest has taught me to notice a lot. I wanted to hug them instead of the kids...and tell them I understand."

The curricula at the deaf school expanded as enrollment increased---by 2004, there would be forty-two children from three to ten years of age, coming from poor families all over Thailand. Now they were taught the English sign alphabet as well as the Thai (sign varied somewhat from country to country), along with lessons in "living"---manners and hygiene---the latter added when it was discovered that because they couldn't hear, and some families thought their children were "idiots"---Father Ray's word---they hadn't been taught even the most basic day-to-day stuff. The children also were instructed in lip reading and, when possible, given vocal training.

Friends and co-workers say Father Ray was fascinated by the deaf children, wondering what "language" they thought in. He never learned more than a few signs himself, so when he asked the teachers to ask signing children how they thought when they were young, they said they didn't remember. Academics say, unsurprisingly, that thought was comprised of images, so for the deaf it was a visual language that comprised their thought, images that were replaced, more or less, once the child learned how to sign, thus learning something that remained visual yet fitted more conventional language parameters.

For some common types of communication, there was no difference between the deaf and hearing worlds. "It has always amazed me," Father Ray wrote in 1983, "that although they cannot hear, the two sounds they make like any other human being are a cry or a laugh. If you heard them laugh, you would not know they cannot hear. The laugh is real and full of joy."

Chapter 10

It's not the worst jail in Thailand, far from it. But a jail is a jail is a jail, after all, and when Father Ray heard about a Nepalese man who had been locked up in a cell at the Department of Immigration in Bangkok for twenty-six years for nothing except entering the "Land of Smiles" illegally, the priest decided to do something about it.

It was 1980 and the immigration jail was then, as it is now, where what are called "illegal aliens" were kept prior to deportation, usually for no longer than a few months as the paperwork moved slowly through the Thai bureaucracy. Then they were free to leave both the jail and Thailand, presuming they had the money for transportation and a country to go to and, perhaps, an embassy to help.

In fact, many embassies didn't consider it their responsibility to look after their citizens, or apparent citizens, in foreign jails. Even if they do, they lose interest if the person is poor and has no record anywhere of his birth or residence, as is often the case with old people born in parts of Asia. In addition, many minority people in Asia are still stateless in the countries (Thailand among them) where they and their ancestors have been born and lived for generations. The officials of their countries of residence feel little or no responsibility for such minority people when they are home, never mind if they stray beyond their borders.

The old Nepalese man was in just such a bind. He had no proper identification---thus, officially, he didn't exist---so he could neither leave

Thailand nor pass through an immigration checkpoint to enter another country. He was a man without a country.

"This poor fellow never committed a crime," Father Ray said, "but simply did not have a passport. For those twenty-six years he was in immigration jail, he had not been outside even once. When I drove him from Bangkok to the Orphanage, it was like sitting in a car with Rip van Winkle. Everything was new to him…everything was beautiful…everything was breathtaking. He cried for a bit. I don't know if it was from happiness or frustration from losing so many years of his life.

"When I finally brought him to the Orphanage, I gave him a room and told him to make himself at home. I told him what time breakfast and lunch was served, and the time of dinner. I left him alone to his own doings and returned to my office to do some work. Late in the evening, the cook called and informed me the fellow had not come for lunch or supper. I immediately went to his room to find out why. He was still sitting in the same chair I put him in…in total darkness. He was afraid to turn on the light or leave the room because he thought he needed permission to do so. He was frightened. My heart bled for him when I realized how 'conditioned' he was. However, I am now very pleased to tell you he is doing well…out of his prison attitude, and even joking and laughing with the other old people.

"Each of the old people gets a private room, good medical care, and, of course, food and clothes. I give them each one hundred baht a week for their personal spending. When one of them dies, we cremate the body and put the ashes in the St. Nikolaus Cemetery. After every funeral, we bring the old people out for a meal. And to overcome their grief, we have some cold beer."

Although he had to post a U.S. $2,500 bond for each of the prisoners released to his care---a sum that was to be returned, without interest, upon the individual's death---Father Ray considered the responsibility a gift. "When I bury him, I want him to have spent his last period on earth enjoying the beauty of birds in flight, in the peace of a green shady tree."

Father Ray seemed enchanted by the old-timers and over time, they became running characters in his newsletters. The man who was incarcerated for twenty-six years was covered with tattoos. "From his neck to his ankles is a solid mass of purple dragons, mystic signs, birds, Buddhas, and even sacred writings in Sanskrit. One day I was looking at this living picture gallery and I asked him why he ever allowed himself to be decorated for life with tattoos. Although he is about seventy years old...a boyish, devilish smile came over his face. Then he told me (with a spry wink of one eye) that in 'his day' it really turned the girls on!! I never expected an answer like that, and I had to laugh. 'Yes,' he said, 'we didn't have television or even a radio in those days, so we did things people don't do today. We were able to show the girls how manly we were by having tattoo on our body. Sure, it hurt...but we pretended it did not just to impress the village girls of our virility. I had my whole body covered and let me tell you...the girls went crazy over me.' "

Another stateless resident came to Thailand from Vietnam after World War Two, walking across Cambodia, escaped detection for fifteen years, and then was arrested for having no documentation. A woman with the same legal problem had only one leg, and in her homemade wooden one where "she keeps her sewing kit, her money and other odds and ends which are important to her. She told me it is very convenient and better than a purse." Another man, who said he was Malaysian but had no papers to prove it, had a bad leg, as well, and one day decided he wouldn't walk again, remaining in his room for ten years.

And then there was Jimmy Exes, who drank. "We took the old stateless people out for a meal recently," Father Ray wrote. "As usual, it was a great success. Because they have not got good teeth, we have to order soft foods. Some of them would prefer the softest of foods...beer, without food. We had both. Jimmy, eighty-seven years old, kept stealing the beer of Miss Prani, eighty-three years old, who finally whacked Jimmy over the head with a big Chinese spoon. Blood came, so I had to run to the car for the first aid kit. Jimmy continued directing his criminal activities toward the others. Before the meal ended, Jimmy fell asleep at the table amidst the complaints from the others that he had consumed their beer. It was a picture to behold…a big band-aid on his bald head, slumped over in deep sleep with a satisfied but wicked smile on his face."

If the pace was understandably slow in the small building that housed the dozen or so residents, it also was sometimes confused. The married couple who ran the home, Pranom Taowlim and her husband Amnoy, had been with Father Ray for as long as he had the home, joining the orphanage family in 1980. They were still there in 2004. Initially Amnoy was a general handyman, Pranom a caregiver in the baby room. Both took full-time supervisory positions at the stateless in 1987. They described the home as a mini-United Nations. Jimmy, the drinker, was an Australian. The man who stayed in his room for ten years was Malaysian. Others were Burmese and Chinese.

Father Ray told a story about one of them: "Did you know there are so many Chinese dialects that people from different parts of China cannot talk to each other without using a pencil and paper? The written Chinese language is the same…but the spoken is different. Hence you can understand the difficult problem we have with one of our newly arrived old people. He only speaks one language…Chinese! But it is a rare dialect of Chinese and only one other old person is able to understand it. That other old person only speaks two dialects of Chinese and nothing else. So after he gets a message from our new arrival, he translates it to a third Chinese who speaks one dialect of Chinese and English, but that latter person cannot speak Thai! So the third person tells me in English and I translate it into Thai for the nurses. Five people are involved in the whole translation. Have you ever played the game where the first person whispers into the ear of the person next to him, and it is passed down the line until the end? If so, you will understand the strange request I received for a case of very sharp swords!! After lengthy interrogation, the poor man simply wanted a package of razor blades."

Another time, Father Ray reported that the stateless people "get into arguments almost every day. The latest was over a picture frame that somehow became crooked on the wall. It was a simple matter to just straighten it again…but they decided someone had to be blamed for making it crooked. They blamed a poor fellow who is confined to a wheelchair as the guilty culprit. The guy could not even reach the picture if he stretched his arms up to the fullest. When I asked how he could possibly be the guilty party, there was silence. Then someone spoke up and said he does it when he slams the door of his room. 'He does not know how to close a door, he can only slam it.' I straightened the picture, opened the refrigerator and gave everyone a nice cold beer. Fellowship blossomed."

It sounded like the premise for a Broadway play, a television show, or a film, something like Neil Simon's hit of a few years earlier (1975), *The Sunshine Boys*. This was a play that started on Broadway and moved to Hollywood with Walter Matthau and George Burns playing two cranky ex-vaudevillians who are persuaded to re-team for a TV special. Simon used the same premise earlier in *The Odd Couple* (1968) and someone else took the winning formula back to the big screen in two films, *Grumpy Old Men* and *Grumpier Old Men* (1993 and 1995), all starring Jack Lemmon and Matthau again.

Father Ray's version could have been a big hit, too. As cantankerous as Walter Matthau. With palm trees and tattoos.

Chapter 11

In 1983, a writer for *Reader's Digest* counted on the Orphanage grounds seven-hundred-and-fifty chickens (producing between three-hundred and four-hundred eggs a day; the eggs not eaten were sold to pay for the chicken feed) along with fifty-eight pigs, forty geese, thirty ducks, eight cows, a pond full of catfish, and approximately ninety children. Many of the children helped with the livestock under the guidance of salaried, professional staff. When visitors came to the Orphanage, the youngsters clamored to be the ones to take them to see the animals.

"I feel so far this year, it has really been a 'heart rewarding' six months," Father Ray wrote in the summer newsletter. "The children are a year older and I am a year younger." He then added that "we are going through a 'tooth losing' period, as the younger children are surrendering to new strong pillars of munching power, which are pushing their way up looking for space to grow. We have no Tooth Fairy in Thailand, so there is no coin under the pillow in the morning. But we have a prize for the owners of such marvelous discarded dentals … a trip in my car with me and no other kids. They think that is a really great treat. Perhaps we will only go to the market or the post office, but we have gone alone, special like!! Of course, it usually means some kind of a treat, too…but that is incidental."

The older children were more numerous now, going off to government school in clean uniforms every day, Father Ray often driving the rickety old van or bus, and when they returned from class, several went not to the old dormitory they had inhabited, but to rooms with a double bunk, located in a new building. "One problem is who will sleep with whom," he wrote. "That is not an easy thing to solve. But the biggest problem is keeping their rooms tidy. Today, I went on 'inspection,' like the army. It was hilarious. There was a great rush to get into the rooms before I got there. I heard hasty noises such as drawers opening and things being stuffed inside. Also, brooms being used as secretly as possible. It was the first of many more inspections I will make, but they will never know when I will come again. It doesn't make any difference anyway, since whenever I tell the children I am 'VERY ANGRY,' all they do is laugh."

On days when the kids were to be tested at school, they rubbed the priest's ample waistline before leaving the Orphanage grounds or leaving the bus, rather in the same way the round belly of the Happy Buddha is touched to bring good luck. "They love to pat it and comment on its girth," he wrote. "Their eternal question is what do I eat to get such a big stomach. The real answer is Thai beer, but I can't tell them that. So I tell them various things like 'I eat little boys and girls who do not get good grades in school'! Of course they laugh at that, but I have noticed their grades have improved!"

The same year, 1983, the Orphanage experienced its first crib death. The child was one of those whose parents were in jail. "Of course, we worried the mother would think we simply did not take good care of the child," Father Ray wrote. "However, the opposite happened. The mother said she knew we were taking excellent care of the child and she doesn't hold us responsible in any way. I was very grateful to her for those words of comfort. It's strange, we went to comfort her...and she ended up giving us comfort."

The population overall was growing, too. Nearly all of the cribs were double occupancy and the increasing numbers of school-aged children could be explained in part by the continuing problem of obtaining documentation of birth, which was required for adoption. (Father Ray negotiated an off-the-record agreement with the local school system to accept those kids without the papers.) Without a birth certificate, no government identification card could be issued until the child was fifteen, by which time he or she was considered unadoptable. Few potential parents wanted a child older than three.

Moreover, Thais themselves rarely adopt a Thai child. This may sound odd to outsiders, but it was commonplace, rooted in the belief that some of the parents might be unmarried or engaged in prostitution or other crimes---too often true!---and that they might inherit the same tendencies. Others believed that the child was an orphan for the same reason a disabled child was disabled, the karmic consequence of misdeeds in an earlier life. Thus, an adopted child might bring bad luck to a family. Thus, the number of adoptions was low, as more and more children arrived.

"So far this year," Father Ray wrote in the summer of 1984, "five children have left the Orphanage for new homes. We have no Thai people asking to adopt this year. We have some considering to do so…but nothing firm. According to the regulations of the Thai authorities, we are allowed to have only eight children adopted by foreigners per year. We will certainly fill that quota."

Occasionally, Father Ray received letters from former American servicemen who admitted to having abandoned the children they fathered with Thai women. The priest's reaction was to try to shame them into helping, maybe even to the point of taking their kids to the United States. Some of the runaway fathers sent money. None showed any interest in assuming any more responsibility than that.

Pee was only a month old when his mother left him with a neighbor and said she'd return the next day; she did not, so the boy was sent to his grandmother, who was too old and poor to care for him. She took him to the local Catholic Church. Sao was born deaf and left at the Orphanage when his mother died. Bew's father deserted his wife while she was pregnant. Pao's father died before he was born; the mother already had seven children when Pao arrived and sales of green papaya salad at a roadside stall didn't provide the income for any more mouths. Dew's parents separated before he was born and he was in such poor condition when he arrived in Pattaya, he had to be given physical therapy in order to walk. Manit was in even worse health when he came, so he was hospitalized and the doctor didn't think he'd survive; he was in and out of the hospital for a year, recovering gradually.

Another boy arrived at the Orphanage so crippled that his legs were folded against his stomach. "We have had several operations on the child," Father Ray wrote, "with at least one more to come. His legs had to be put in plaster casts to straighten them out. He also has to wear special shoes. Now he walks, runs, jumps, and plays games just like any ordinary kid. A few days ago, we had games for the children...and one of the contests we had was in a three-wheel bicycle race for little kids. Believe it or not, the little fellow won."

In mid-1983, Father Ray composed a tribute to his own good spirit and health: "My heart is very young...and hence I have a feeling I will live a hundred more years. That is, of course, impossible, but although my intellect tells me so, something inside me whispers, 'Don't believe it!' I prefer to listen to the whisper. If I could tell you of my dreams, you would either think I was literally dreaming or just plain loco. A man needs a bit of both, especially in my job. A cool beer in the dead of the evening usually makes the dreams seem easier to accomplish!"

The truth is, his health had begun to slip, the years of cigarettes, over-eating, and lack of exercise had begun to take their toll. He had been in Asia for twenty-three years now and on his first holiday home leave in five years, as usual he visited family and friends, but this time he also sought medical care. He joked about his attempts to change his diet and quit smoking, but in what he called "the land of the big hamburger and malted milks," where everyone invited him to belly up to the table or bar, the man hardly ever said no and inevitably he returned to Thailand heavier than he was when he left.

A big man with a big heart is the way many described him. One of these was Sister Michelle Lopez, one of the Good Shepherds Sisters, an order based in France whose service was dedicated to oppressed women and children. Born and raised in Malaysia of Indian parents, her surname was that of the Catholic priest who converted her ancestors, an old practice in India when conversions took place.

The Mission of the Sisters of the Good Shepherd is 'to be a presence of Jesus the Good Shepherd' who approached each person with compassion, gentleness, acceptance and respect. The Sisters believe that through this approach they can awaken in those wounded by injustice, oppression and alienation a deep sense of their infinite worth and dignity as persons and instill in them a hope for the future

Sister Michelle was sent to Thailand in 1975. In 1988, she went to Pattaya. That was when an American who ran a bar called Two Buffaloes walked into Father Ray's office. Unannounced and apparently somewhat inebriated, he said he'd had enough of Thailand and he was going home and he wanted to give the priest his bar. Father Ray told him to think about it and if he still wanted to do it, to come back the following day. The man returned, sober, and said he hadn't changed his mind. He then signed over the lease to a three-story shophouse in central Pattaya in which his bar was located and walked out. Father Ray never heard from him again.

Though he would have found ready use for the building if it were on the Orphanage property, he didn't need space downtown. He had met Sister Michelle, who had talked about opening a drop-in center that taught English and sewing to prostitutes, so he gave her the lease. The Fountain of Life Women's Centre was thus founded in 1988, as a Non-Formal Education center providing information on a wide variety of subjects such as trafficking, HIV/AIDS, women's empowerment, language proficiency, computer skills, literacy classes, dressmaking, hairdressing and Thai language. The truth was, Sister Michelle said, "we wanted to give them dignity. Poverty without dignity is the worst."

In the early days, she and a Buddhist nun walked along the Pattaya beachfront and went into the bars to tell the women about The Fountain of Life. "The women who came were so thirsty for so much and they felt so refreshed after visiting us," she said. "And they were a reminder to us that we needed to be refreshed as well.

Father Ray was a person-centered person in a most unusual and creative way. He came to the center and listened to the women. We could not have done it without his love."

Nor did the priest believe that he could have accomplished what he did without help, and he was always ready to say thanks. "Whatever gets accomplished over here, you share the good that is done," he wrote in a typical note. "It will probably interest you to know that I daily remind my 'Boss Upstairs' of the people helping me. What he does about it, I don't know. But if he does something at my end, he must be doing something at your end. I keep reminding Him it's a 'package deal.' He has not complained yet!"

In nearly all his newsletters, and in his personal correspondence, Father Ray referred to God as The Boss Upstairs, and sometimes as The Big Boss Upstairs. "I have asked The Boss Upstairs to credit your heavenly account," he wrote in one letter of thanks. Another time: "The Boss Upstairs says He will not forget you, and I can assure you He is very reliable." Again, during a period of extreme drought, he wrote, "I don't expect The Boss Upstairs to give me a miraculous spring like Lourdes...but a little more rain would help."

It was almost Disneyesque and some might have said that he was trivializing God, giving him such a cartoonish nature, but Father Ray was not being disrespectful, he believed he was only making Him more accessible.

"God is good!," he wrote. "So between His help and yours, we got it made!"

"God bless you...keep me and the kids in your prayers to The Boss Upstairs."

Chapter 12

However strapped he always was for cash, there was something Father Ray put at the top of the year's calendar for which he spared little energy or expense. This was Christmas, the day that topped the Christian year and the one that brought back so many memories of his school holidays in America.

Even when he was still the parish priest at St. Nikolaus, up until 1978, Father Ray went all out. Of course, all Christian churches do strut their stuff a bit for the celebration of Jesus Christ's birth. But the prankster from Chicago usually went the extra mile. Betty Roy remembered one Christmas Eve when he ran a wire overhead running from one side of the church to the other. On a signal from Father Ray, using a simple pulley, someone standing below was to pull on a rope and a star would travel along the wire. At the halfway point, it fell, crashing in front of the pulpit.

"Another time," Betty said, "Joe [her husband] was asked to play his trumpet to accompany a Thai choir from Sri Racha when they sang Christmas carols, in English. Well, there wasn't any rehearsal and the choir mispronounced all the words and couldn't sing on key. That was the year Father Gautreaux gave the sermon and told the story of Christ's birth. Father Brennan had it all set up and five fireworks fountains were to go off on each side of the church, outside in the garden. This was supposed to happen just as Father Gautreaux got to the part about the child being born. But they didn't all go off. They kept going off all through the rest of the sermon. Father Gautreaux made a good recovery. After the last of the fireworks, he asked everyone to sing 'Silent Night' together in their own languages."

At the Orphanage, no less effort was expended, although generally there were no stunts or attempts at special effects. For Father Ray, as for most Christian families, Christmas was a time when relatives gathered together…and that generated enough excitement by itself. The Orphanage was well established in both its rhythm and reputation by the time Father Ray left St. Nikolaus, and its occupants may have been half a world away from the Brennans and O'Connells in America, but they comprised a true family for the priest and he was its undeniable patriarch.

A majority of the children were born into Buddhist families and no attempt was ever made to convert them to the Catholic faith. Yes, Mass was said for the numerous Catholic children in his care, and all were taught Christmas carols and the story of Christ's birth. There were other occasions when the priest wore his collar or robes rather than the usual slacks and polo shirt. Nuns in their habits served as teachers and caretakers. And there were Christian crosses and other religious reminders in his office and hanging on the walls. In many ways, it was clear that this was an organization with clear and strong Catholic connections.

However, Father Ray often told interviewers who asked about attempts to convert that he wasn't the least interested in trying. "There are enough halfway Christians in the world already," he said, "and if the kids are good Buddhists, I'm perfectly happy."

Because Father Ray wrote a newsletter every year at Christmas time, the details of that holiday were amply chronicled. In the early years, he talked of the Orphanage's rickety movie projector, always repaired in time for Christmas…of the effort that went into purchasing or acquiring gifts (about US$20 was spent on each child, far more than was spent outside the Orphanage)…and of the various ways Santa Claus arrived on Christmas morning to help distribute the gifts. Father Ray by now needed no extra padding to fill the red and white suit, but the year he arrived in a hot air balloon; in the excitement, he'd forgotten his beard.

Next to the gift-giving, surely Father Ray's favorite celebration was in what he called "The World Famous and Stupendous Brennan Christmas Singing and

Dancing Children's Troupe of Pattaya." This became a tradition, too, and from the 1980s onwards, he took the children to many of the tourist hotels in Pattaya to sing carols. It was an exercise that, for the kids, was great fun and a confidence builder as well. It also kept the Orphanage in the public eye, inspiring both local businesses and visitors to contribute in some way if they could.

Father Ray wrote in the 1985 newsletter that "Jingle Bells" and "Silent Night" were being performed in sign language by deaf children, an effort that was "louder than the combined voices of the La Scala Opera Company. People sit in reverent silence while watching them 'sign' a song with their hands. When the applause comes, even though the deaf children can't hear it, they are thrilled and even shake with excitement. Of course, the deaf kids are only a part of our great little Christmas show, which we do in the hotels. The real showstopper is the little orphans singing and dancing."

"Hotels put us in the middle of their Christmas Eve show. By the time we have finished our little fifteen-minute performance, people have been injected with a Christmas spirit only children can give. The hotel guests are standing on their chairs applauding and roaring, 'Bravo!' The entire place goes wild. I pity whoever follows us on that stage."

Shopping for presents began months ahead of time and so no children could stumble upon them---or find them in a search---many were stashed in Father Ray's modest quarters, which were off-limits to virtually everyone, and in locked closets.

"We start wrapping presents in early December and do not finish until just about a day or two before Christmas," Father Ray explained. "My bedroom is filled with model boats and airplane kits, cherry-cheeked dolls of all sizes, wind-up toys, Chinese checker games, model race cars, pickup sticks, etc. The girls will treasure the sample perfume bottles [contributed by wholesalers and shops], along with the dainty hankies and scarves.

"The older girls are becoming very sophisticated now and have expressed a desire to pick out their own Christmas gifts. (They say I have no 'taste'!!) So we are bringing them to Bangkok for their shopping spree in a big department store. I [no longer] accompany them since they tell me I am useless. Whatever dress they try on, I always say it looks nice. (It does, but they don't believe me!)."

For Father Ray, Christmas was a marathon. On Christmas day, following an eve of leading his charges into half a dozen hotels and giving a midnight Mass and falling into bed about 1:30, he drove the kilometer to the Orphanage. The gifts were arranged on long tables. The kids were served breakfast, caring little about the food, eyeing the array of colorfully wrapped bags---and in later years, large boxes---each full of presents, one for every child. Christmas songs were next, drawing out the suspense to the almost unbearable.

Finally, after Father Ray said a few words, the children's names were called out and the gifts were finally---finally!---distributed. Every kid got one big present and many smaller ones, along with any gifts that were sent by a child's sponsor.

What came next was akin to bedlam, as Father Ray described the scene. "[T]o see little tykes lugging away boxes almost as big as themselves, then to watch the suspense and happiness on their faces as they savagely rip off the colored paper and dig into these wonderful 'goodies' that are all theirs...as more and more children receive their gifts, the room where everything gets unwrapped gets fuller and fuller.

"It also takes on all kinds of sounds besides the ripping of gift wrapping off the boxes. All sorts of mechanical toys start to whirl and whine. A new atmosphere develops, as each child cannot wait to show someone, anyone, what they have received. At that time, an adult has to make sounds like, 'Ohhh, wow, etc.' In the meantime, the other kids are trying to push that child out of the way so they can show what they received.

"It does not take an hour from the time the children receive their gifts till there is a line of kids wanting new batteries. Everything nowadays seems to need a battery. I would like to suggest to the toy makers they work on making solar powered toys. When you have a couple of hundred kids running their new toys until the battery gives out, it's time to think of a different power source."

As the years passed, and some of the children reached adolescence, their desires changed along with their height and level of sophistication. "This year [1991] I had the kids write down in priority three things they wanted for Christmas. I told them they would not get all three…but they had a good chance of getting at least one item on the list. What they wrote surprised me, to say the least. I suddenly realized that some of my kids were not kids any more, but young adults wanting young adult things. I was thinking of toy airplanes, rockets, cars with flashing lights, etc. They were thinking of imitation Walkmans, waterproof backpacks, soccer shoes, waterproof wristwatches, a table lamp, and specific books about the 'Green' movement, anatomy, and space. It was somewhat of a shock to me…but a pleasant one. How come they are getting older and I am not?"

Chapter 13

The Orphanage's Mother Superior was also a superior object of the jokes, an innocent "victim" of Father Ray's schoolboyish sense of what was and wasn't funny.

"If only," Father Ray wrote in 1984, "she had a sense of humor. I was fixing toys with that marvelous strong glue when she came into my office and put her clipboard down. She placed it on a big circle of glue I had just mixed. I tried to stop her, but it was too late. Before I could speak, she saw I was excited about something, so she immediately put the board on her lap. Naturally, the glue stuck to her robes. Then when I explained about the glue, she tried to use her hands to wipe the glue off the back of the board. She did not know that epoxy glue can only be taken off with a special solvent. By the time she left my office, she was a total wreck. The super glue was on her shoes, her hand, her robes and even on one ear. For some reason she would not let me use the solvent on her. She said one of the other sisters would do it. After warning her that this is a super fast-drying glue, she took the solvent and ran. Ever since that day, she has never been the same when she comes to my office."

In this fashion, Father Ray used Sister Nomchit Aripak for comedy relief, not only in his newsletters but also as respite from the stress and sadness that accompanied the joys associated with the daily operation of the Orphanage. He always wore a happy face in the letters, but it didn't take great effort to see the grim harshness of reality, and the letters reflected that, too.

In addition to young refugees, by the 1980s Father Ray was accepting the children of women being held in Thai prisons. By Thai law, women who were detained while pregnant were permitted to keep their babies with them for a year, but then the children had to go. Some went to Father Ray.

As the priest so often said, every child had a story. For example, the hospital in Sri Racha said it had no information about Narin's mother, who simply got out of bed and walked out of the building without anyone seeing her leave; the hospital kept the boy for a year, thinking his mom would return, but she did not.

"Phaiboon's parents are both construction laborers who lived together for some time before the father decided to go his own way, leaving the mother soon after she discovered she was pregnant," was the way one of the case studies of the other orphans began. "In the later stages of pregnancy, she became unfit for work, so some of the other laborers took care of her until the baby was born. When the mother became strong enough, she decided to go back home to the north of Thailand with the baby. The laborers all chipped in and gave her money for the bus fare. On the way from Rayong to Bangkok, she saw the Pattaya Orphanage sign from the bus. She brought her baby in…"

Ping's mother didn't have enough milk to feed her. Sao was born deaf and was left at the Orphanage by his father when the mother died. Sang's mother was almost always ill and found it impossible to raise the child; relatives refused to take the girl into their care. Tae and his sister Bim came after their blind parents divorced. Pee's mother left him with a neighbor a few days after his birth and never returned. The illegitimate children of Pattaya prostitutes provided another steady source. One newborn was found abandoned in a dumpster.

The stories went on and on. Each child was different, as was his or her story, the details of which for many would always remain a mystery. But the patterns of poverty and need were common and set, unchangeable.

Mother Superior was now called Sister Shark by Father Ray because if her surname was slightly mispronounced, it sounded like the Thai word for shark. Besides her level-headed administrative skills, she also provided a sort of comic relief, both to Father Ray and to the growing numbers of people on his newsletter mailing list. Frequently, he made himself the butt of the joke.

"Mother Superior has taken a new tack with me," he wrote. "As most of you know already, Mother Superior considers me one of the children, a bit more advanced than the ordinary orphan, but still retarded for my age. She has recently begun to repeat things to me, the second time more slowly than the first time. She also has developed the strange habit of looking at the ceiling when she repeats things. The second time she repeats, the words come out not only more slowly but louder. Like she is talking to God up there, and He is partially deaf. I accept these strange new foibles because they are rather harmless. It keeps her quiet and probably helps her feel fulfillment. I just look at her and smile. It's the same smile I have learned off the kids."

On a trip to Europe he bought her a box of chocolates several months in advance of her birthday. Father Ray confessed that he'd forgotten that because of the heat in Thailand, locally-made chocolate contained vast amounts of paraffin so it wouldn't melt, while European chocolate did not. So when Sister Shark was given the present and she opened the box, what appeared to be a thousand ants were dining happily. She thanked him for the "kind thought," the priest reported, and as he was leaving her office, he "saw her give the other Sisters a look of exasperation, the kind she reserves for children who have flunked their grades or immature priests."

Following another home leave, Father Ray wrote, "Ordinarily when she has some business with me, she simply comes to see me when it suits her convenience. However, when she asks for a formal appointment (she is the only one who ever asks for one), I prepare myself by doing such things as drinking a cup of battery acid, chewing up and swallowing a dozen steel ball bearings, and finally, just before she arrives (on time! As you would expect) I begin practicing my growling and coughing routine...

"I hear the sound of determined black leather clad celibate feet zeroing in on my office door. Suddenly, as they reach the front of my office, they stop and there is silence.   Perhaps she is readjusting her robes or whatever…but there is a sudden dead silence. I now understand how the English people felt during World War Two when those V[1] rockets abruptly cut their engines and began their silent downward plunge of destruction. There is a gentle knock on the door and I rise to receive Her Majesty."

Chapter 14

When the American couple came to Father Ray in 1977 to adopt a child, they---and even Father Ray himself---had no idea how many hurdles would have to be leaped, how many hoops would have to be jumped through.

By the late 1970s, the routine of adopting a child was just that, routine, but it also was rigidly regulated by law, and where the "adoption" of children in some other Southeast Asian countries was no more complicated than knowing where to go and how much to pay in the babies-for-sale underground, Father Ray insisted that everything be done by the book, satisfying the laws of the adoptee's new country as well as those of Thailand.

One of the first things done when a new child arrived at the Orphanage was to learn as much as possible about his or her birth. This was, and always would be, difficult in many cases and impossible in some, such as when a child had been abandoned, or when the mother gave birth at home, or when a mother left the hospital with the infant before bothering to fill out the required documents (often because she didn't have the money to pay the small hospital bill). In these cases, the birth was never registered. In addition, many of the births were illegitimate---that is, there were no fathers standing by and willing to take some credit and responsibility---and that gave many of the mothers another reason, out of shyness and shame, to fail to take legal steps. In still other cases, the mothers didn't know who the fathers were.

Without proper documentation, a child born in Thailand was regarded as a non-entity. He or she could not attend a government school or, later in life, own property. Without an official identity card, age couldn't be proved, which meant the individuals could be prevented from entering a bar or driving a car or voting. Many job possibilities would be closed to them. And they couldn't be adopted.

According to Thailand's Child Adoption Act of 1979, all adoptions by foreigners living abroad had to be processed through the Public Welfare Department or a legally authorized child welfare agency and then approved by the Child Adoption Board. Numerous documents were required, including not only a home study report, but also a statement asserting that the applicants were "legally qualified according to the adoption law of their country and are suitable to be adoptive parents of a foreign child according to the social standard of their country."

Further, the would-be adoptive parents had to submit a medical certificate "verifying good physical health and mental stability, and, in some cases, an indication of the applicants' infertility." Documents certifying marriage and occupation and income and financial status and assets were demanded. Two references were needed as well, along with a letter from the foreign country's immigration authority approving the child's immigration.

Once all this paperwork was assembled, every certificate, form, and report had to be "certified by the Thai embassy or consulate in that particular country" and documents in foreign languages were required in Thai or English translation along with the originals. In sum, it seemed almost insurmountable.

When Thom brought her infant son to Father Ray in October 1977, she provided a birth certificate, along with a story the priest and others at the Orphanage had heard too many times. The nineteen-year-old mother said the boy's father---to whom she was not married---had abandoned her and she was unable to support the child, named Khalom Priyakoot (the surname was the father's, as shown on the birth certificate), then just three weeks old. A resident of Udon Thani in Thailand's poor Northeast, she readily agreed to surrender all rights to "further guardianship and care...in any event whatsoever." This gave Father Ray the right to put the boy up for adoption.

In 1979, Danny and Harriet Scott from Columbia, the capital city of South Carolina, in the United States, expressed an interest in adopting Khalom. He was then eighteen months old, one of dozens of children his age in what by now was being called "Pattaya's largest family." Mr. Scott was a partner in a law firm and Mrs. Scott owned two shops that sold children's clothing. They had one child of their own, a daughter, then seven, named Riley.

Most adoptions took at least a year, and in this case it was three years before all the legal requirements were satisfied. During this time, following a visit to the Orphanage, the Scotts were kept advised of the child's development through letters and photographs. Then suddenly, with only eight days' notice, placement was approved. This was the next, but not the final step. This was "placement" only, not adoption.

Mrs. Scott flew to Thailand to get the boy and upon the five-year-old's arrival in South Carolina, in February 1982, the arduous task of adapting to a new culture and country for began. Over the next six months, visits to the Scott home were made by the Children's Bureau of South Carolina, a state-operated social welfare agency, with reports going back to Father Ray. In the second of three, written in June, it was reported that Matthew, as he was renamed, though small for his age, had grown two inches since the first home visit, and his English was improving.

It also was reported that he was to be tutored before entering kindergarten in the fall. The boy sucked his thumb, sometimes he went to his sister's bed in the middle of the night, and he hadn't yet accepted beef, the social worker wrote, but he was showing some interest in bread.

In the final post-placement visit, in September, Father Ray was told, "We arrived at the home as Mrs. Scott was bringing Matthew and two of his friends from kindergarten. Matthew appears to get along with these boys, and during my visit he was back and forth to their homes next door. The Scotts feel Matthew's adjustment is far better than they had anticipated. He makes friends easily and you sense that he feels himself a part of this family group. Mrs. Scott served ice cream and Matthew brought most of the plates to the table, folded the napkins very carefully and placed the spoon on top of the napkin."

A medical report showed the youngster to be in good health. His teacher said he "really fits things together well." And the report concluded, "We believe the bonds of love and affection have been established between the parents and this child, and we are recommending that legal adoption proceedings be initiated if you concur."

More time passed before the last documents were stamped and filed. To satisfy South Carolina law, the boy's natural father had to be located (as his name was on the birth certificate) and he had to agree to waive all his rights. He was found and he agreed and finally the adoption was approved and Khalom Priyakoot legally became Matthew Daniel Scott.

This was not the last to be heard from the boy. Years later, Matt returned to Thailand on a search for his biological mother and found himself splashed all over the front pages and making TV news. The story will be continued.

(Above) Father Ray's parents, Norrine and Walter Brennan; this photograph was in his office until he died and remains in place, although the office is now used as a conference room

(Right) Ray at his First Communion, about age seven

(Above) First row, second from right,
Fr. Leo McNamara (Father Mac), a
close family friend, other men are
unidentified; second row left is Fr.
Thomas Conlin, another friend,
Father Ray in the military uniform,
aged thirteen; mom is holding his
sister Sharron; in the rear is
Jerome McNamara, Fr. Mac's
brother and Sharron's godfather

(Right) Ray in his military school
uniform, about age nine

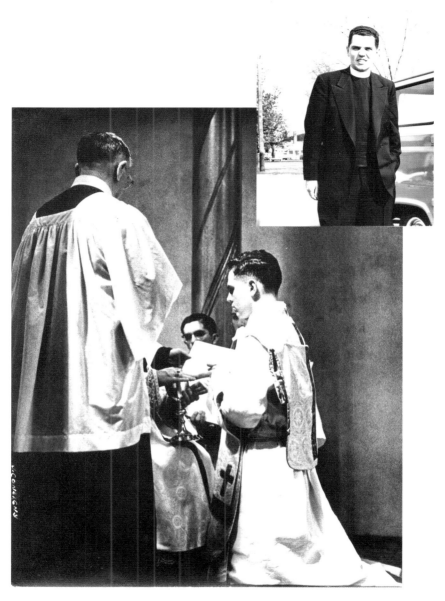

(Above) Father Ray is ordained in
Oconomowoc, Wisconsin, July 2, 1959

(Inset) Undated photo of the young priest

Father Ray meets with villagers in a
remote village in northeastern Thailand
in the late 1960s, in what is called a *sala*,
an open-sided structure with a grass roof
and plaited coconut frond back wall; the
stilts and ladder give the *sala* protection
from flooding and snakes

(Above, left) Father Ray with the methane generator that turned elephant poop into cooking gas

(Above, right) An old concrete mixer was used to wash diapers

(Left) Father Ray with an unidentified woman outside the trailer that served as his first office and was "donated" by a sympathetic American soldier in a nearby military base

The sign prominently displayed on his
desk reveals Father Ray's philosophy
and the permanent state of his desk

(Above) St. Nikolaus Church, showing typical Thai architectural design

(Right) The leafy Orphanage grounds make children from villages feel at home; the first Orphanage structure is in the rear right

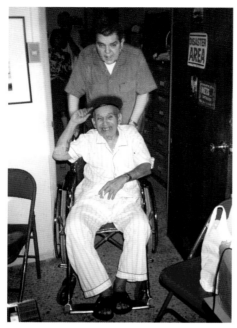

(Above, left) Father Ray assists Jimmy, one of his elderly charges from the government's Immigration Jail

(Above, right and left) Two young orphans being comforted by their friends

(Above and right)
Two snapshots in the baby room, showing the cheery atmosphere, the rows of cribs, and bottle preparation at feeding time

9

Father Ray's whimsical chapel, constructed in traditional Thai design, its exterior walls decorated with broken pieces of tile and porcelain, an architectural eccentricity introduced in the 19th century by King Mongkut to one of the most famous temples in Thailand, Bangkok's Wat Arun; notice the full plates beneath the eaves

The interior walls of the chapel were covered,
in the style found in Thai temple murals, with
illustrations telling some of the best-loved
Bible stories, always remaining faithful to
Thai settings, hairstyles and dress; here, Jesus
is turning water brought from the river in Thai
clay jars into wine

(Above) Jesus sits in a Thai village after producing "loaves and fishes," another New Testament miracle given a Thai spin in the chapel

(Right) The familiar crenellated walls that surround the Grand Palace in Bangkok and many other official and religious compounds throughout Thailand come to mind in this gathering of worshippers

(Right) Jesus is crucified
and, in what perhaps was
the most startling scene
(above), is carried to
Heaven in the chariot of
the Hindu god Krishna,
drawn by four white
horses

Father Ray met Mother Teresa in Calcutta

Chapter 15

In the beginning when there were medical problems---and with abandoned infants, there were almost always problems---Father Ray took the children to local clinics or, in an emergency, to the hospital in Sri Racha. The hospital in Pattaya was regarded as too expensive. A year before Father Ray accepted the first child, a young pediatrician named Sophaphan Puenpatom was at that Sri Racha hospital, but it would be several years before they met.

Dr. Sophaphan was trained at Siriraj Hospital in Thonburi, across the Chao Phrya River from Bangkok, and following graduation went to the United States for pediatric training at Philadelphia General Hospital, an institution that was connected to the University of Pennsylvania and its medical school. There, she trained for five years, serving her internship and residency, specializing in neonatology, the care of newborns.

A classmate in Thailand who was four years her senior, Mesyon Puenpatom, accompanied her to America and after spending some time in Salt Lake City, he went to Philadelphia and worked at Hahnemann Hospital. He was an anesthesiologist, but had some pediatric training. When the two young doctors returned together to Sri Racha, both were offered jobs with housing at Sri Racha Hospital, an institution founded by one of the wives of King Chulalongkorn, who reigned from 1868 to 1910. It was considered the most beautiful care center in all of Thailand and one of the most modern.

But it wasn't until the 1960s that the hospital began to add medical specialists to the staff. Dr. Sophaphan and Dr. Mesyon, soon to be married, were among the earliest. She opened the hospital's first clinic for kids and was the hospital's first doctor trained abroad. That's when she began seeing the children from the Orphanage and in 1979 or 1980---she doesn't recall exactly---she was asked to join the Orphanage staff and she said no. But she volunteered her time, without pay, one day a week, on Saturdays…and, she added, during the week she would continue to see the orphans at the hospital clinic. She also gave Father Ray her home telephone number for emergencies.

Father Ray said he didn't want Dr. Sophaphan's charity; he wanted to pay her. Again the pediatrician refused. He asked her to take a dozen eggs a week, said he had a surplus, and again she said no. Not only that, she began bringing her husband to the Orphanage too. Neither of them, she hastened to say, was a Catholic.

This bears remarking. From the Orphanage's beginning, many of the teachers and caretakers, paid and unpaid, were not Catholic, and this would characterize Father Ray's organization and efforts for more than thirty years. An individual's specific religious belief was irrelevant, to Father Ray and to those who chose to help.

"Father Ray came here, a foreigner, and he gave so much to Thailand," Dr. Sophaphan said. "It didn't cost me anything. I just brought my brain and my skills and it made me feel better to do what I could."

She was provided with a high-ceilinged space on the ground floor at the back of the Orphanage building, adjacent to the baby room. It measured about six by ten meters (eighteen by thirty feet) and had big windows on two sides that let in soft light, muted by tropical trees. The floor was tiled and the furnishings were basic, including an examination table, a few chairs, a sink, a shelf for medication and other supplies. It would be years before there was a cabinet with a lock to house the medicine. The cries of babies provided a background that subsumed the sound of an overhead, racketing fan.

Dr. Sophaphan recalled that there were well under a hundred children at the Orphanage when she started. She administered to them all, as well as the children at the deaf school. The most common complaints were upper and lower respiratory problems, pneumonia, bronchitis, chicken pox, measles, and diarrhea. Measles was accompanied by high fever and that sometimes led to pneumonia, which sent children to the Sri Racha hospital. She saw the newborns and babies, and her husband treated the older children. Together they saw as many as fifty to sixty children every Saturday.

Not all of the children they saw were sick. When one was being adopted, Dr. Sophaphan did the required medical examinations and reports. When children arrived at the Orphanage without birth certificates and none could be found, she estimated a date of birth and, in time, that was accepted by the government. She also advised the kitchen staff on nutrition.

"Rice and banana at the start," she said, "adding eggs at about five months. Then agar at seven months…" And every child was given vitamins.

It wasn't always easy. "We didn't have any information about many of the children, didn't know their family or medical histories. If children got early care, they didn't have so many problems later. Many, if not nearly all, of the children that came to us had problems when they arrived."

Later, she said, as the baby room filled, the cribs were lined up like open shoe boxes on a shelf, and most were double occupied. That meant that when one infant got sick, the illness moved rapidly along the line of cribs, infecting dozens, sometimes the entire ward.

"In a hospital, there are regulations about separating the cribs by at least one meter," Dr. Sophaphan said. "We didn't have that kind of space."

In 1979, Father Ray reported in his newsletter, "One of the babies broke out with measles. We isolated the child immediately, but as more children became affected, the doctor advised us that we might as well let it run its course since there was no way to control it. Eventually, every child in the babies' room, forty-four of them, caught it and was sick. Many developed complications and here was a steady stream of babies going to the hospital thirty kilometers away for special attention. But like all unpleasant things, the measles passed and it was a joy to see the children bounce back with smiles on their faces and livelier than ever. Many of you have experienced measles in your family. Can you imagine what it is like when forty-four children come down with them more or less at the same time? This crisis descended on the new Sisters just a month after they assumed care of the children. It was their baptism under fire!!"

A few years later, in 1984, all the kids in the deaf school got measles as well and were sent to their homes for two weeks.

As more visitors to the Orphanage arrived and were taken on a tour, unknowingly they sometimes brought germs with them, Dr. Sophaphan said, and that added more risk to the equation. Father Ray figured the physical contact, the love that was given to the infants by these visitors, and by a growing number of volunteers, was worth any slight jeopardy.

Every Saturday, the older children lined up with the week's new infections and for a check of any broken bones that might have been set earlier at the hospital. Dr. Sophaphan said that, especially amongst the older boys, there were a lot of fractured arms and legs.

"After watching the movie Superman," Father Ray wrote in a newsletter in 1996, "one little tyke put on a red cape and proclaimed himself as the 'Orphanage Superman.' He raised his arms into the air and shouted, 'Superman can fly like a bird!' He then bravely jumped from the second floor and broke his leg."

Chapter 16

It was one of the twentieth century's most recognized names in religion, Monsignor (later Bishop) Fulton J. Sheen, who suggested the unique style of the Holy Redeemer Church, the massive building constructed by the Redemptorists in Bangkok as their primary place of worship. On a visit to that city in the early 1950s, the monsignor told Father Roger Godbout, "When you get around to building a church, why not build it in the style of Thai architecture?" The Redemptorists accepted the advice and in 1954, what became one of the largest Catholic churches in Thailand was blessed.

"Put very simply," Father Pat Morrissy wrote in a small book, published in 1998, commemorating the Golden Jubilee of the Redemptorists in Thailand, "it looked like a Buddhist temple, with a tiered and slanted roof of multi-colored tiles. The doors were framed in gold leaf and only a cross over the front gave a hint to its actually being a Catholic church. It was an idea that received opposition from Thai and foreigner alike at that time. But Father Godbout has been proved absolutely right in taking the course he did." However controversial its design, it fit perfectly in a city scattered with similarly styled Buddhist temples.

The same approach was taken when St. Nikolaus Church was designed in Pattaya and, later, when Father Ray decided to build a chapel on newly-acquired property that would house the Redemptorist Vocational School for the Disabled and a hostel with facilities for conferences. But now he wanted to go a step further. A giant step further. He wanted to do something that had never been done. Not only did he want Thai architectural design for the building itself, he also wanted the exterior walls to be decorated with broken pieces of porcelain, an architectural eccentricity introduced in the nineteenth century by King Mongkut to one of the most famous temples in Thailand, Wat Arun…and, more radically, he wanted the interior walls to be covered floor to ceiling in the Thai fashion with minutely-detailed murals. Such elaborate artwork depicting the Buddha's previous lives was commonplace in Thai temples, so, Father Ray decided, his chapel walls would illustrate various scenes from the Bible…andthey would be executed by a Thai artist in traditional Thai style.

The result was as shocking as it was beautiful.

Typically, when it came to the execution of his dream, Father Ray was forced to scrounge and improvise. When King Mongkut embedded the Khmer-style tower of Wat Arun in the mid-19th century with a mosaic of broken, multi-hued porcelain, he had the use of tons of old chinaware brought to Bangkok as ballast in Chinese ships then trading with Siam. No such source existed in the 1980s, so Father Ray went to a manufacturer of floor tiles. He pointed to some with flowers painted on them and asked the price. Stunned by the cost, he looked around the warehouse, finding a pile of broken tiles.

"How much for them?" he asked. The salesman laughed and said he could have them. A gift. Just get them out of here. Within a few days, Father Ray had people cutting the broken tiles into smaller pieces that took the shape of flower petals and naga figures that resembled hooded snakes. These then were pressed into fresh plaster as it was spread on the building's exterior wall. For a lark, here and there, up high so you had to search and couldn't quite believe your eyes when you spotted them, he embedded entire ceramic teapots and soup bowls and supper plates. Tea kettles and dinnerware adorning the walls of a place of worship? It was as if Father Ray had become the Mad Hatter in *Alice in Wonderland* or, perhaps, a Redemptorist Dr. Seuss.

If the exterior presented an imaginative and amusing surprise, the interior truly halted the mind. Recruiting artists from the art department of a university, he carefully explained what he wanted. He was going to tell the story of his Lord,

Jesus Christ, he said, and he was going to do it using the cartoon-like style of Thai mural painters…and, he said, though the scenes would be inspired by 1st century Jerusalem, the thousands of human figures in the paintings that eventually would cover the walls, would be Thai, wearing the traditional hairstyles and costumes of eighteenth and nineteenth century Siam, as often can be found in old Buddhist temples.

Father Ray worked daily with the artists, providing sketches, feeding them ideas. Father Frank Gautreaux said, "He told the artists what to draw and they did." Betty Roy remembered that Father Ray would tell the story of one part of Christ's life, the artist would make some drawings, and Father Ray would approve them or not, offering suggestions. Father Morrissy said Father Ray went so far as to outline some of the scenes on the wall, letting the artists fill them in. He said, "The colors, every detail was all Father Ray's and he was in and out of the chapel several times a day for months."

By all descriptions, it became Father Ray's great passion---of the sort another man might have for a woman, a scholar for study, a musician for rhythm and melody, an artisan for craft and art. Early in the morning, before traveling to the Orphanage to say Mass, he visited the chapel site, envisioning the time when he would say Mass there. In the evenings, when returning to his room, he checked again. Each time he visited, friends said, he made notes to have small changes made and imagined more eccentricity, all adhering to Scripture, but with Father Ray's spin, or twist.

Jesus' birth, His tossing the money lenders out of the temple, His miracles, His preaching to his disciples, the Crucifixion and Resurrection…all were painted as if He had been born, raised, and died (and experienced His own sort of reincarnation) in Buddhist Siam rather than in what is now called the Middle East. The panel showing the birth of Jesus included female attendants shading Joseph with an ornate Thai umbrella and cooling Mary with a teardrop-shaped fan of the sort used for Thai royalty. The angels hovering overhead wore the gold costumes and pointed headdresses of Thai dancers and their halos were shaped like nagas. The Three Wise Men approached on elephants rather than camels.

At the front of the chapel, over the altar, was the most unusual panel, linking Christianity with Asian religion in a way that startled even those accustomed to Father Ray's odd and predictably unusual ways. This depicted Jesus being carried to Heaven in the chariot of the Hindu god Krishna, drawn by four white horses. Father Gautreaux said, "I told him, 'Jesus didn't have his hands on the reins in a chariot!' and Father Ray said, "The power of the Lord, you dummy!'"

The village homes had thatched roofs and the women wore straw farm hats and there were lotus ponds in ancient Israel. A woman suckled an infant while sitting next to a Thai sling hammock. In the trees were monkeys and bears, animals not found in the Middle East. Children played traditional Thai games. When Jesus changed water into wine, he did it using Thai water jars.

There was shock and titillation as well. A man was seen using an Asian squat toilet. A small boy urinated in the woods. In one panel, people ate, drank, and vomited into a pond. In another, adults killed children with swords and clubs.

In addition to the fourteen stations, there were two other panels showing modern day Catholics. On the same wall where Jesus told Peter to be the "rock" upon which He was told to build His church, beneath it was an illustration showing a procession of modern day Catholic Cardinals entering the Vatican to elect a Pope.

"The bravado of that chapel, the daring, the genius, to dare to do that," Father Joe Maier said, "that would have gotten anybody else in trouble. He really went against the establishment in everything he did. He was always on his own. If the fundamentalists saw that painting of Jesus going off in that chariot, it would be a scandal that would go on for the next ten years."

The chapel was not a prank, nor was it a thumbing of his nose at the establishment. Father Ray genuinely believed that when the tall wood Thai doors were thrown open in 1987 and the first worshippers passed between the Chinese lion-dogs guarding the entrance, what they were experiencing a denial of Rudyard

Kipling's poetic claim that East and West would never meet.

It would be here, in the dim light of a large room furnished with low tables and cushions (and a collection of Christian icons from Russia, taking the place of a Thai temple's Buddha images), that Father Ray would now start his day with a morning Mass for most of the rest of his life.

The chapel was a gem in a tropical garden, constructed on a seven-acre parcel of land donated to the Redemptorists by Sumalee Pattayanond in 1986. When the chapel was officially opened a year later, it accompanied the blessing of the Redemptorist Center itself, a hostel that eventually would offer one hundred and forty-four air-conditioned rooms with cable television, refrigerator, telephone, and Internet service. (Forty-four of the rooms were equipped to be fully accessible.) There also were four conference rooms with an auditorium that seated nearly three hundred, along with a library, a large kitchen and dining room, and a swimming pool. It was a place designed for thought-provoking and contemplative retreats.

The walls of the common areas of the main buildings---the lounges, the hallways, the staircases, the dining room, the toilets, and so on---were painted in color combinations selected by Father Ray. Rarely did they complement each other in the usual "interior decoration" sense. A blue wall abutted another in Chinese red and the four sides of the pillars holding up the ceiling were painted in four different tints. So conflicting were the juxtapositions, some people thought Father Ray was colorblind. He was not. He said he liked the colors he used and, besides, he was using the cheapest paint he could find, much of it the odds and ends of lots left over following a commercial job elsewhere in Pattaya.

In addition, there was a printing business. Not many knew it, but the Redemptorists operated the largest Catholic publishing house in the world, in Liguori, Missouri, a town named for the order's founder. "In Pattaya", said Father Morrissy, "We wanted to spread God's word of the Gospel, so we called it the Apostolate of the Pen. We produced Sunday church bulletins and sent them to the parishes. We'd provide a single sheet folded down the middle. On the front and back we'd have a message that we wrote here in Thailand or came from Missouri. Then the parishes would have the inside two pages where they printed their announcements and order of their services. We even had some Protestant churches taking them. We printed the bulletins in English and in Thai and at the peak we were producing ten thousand copies a week."

Profits from the printing business and the Center itself were pumped into the vocational school.

And the chapel became one of those little-known "tourist destinations" for people visiting Pattaya, described in guides and maps as "worth a look."

Chapter 17

Father Ray moved from his original office in the donated trailer from U-tapao into a small space at the rear of an administration building that was constructed only a few steps from the original Orphanage building. It was only marginally larger than his first office, measuring just four meters by four meters (twelve by twelve feet), and was situated at the back end of the building about twenty meters from the front door. There were bookshelves and a desk and chairs and, in one corner, a door that led to an adjoining cubicle that offered a small washbasin and a flush toilet.

The first thing a visitor noticed after passing through the always open door was the clutter created by a lifetime of Father Ray's disregard for the tidiness of his immediate environment and, adding to this, the amount of furniture and other things that were packed into such a small space. The desk was a standard-issue piece of furniture no different from those seen in government offices. There were the predictable files, letters, and other documents that went with running an orphanage atop the desk. There also was the obligatory telephone, a battery-operated desk calculator, an outsized coffee cup stuffed with pens and pencils, and an overflowing ashtray. A supply of his L&M filter-tipped cigarettes was stacked on a shelf nearby, next to a jar full of candy or maybe a box of chocolate bars. In the early days, his old Olympia manual typewriter was on a small table nearby, years later to be replaced by a computer.

On a shelf on one side was an eclectic collection of books that included an anthology of Irish blessings ("May you be in Heaven a half hour before the Devil knows you're dead"), *The Rubiyat of Omar Khayyam*, a handbook titled *The Priest's Ritual* (providing the text for the rites of marriage, baptism, anointing the sick, last rites, etc.), another instruction manual called *The Pastoral Care of the Sick*, and a slender volume of *Jokes Priests Can Tell*, a collection of simple innocence that must have been a gift from a friend who knew that Father Ray's personal repertoire of jokes ran in a far bawdier direction.   No surprise, there was a copy of the New Testament and a Thai dictionary.   Additionally, there were religious beads and crucifixes and small bottles with labels saying they contained holy water.

What made a greater impression than the disarray were the things to play with rather than work with: toys and games of an ever-changing variety and in such number it sometimes appeared as if Santa Claus had dropped his sack through the building's roof from a considerable height, making it look at other times as if a bomb had gone off in Toys-R-Us.   Father Ray loved toys and what were called when he was a kid "gags", especially those that were now, simultaneously, simple and sophisticated.   Simple in remaining true to the slapstick level of humor or play that Father Ray so adored, modern in the need for batteries and remote-control devices.

"The orphans find my office a constantly changing, wonderful place to find all sorts of things," he wrote in one of his newsletters.   "They come in and feel a compulsion to start looking on my desk for things to play with.   As a consequence, I keep all sorts of crazy things on the desk in the hopes they won't play with my important work.   As I write this letter, I have a plastic dog that bites when you press its teeth, a back-scratcher that whines when you use it, a monkey holding a coconut, a thing with hundreds of little wires attached to it, a draw poker machine which is now broken, and a variety of things you turn over and little drops of color come floating down."

There were Santa Claus and Snowman dolls that harmonized when you switched them on.   In a drawer were coins and cards for magic tricks.   For a time, there was a popcorn machine.

"I have a wind-up mouse that skitters cross the floor like a real one. I am surrounded by pen-size microscopes, two rabbits made out of washcloths, magnetic fish that move in the water without any visible control, and a box of pick-up sticks. Behind me is a life-sized baby baboon that looks so real it scares visitors when they enter my office. (Mischief makers on my staff put it in my chair when I'm out and leave the door open!) Above my head is a crystal ball that has something in it that changes colors as you move it. Without a doubt, my office is kids' paradise. And I am in Heaven watching them explore its depths. The little Devils!!"

There were reminders from home as well. There was a small, framed snapshot of his parents near his desk, looking formal and as stout as his siblings had recalled, and on a wall was a phony newspaper front page that had been sent to him by his sister Sharron. The headline across the top read, "FATHER RAY MARRIES LAS VEGAS SHOWGIRL." And on every open space on the walls were cornball signs that reflected both his humor and philosophy:

A CLEAN DESK IS A SIGN OF A SICK MIND

YOU TOUCHA MY DESK, I BREAKA YOU FACE

CHOOSE A JOB YOU LOVE AND YOU WILL NEVER HAVE TO WORK A DAY IN YOUR LIFE

I'M TOO BUSY TO GET ORGANIZED

EVERYONE HERE BRINGS HAPPINESS---SOME BY ARRIVING, OTHERS BY LEAVING

HOW MUCH CAN I GET AWAY WITH AND STILL GO TO HEAVEN?

EVERYTHING I LIKE IS ILLEGAL, IMMORAL OR FATTENING

JUST ABOUT THE TIME YOU THINK YOU CAN MAKE BOTH ENDS MEET...SOMEBODY MOVES THE ENDS

Other bumper-sticker type slogans were more serious, sounding like titles of sermons frequently seen posted in big letters outside churches in the United States:

YOU NEVER FAIL UNTIL YOU STOP TRYING

WHEN GOD MEASURES A PERSON, A TAPE IS PUT AROUND THE
HEART INSTEAD OF THE HEAD

BLESSED ARE THE SMILE MAKERS

THE BEST SERMON IS A GOOD EXAMPLE

THE THINGS THAT COUNT THE MOST ARE THE THINGS YOU CAN'T
COUNT

FAITH IS NOT BELIEF WITHOUT PROOF, BUT TRUST WITHOUT
RESERVATION

And of course the kids got their share:

I CAN HANDLE ANY CRISIS…I HAVE CHILDREN

DISCOVER WILD LIFE---HAVE KIDS

GOD'S BIGGEST BLESSINGS ARE THE LITTLE ONES

The smell of cigarettes was always present, yet when the window at the rear wall was open, the fragrance of a nearby frangipani tree sneaked in. Not missing were the scents of Aqua Velva after-shave and Vitalis hair tonic, bottles brought in by friends from the United States and placed on a shelf beside dietary supplements, manicure implements, lip moisturizers, and dental floss.

One reason such items were in his office was that the room where he now slept, in the recently constructed Redemptorist Center, was so small, offering insufficient space for necessities. (Especially before Christmas, when so many of the children's presents were hidden there.) Not much larger or better furnished than the proverbial monk's cell, it measured about three meters by two and a half (nine by seven feet). His bed looked as if it had been salvaged from a provincial hospital, too narrow for him to sleep on his back. There was a small table next to the bed and on the other side of it an armchair where he sat while reading and watching television. Near a small wood desk and stool was a tiny refrigerator---the TV was on top of it---that was stocked mainly with cans of vegetable juice and, not unusually, cans of Singha beer. He had no dresser or wardrobe, only shelves for his clothes, plus a small storage closet where he kept his luggage and clothing that often didn't fit as his weight rose and fell from dieting.

The bathroom was about one meter by a meter and a half (three by four feet) with a low toilet, a bucket of water with a plastic scoop to flush it. There was a washbasin, not much bigger than his two hands, attached to one wall and a hose pipe served as a shower. It was a space so small, one of his friends said, "You had to know what you wanted to go in for, so you went in face front or backwards."

Father Ray began his mornings by saying Mass in his beloved new chapel. After, he often walked the grounds, checking on new construction. Once the Center's dining room was up and running, he ate some of his meals there, but more often ate at his desk at the Orphanage, consuming the same food that was being served to his kids.

Chapter 18

Father Ray said it was difficult to witness the physical deprivation endured by the disabled people. Yes, the orphans' loss of family was paramount, but many of the handicapped were orphans or abandoned, too. And always treated "differently." Even when they had parents, people who are in today's politically correct world called "challenged" were set aside by Thai society. They were pariahs. Scorned and left alone.

While professionals in the field argued that a severe hearing impairment was, in fact, a greater loss than blindness, at least deafness usually was invisible to others. And when Father Ray burst into the deaf school classrooms on his frequent and unplanned visits, disrupting the instruction irretrievably for so long as he remained, performing magic tricks, disappearing coins and retrieving them from the children's ears, he knew that he could not do the same for the blind children in his Orphanage.

It was not much easier at the Redemptorist Vocational School for the Disabled, a venture being planned the same year the deaf school opened, but delayed for several years. This school was to serve the physically disabled seventeen years of age or older---young men and women with birth defects, or crippled by disease (mainly polio, which had not been eradicated in much of the undeveloped world despite the great success elsewhere) or victims of accidents.

Those who were impaired from birth or childhood never held jobs, remaining at home, essentially abandoned, or were put out on the street to beg. In addition, many accident victims who had been gainfully employed lost their jobs along with their arms and legs, no longer able to perform their tasks. Father Ray's wish was to teach such disabled young adults a worthwhile occupation. Again, the students had to be poor, and room and board was offered along with the instruction.

Initially, Father Ray planned to offer classes in ceramic tile-making, electroplating, computer skills, and, possibly, bee culture. By Christmas 1983, successful pilot programs were under way and the priest was hoping to begin instruction the following year.

"Remember," he said in a newsletter, "we are using homemade things. So if you would look at our electroplating outfit you would think you were in the lab of Doctor Frankenstein. We have various solutions in blue and pink plastic baby bathtubs...with electrodes and metal chargers stuck on to the object we are plating by clothes pins! Anyway, the important thing is the bottom line...and that line says it works! We have just completed gold plating four hundred small Thai orchids. They are beautiful!"

Other crafts were proposed as well but, in the end, it was decided that skills for which there would always be a demand related to computer science and electronics. There was hardly a business in Thailand that didn't need programmers and repair technicians. Such skills not only would give the disabled a modern, high tech craft, but also generate heretofore unimagined self-confidence. Father Ray also believed that every graduate should be taught to speak, read, and write English, not just because most of the textbooks and other learning materials were written in what was now the international language of business, but also because English mastery would move the handicapped still another step toward self-reliance and self-worth.

This was when luck or fate intervened---Father Ray always insisted it was providence---when a young American who had been trekking in Nepal decided to visit Thailand on his way home. Ron Small visited the Orphanage after seeing an advertisement in a weekly magazine and Father Ray took him on what was by now a practiced tour.

"After an entirely wonderful two or three hours that included sitting in Ray's office listening to all his plans and wishes for the children, I said goodbye and, reaching for my wallet, asked Ray what I could do for him to thank him. I expected a disclaimer about giving a donation and never expected the answer I received. 'When people ask what they can do for me, I always tell them what I need most and God often provides solutions,' he said. 'Right now, I'm trying to start a school for young handicapped here in Thailand. I have the idea that if I could give them training in computers that they could get good jobs. I need to find someone with experience in teaching and knowledge of computers.'

"I was completely astonished," Ron said. "I had not spoken a whit about my own background at all. And here is this gruff Irish priest describing my background perfectly. I had helped start a computer software company and throughout my career had always spent additional time volunteering to teach at both university and high school and grade school level functions." He'd also taught at UCLA, the University of California at Los Angeles. It seemed a perfect match.

"Well," Ron replied, "I can give you a hand with that. Let me adjust my departure and I'll stay for a while and help develop some lesson plans and help find staff to do some teaching." The 'for a while' ended up being two solid years and then another ten years of part-time work for Ron assisting at what became a very successful school, serving as the first dean and eventually as Dean Emeritus.

Not to push aside Ron Small's great contribution, another of the reasons for the school's immediate success was Father Ray's decision to guarantee jobs to every graduate. To accomplish this, he put on all his priestly robes and sashes and medals and chains, a huge crucifix as the centerpiece, inappropriately overdressed by Catholic tradition, and appearing a bit like a priest might look if he were a character in a Gilbert & Sullivan operetta or a film by Monty Python.

He then called hotel general managers, company chief executives, everyone he could think to ask for a meeting who was in a position to hire one of his students. Once given an appointment, he showed up early and while sitting in the reception room, where he humbly dropped his head onto his chest, began running the rosary beads through his fingers, and prayed audibly. When finally he was ushered into the office, knowing that the person he met expected him to ask for a cash contribution, instead he talked about his new school and said he wanted a job for one of his graduates. The executive was so relieved to hear the request was not for money, offering a job was easy.

Father Ray made it even easier. Suspecting the business person subscribed to the common superstitious Thai belief that a disabled person might bring bad luck to the company, the priest suggested that the young graduate could be hired for six months on a trial basis, and if the individual didn't come up to expectations, his or her employment could be terminated.

More employers went for it than did not and in 1987, Father Ray wrote, the first class trained in electronics repair left the school "to do an apprenticeship in various radio shops all over the Kingdom. After the six months are up, they will have to return with a letter from the owner of the shop giving a favorable appraisal of their ability. If everything is as we expect it to be, they will then receive their diploma as an electronic repair person."

By which time, Father Ray figured the former students would have proved their value to the businesses that had hired them. As he suspected and had confirmed in the years ahead, many of those employers admitted to offering the jobs as an act of charity, but then returned again and again, asking for more, because not only were the graduates well trained, they were more motivated than others with the same skills.

"You have no idea how proud I was to see them finish the course and get their very first job of their life," Father Ray wrote. "More than half of them have previously begged on the street. Some even had to steal in order to get enough to eat. They would never have been able to take a course like this if we did not give it to them. A course such as ours, with room and board, would be only a dream, an impossible one at that."

The same year, Father Ray told a story about a young man he interviewed.

"The poor lad has no feet! He has legs and at the end of the legs is simply a little round ball resembling a heel. In other words, he has no toes or arches … only a heel on each leg. One of his arms is cut off at the elbow. The other arm is whole, but the fingers are mangled. When I interviewed him, I tried in the nicest way possible to tell him he could not be accepted into the electronic repair school because he simply could not lift the guts of amplifiers or TVs out of their housing…and certainly could not handle them even if someone else took them out for him. I tried to tell him to wait for a year, when we will be starting a different kind of job training, which would be easier for him…such as learning how to grow house plants for sale to the public.

"When he caught the drift, he stood right up in front of me and said, 'Father, look at me. I am so ugly that wherever I go, people move away from me out of repulsion. If you do not take me into your school, I will probably kill myself, since I cannot stand it any longer.' When I asked him what it was he could not stand any longer, I expected the answer to be severe malformation of limbs. However, what he finally answered moved me so much that I accepted him into the school.

"He said, 'I can stand the stares and fear of normal people when they see me…but I cannot stand my own lack of self-respect. I need this opportunity from you, Father, to make me look at myself in the mirror and say I am good for something!' "

The young man was enrolled and after a dentist had devised a special appliance, he was taught to type with the appliance held between his teeth.

"The sight which always gives me a shudder happens every evening when the students go to bed," Father Ray wrote. "They take off their artificial legs, arms, braces, etc., and put them on the floor next to their beds. Walking through the dormitory at night gives one an eerie feeling until one gets used to it. In the morning, there are all kinds of click and clack noises as the braces and limbs are snapped, strapped, and buckled."

In 1989, Father Ray got his pay-off, a reward that he could have imagined only in his prayers to The Boss Upstairs. However skilled the school's administrators thought its students and staff, Father Ray had contracted with a company in Bangkok to keep the school's computers and other electronic equipment in tip-top shape. The company sent someone every month on a maintenance visit.

"I always looked with awe at these particular service men since they seemed to know a computer backwards and forwards," Father Ray wrote. "They take this and that out of the machine, clean it, discard faulty parts, replace new parts, and in general keep our computers in first class condition.

"Just a few days ago, the service man showed up with a big smile on his face. At first, I did not understand why he was smiling at me…and then it hit me. It took me at least fifteen minutes before I finally realized he was one of our handicapped graduates from our own electronic school!! When he saw that I finally understood the meaning of this smile, we hugged each other like two long lost friends."

Chapter 19

Father Ray often said that when he needed someone, The Boss Upstairs was listening, had someone ready to send in, like an understudy to save the Broadway show when the star got sick, like a bench-warmer on a sports team who made an impossible catch or hit or kick and won the game. One of these was Tom Vincent.

He was a retired American industrialist; a university dropout who started his career with The Martin Company (now Martin-Lockheed) and in the years following worked for other aircraft companies and firms that manufactured oilfield and air-conditioning equipment, and concrete, moving up the corporate ladder as he developed what he called "an ability to solve problems." One of his bosses along the way, early on, said he wanted to underwrite his return to school to get a master's degree. The fact that he didn't have an undergraduate degree somehow was put aside and Tom said he might have been one of the first to get a Master of Science degree as an Alfred P. Sloan Fellow at the Massachusetts Institute of Technology with only two years of university.

The quick rise to CEO status followed, as Tom moved from job to job, most of them managing subsidiaries of Fortune 500 companies that were determined by corporate headquarters to need a "troubleshooter," a turnaround guy. He spent much of his time flying all over the world, but not seeing much of it, traveling from Los Angeles or Minneapolis (or wherever his employer was based) to South Africa to Brazil, always on the move, but never seeing anything but airports, airplanes, taxi cabs and limousines, hotel rooms, offices, and factories. That, he said, was why he now took a cruise aboard a ship to some exotic part of the world every year or so, so he could see everything he missed the first time around.

Tom retired in 1988, the same year he heard about Father Ray on one of his frequent visits to Thailand. By now, he had homes in Florida and Hawaii and soon bought a condominium in Bangkok. He didn't recall how he heard about the Pattaya priest, but he said he was impressed enough to hire a car and driver to take him to Pattaya, where he found the Orphanage, walked through the priest's open door, talked for a while, and was taken on a tour of the grounds. Everywhere they went, the kids rushed to Father Ray and clung to him.

Tom was impressed. And in the following years, he returned, wanting now not just to visit, but to participate.

In 1992, noticing that some of the youngsters who'd spent virtually all their lives in the Orphanage were nearing university age, he set up an endowment fund to provide higher education for those who wished to continue in school---to pay all tuition, housing, and other costs for however many years it took. In the next decade, the Thomas J. Vincent Foundation put eight orphans through university. In time, that also would finance the research, writing and production of this book, with all profits from the book's sale pledged to go into the same fund.

Eventually, Tom realized he was spending more than half of every year in Thailand and as his friendship with Father Ray grew, so too did his support of the priest's work. After the country's economy collapsed in 1997 and the disabled students at the Vocational School found good jobs more elusive, he bankrolled an electronics repair shop in Pattaya that employed three of the institution's graduates, calling it a "pilot project" that could, if successful, lead to the opening of additional stores. Father Ray withheld his approval, believing it wasn't fair to other students who didn't get the same "break."

In the end, Father Ray said yes and equipment for repairing computers and electronic products was moved into a shophouse on one of the main, north-south Pattaya highways. Flyers were distributed; small ads were taken out in the local press. Hotels were solicited and a few of them sent TV sets for repair that they didn't want their own high-priced employees to bother with.

Tom also talked to his tailor, Raja's Fashions in Bangkok, and got Raja and his son Bobby to donate, over a period of time, more than two tons of clothing. Another friend who made shoes for export cleaned out his sample room; many of the shoes were "singles," but Tom had them taken to Pattaya because many of the disabled people had only one foot. Stuffed animals came from a manufacturer he met casually. Hundreds of pairs of running shoes and thirty-nine large cartons of jackets, pants, shirts and other clothing were donated by Nike, the result of another chance encounter.

"The kids were wearing $160 Air Jordans!" Tom said. "And they knew who Michael Jordan was! Imagine what the other kids at the schools the kids attended in Pattaya had to say about that!"

Tom was still a businessman, with an interest in a couple of medical clinics in Florida and other investments, but more and more of his time was devoted to Father Ray's projects. There was a library at the Street Kids Home, but there was no allowance for books, so he asked a friend, David Duesler, who taught at Chulalongkorn University in Bangkok, to put up notices on bulletin boards soliciting books. More flyers went up in his and friends' condominium elevators asking for used TVs and other electronic equipment that was either repaired and resold at the electronics shop or "cannibalized" for spare parts.

Tom also participated in Father Ray's program that enabled orphans to live for six months to a year with English-speaking foreigners. Tom took two boys, aged fifteen and sixteen, back home to Hawaii and in the eight months that followed they studied English for long hours with a tutor, went to Disney World and other tourist attractions in Florida and Washington, D.C., took a ride on the Chesapeake Bay in a Cigarette speedboat belonging to one of Tom's friends, and stopped in Las Vegas on the way home, where the boys were told to *keep walking, don't even pause* when moving through the casino to the elevators.

Tom also brought packages back from the U.S. to Father Ray, things the priest said he couldn't find in Thailand: Vitalis hair tonic, Cheese Whiz, butterscotch liqueur, and jockey shorts in size XXL. Tom said Father Ray always asked for XL, but he always bought the more realistic, larger size.

"Vitalis!" Tom recalled. "I told Father Ray I didn't even know they still made that stuff. I had to go to five shops before I found it. And," he added, "liqueur made from butterscotch? How could someone drink that?"

*

Father Ray considered Bill Mangelsen another gift from The Boss Upstairs. He, too, was a businessman, based in Omaha, Nebraska, and running a company that imported arts and crafts items manufactured in China. As the business grew, in 1979 he opened an office in Hong Kong. And then he twice suffered a great personal tragedy. His oldest daughter Mary, thirteen, died suddenly of myocarditis (inflammation of the heart muscle), and seven months later his son Paul, ten, was killed in an automobile accident. In shock, but determined to go on, he started the Mary and Paul Mangelsen Foundation, named for his children, and started sending contributions to the Save the Children Fund and other similar agencies.

On a trip to Bangkok to buy artificial flowers in 1984, he bought a copy of the *Reader's Digest* at his hotel. He said he'd never bought the magazine before and didn't know why he did so now, but he read a story in it about Father Ray. Once back in the United States, he wrote a letter and sent it to the Redemptorists in Bangkok.

"One of the priests at Holy Redeemer Church gave me your name and address," Father Ray answered in a letter than ran to two single-spaced pages---typical for Father Ray in answering such inquiries. "He said you wanted to know something about the work for children which is being done by this Orphanage. That is a big order...but at least I will give it a try.

"First of all, in this letter you will find two information sheets. One about the Orphanage and another about the deaf school. These two papers should give you some idea as to how we help the kids. However, besides that I would like to give you a complete list of our present work."

In the paragraphs that followed, Father Ray mentioned programs that gave money to mothers who wanted to give up their children "if the reason they are giving the child is an economic one," and that helped Burmese refugees and old people from immigration jail. There was "a schooling program for young people who have brains, but their parents do not have the finances to send them to higher education."

The vocational school for the disabled young people was mentioned too, as was still another program to support children whose mothers were in jail and whose fathers were unknown or uninterested.

Father Ray also told Bill about the crippled boy who, after having several operations on his legs, was able to join the other children in play.

"I hope this 'brief' letter gives you the information you need for now. I will be very pleased to send you more if you want it."

On his first visit to the Orphanage, Bill, too, was taken on a tour, during which he met an elderly man who came to the Orphanage every Sunday to teach the kids guitar and refused to be paid when pay was offered. Bill also remembered watching a truck full of chairs unloaded, a donation from a hotel, the chairs to be used wherever needed.

When the arts and crafts "entrepreneur" (the word he used to describe himself) returned to Omaha, he started sending donations, some of them in the five-figure range. He also got involved in a number of well-meaning schemes, some that never materialized. When Father Ray thought it might be a good idea to add turkeys as an alternate protein source to his chickens and ducks and pigs---and because there were no live turkeys in Thailand, so far as Father Ray could determine---Bill found a farmer in Nebraska who could provide the fertile eggs and got a major airline to "hand-carry" them to Bangkok. But at the last minute, it was decided that Thailand's climate might be too hot. Bill also located some special gold paint for the mural in the chapel when it was in process, but this time the airline said no, because the liquid was too flammable.

He continued to send checks. "You know I start projects but must honestly admit I usually don't know where the money will come from to pay for them," Father Ray wrote Bill in 1991, acknowledging another generous contribution. "Keep me in your worthy prayers, as I need a lot of help from The Big Boss Upstairs. Sometimes He sleeps on the job and has to be reminded now and then."

Chapter 20

One of the things Father Ray did best was to write letters. Day after day after day, even when ill, he drove or was driven from his room at the Redemptorist Center to the Orphanage, where he proceeded to his office and between juggling crises (usually financial) and meeting visitors and welcoming kids who wanted nothing more than to climb onto his lap---he read letters that had been sorted and put aside for him by his secretary, answering all that had been addressed to him in a specific, personal way. Often, he wrote at length.

In one letter, he acknowledged a contribution forwarded by the Redemptorists in the United States. When two checks totaling US$10,000 fell out of the envelope, Father Ray said in his response that he "about fell out of my chair. As a matter of fact, my hands started to shake! You certainly realize this will help me make the lives of the children better...but you will never really understand as well as myself what a difference it will make. The donation came as a gift from God at a very difficult time when we needed it the most."

Father Ray then explained in detail how every dollar of the contribution would be spent. "Part of the money will be used to buy the kids a color television set with a big screen. They have been screaming for one and now they will have it. Over here, the price is much higher than in the States. It will cost about $2,100.

"Part of the money will be used for some serious work which has to be done at the Orphanage. The termites are winning the war on the roof beams. There are many interesting things about termites." Shading his words with whimsicality, he continued, at the same time revealing his love of the natural sciences: "They are strange little creatures that are afraid of light. They have an appetite that would put growing children to shame. They can eat through concrete and they have a knack of knowing where to look for their favorite food, i.e., Father Brennan's Orphanage! I have tried to exterminate them with everything except 'yellow rain.' Saint Jude (the patron of hopeless causes) has been invoked, but I hear he always had a special love for helpless animals. God stacked the cards against us human beings when it comes to termites. Since termites are so smart, you think they would be kind enough to refrain from eating orphanage roofs! Anyway, new wood will have to be installed...with the black gooey stuff that is supposed to keep the termites away. That will cost about $5,000.

"The price of rice will be going up in the very near future," Father Ray continued. "As the harvest season grows nearer and nearer...the available rice becomes more scarce. Hence, the merchants hike up the price. I will use about $1,500 to buy fifty sacks of rice to keep in our Orphanage. It will last us until the harvest season when the price gets low again. Just for your information, each sack is one hundred kilo[grams]. We go through one sack every two days! Rice in the Asian diet is equal in our diet to bread and potatoes combined. You simply can't eat without it.

"That leaves about $1,400. That will be used to buy Christmas presents for the kids. I have to start buying early (I started last February) because there are over one hundred and fifty kids that get presents. I keep my eyes sharp for bargains throughout the year...

"There you have the way your donation will be spent. I hope you are pleased with its breakdown. I am...and I thank you for it very much. Not one cent of what you have given will be used in administration. All of it will go to my loveable kids."

Surprising the man who received the letter, that wasn't the end of it. The missive went on for another single-spaced page, talking about how Father Ray viewed his role in life.

"The work I do is admired by people," he wrote, "which always makes me chuckle. People tell me what a wonderful 'job' I am doing, etc. But for me, it does not seem like work. It seems like a hobby or some kind of a great adventure like walking through the pyramids with a flashlight, discovering new wonders every minute. It certainly does not seem like work. I only get frightened when I walk through the Orphanage at night and the children are all asleep. Everything is quiet and dark…their little bodies are twisted every which way in slumber. Some are sucking their thumb while others are half hanging out of bed. That is when I get scared of the responsibility. I have a great confidence in God and the Mother of Perpetual Help. I put it all in their hands, and go to bed myself."

Another letter in his file---Father Ray had written the phrase "THOUGHTS ON FAITH" across an early draft---was written to a woman who had lost her husband. The prose was flowery, some might even say overwritten, but there wasn't a false word in it.

"I have no doubt that from the time you wrote me, until now, it has been very difficult for you. As you can appreciate, it is difficult to write a letter like this to a grieving wife. However, I feel not only that I must…but that I want to.

"You have been blessed with an eternal knowledge. That knowledge is 'true and real love.' Love is not just an emotional twitching of the heart…it is deep down warmth in the heart and soul of a person so that their life is changed. As a priest, I can tell you not many people have had that kind of love.

"Your description of your love life with Jim is beautiful. What makes it beautiful was not just the words you used…but the vibrant life of love which you poured out from your finger tips onto a typewriter so that my eyes could read it and my soul could feel it.

"As I write this letter, I feel a strange closeness to you. It is a feeling I seldom experience when I write a person who has visited this Orphanage. I guess it is a feeling that we both understand more about our life in this world that we can express in words. It is something we want to tell those we love, especially those who are young…but when we try, it sounds trite…and they have heard it before, so they don't listen very well. That only adds to our frustration.

"When I marry young people…and I am standing at the altar in front of those two young, glossy faces, I often wonder if they understand what they are doing. Youth has a way of courage that we older people do not trust. But still I worry for them. I have no doubt their parents in the pews are having the same feelings as myself. Do they know that real love demands self-sacrifice, a total giving of oneself to the other? Have they matured enough to accept that? Will they give each other trust, consolation, and compassion? I finally pronounce them man and wife and when they go down the aisle to begin their new life I stay behind, at the altar, and say a silent prayer for their love…that it may not die.

"Your love for Jim has not died…and that is the way God planned it. That is what love is…an eternal thing. Some day your house will be demolished, the land and properties you own will be sold to someone who, perhaps, is not even yet born. Some day we will both be dead. The only thing we leave behind and take with us at the same time is the love we have had in this world. It cannot die. It is part of the invisible package that God has put inside all of us which stays intact when we enter the new world of God. That is why Christ said the greatest thing in the world is love. You of all people know that!

"I did not find it unusual or morbid that you and Jim should discuss that in the event of one dying, donations should be given to the Orphanage instead of flowers. If I did not know you, I would find it strange. But on the contrary, it is something to be expected of people who can share and who understand life. The most wonderful bouquet of flowers in the eyes of God must certainly be a bevy of little children.

"Nothing has died within you with Jim's death, although you may feel that way. A mother loves the child most, who is the child farthest away, or, who is the sickest at any given moment. Jim is gone, but nothing has gone 'out' of you. Something has been taken 'from' you temporarily. By earth time, that 'temporarily' is an eternity. But by real time, it is the blinking of an eye in eternity. God's promise is that you will have perfect happiness in Heaven…and that would be impossible for you without Jim. Therefore, trust God that you and Jim will share an eternity together with God in more happiness and love than you ever experienced on this globe. What has been taken from you will be waiting to be reunited again.

"One of the great gifts of the priesthood which God has given me is to be able to tell you the above…with absolute certainty that it is true. Love by its nature gives blind trust…that is the reason Christ rose from the tomb…to help us give that trust as a true sign of our love."

Chapter 21

By now, Father Ray was well acquainted with the concept of survival and what was required to make it a possibility; there wasn't always a donor around to bail him out and his experience in northeastern Thailand served him especially well, not only in the Orphanage's early years, but also right up to the end. Improvisation was the name of the game. And begging, if it came to that, as he once did on the streets of Bangkok's business district, standing in his robes on Silom Road with a hat or making a trip to empty collection boxes when the purse was empty in Pattaya.

The pigs and the chickens and the ducks and the sprawling vegetable garden at opposite ends of the Orphanage property only went so far. They were, for a time, not just self-sustaining, but could have been turned into profit if Father Ray hadn't been afraid of alienating local farmers by entering the marketplace. Yet, as the Orphanage population and number of projects grew, Father Ray realized that there had to be an ongoing expansion in resources. If there was one thing he knew, and knew well, it was that all was, always, precarious.

Sometimes, it was the climate that challenged him. "There has been a drought in Thailand for the last two years," he wrote several years earlier. "As a consequence, our wells have gone dry. We had to buy water from trucks, sometimes to the tune of U.S. $400 per month! As soon as I saw that bill, I immediately made plans to dig our own deep water well with homemade equipment. We have one forty-five-meter hole already, which is producing one-hundred sixty-five gallons an hour, twenty-four hours a day. It is still not enough, so we are starting another well.

"After we finish, we will probably use our rig to help other people dig wells, and thus not only pay for our rig, but also help poor people to obtain free water. So you can see, we are not afraid of work, and use your money not only wisely but for the benefit of others. It is another example of how we work to keep expenses to a minimum, yet allow ourselves and others to enjoy the luxury of abundance."

Water and wells were only a part of it. (Eventually, there would be several more wells dug on the Orphanage property; efforts at dousing for water, an experiment that dated back to a visit by Father Ray to Ireland in 1961, proved unfruitful.) Even when food, water, and shelter---the three most needed things for human survival---were assured, there was always a need for cash. Over the years, Father Ray accepted contributions from every source he could imagine and tap, by every means he could devise.

Many charities such as Father Ray's regularly found support in the bars. Let the psychologists explain why so many owners of such establishments found comfort in Father Ray's cause and company, in contributing in some way to his good works. The fact is, it's a fact: as much as Father Ray enjoyed Irish whiskey, the purveyors of the liquid enjoyed him. He could swap jokes and war stories and match the customers drink-for-drink. Thus, it was not unusual when he got a call from Lucy's Tiger Den in the notorious Patpong district of Bangkok.

The Tiger Den was named for the Flying Tigers who flew with the big tiger shark's jaws painted on the American fighter plane's nose during World War Two. Only a handful of those veterans were still in Bangkok in the 1960s and 1970s. By now they had been replaced by former CIA agents and Air America pilots from America's secret war in Laos who decided to stay in Thailand and not go home, along with a contingent of Westerners who worked in bar-free Saudi Arabia and came to Bangkok for their rest and recuperation, commonly known as R&R.

The owner of the Tiger Den was one of Father Ray's supporters and whenever the richly paid engineers and computer programmers from the Middle East arrived, he called Pattaya. Time to make a run to Patpong, he advised the priest, and a few days later, after hanging his belly over the same bar with the workers from Saudi Arabia, Father Ray returned to Pattaya with a pocket stuffed with checks and cash in several currencies. Thus the wealth of the oil-rich sands of the Middle East flowed into Southeast Asia, delivering a different kind of energy to the Father Ray's orphans, blind, deaf, and physically disabled.

Some of the bars in Pattaya responded in kind, as Father Ray became known, and respect for his efforts increased. The Jesters, a local motorcycle club, adopted the Orphanage for an annual fundraising event. Once the Hard Rock Cafe and Hotel was up and running, it sponsored daylong parties for the kids. Local hotels invited the kids to weekday barbecues and, during the off-tourist season, afternoons at the pool. Pattaya markets delivered produce that was still healthy but starting to wilt. Some Thai recording artists released a CD with all proceeds going to the Orphanage.

And Father Ray continued his always well-intentioned but sometimes eccentric experiments. He'd likely never top his attempt to produce colored silk by injecting dye into live silkworms, as he did when serving in Loei, but he did go along with a scheme proposed to breed mutant koi, the large, expensive, multi-colored carp so revered in many parts of the Orient, especially among Chinese and Japanese. When a man came to Father Ray and said he could produce blue koi---normally they are a mottled white, orange, and black---the notion was just cockeyed enough to appeal and because the enterprising fish-breeder said he'd cover all costs, the priest gave him and his efforts his blessing, along with some space in which to conduct his experiment. Alas, it was one of many schemes that never worked.

In 1984, he announced in his newsletter, "We are breeding worms!! You probably have reread that sentence, to make sure you read it right. It's true…we are breeding about five-thousand of them. I have read [that] in some countries, they breed them for food, since they are very high in protein. They make 'wormburgers' out of them. We will not be doing that, although I am tempted to try it once. Instead, we are breeding them for the vegetable gardens. They make holes in the soil and air gets to the roots of the plants. They also leave their droppings which, of course, are a fertilizer. We release a handful of them in the garden each month at night. We dig a hole first, drop the worms in, and then cover them up. By morning, they are safe from the terror of every worm…that is, being a bird's breakfast."

Another plot that wasn't realized was his desire to raise vegetables hydroponically, a soil-free method of agriculture that was modestly successful in several parts of the world. Special shelters had to be erected for the project and a level of expertise was required that the gardeners on the payroll did not have, and the idea was abandoned.

For guidance, he enlisted the help of Bill Mangelsen, the American businessman who had come to Father Ray after reading the article about him in *Reader's Digest* and who bought feathers for the numerous arts and crafts products that he had manufactured in China and sold from his home base in the United States. Bill located and sent a book on turkey farming to Thailand and introduced Father Ray to Loyl Stromberg, a Minnesota publisher of numerous books about poultry breeding, management, and marketing.

"Since my last letter to you, I have purchased a 'small' incubator," Father Ray told his friend after hearing from the publisher. "It holds about two dozen chicken eggs. My geese lay eggs frequently, but they seldom hatch them. Ergo, the incubator. I had to laugh at Mr. Stromberg's [the publisher's] comment about turkeys hatching their own eggs. 'They should follow out their own natural instincts for reproduction,' he says. The book you sent me says that turkeys are sort of dumb compared to the rest of the poultry kingdom. If my geese who won't hatch their own eggs are smarter than turkeys…I'm going to have a problem!!"

The publisher also told Father Ray that although the birds were raised successfully in Mexico and South America and several hot weather states in the U.S., such as Texas and Florida, they had to have a shelter for protection from the sun. Turkeys also needed a higher level of protein in their feed than chickens. He advised that Father Ray add dried fish meal. As for the source of young chicks, he said they were available in Australia and India.

Father Ray was undaunted by the hurdles and when Bill Mangelsen found a turkey farmer in Nebraska who suggested air-shipping fertile eggs, the priest asked Bill to pursue the matter. Quoting the farmer, Bill wrote Father Ray that "during the first several (up to ten) days, the eggs do not need to be incubated. This would allow for safe transportation from here to Thailand." Further calls were made by Bill to the U.S. Department of Agriculture and to his own customs broker, as well as to a friend at United Airlines who agreed to have the eggs "hand-carried" to Bangkok.

Then at the last minute, it was decided that Thailand was just too hot---far warmer and more humid than Texas and Florida, hotter than the parts of India and Mexico where turkeys thrived---and another plot went unhatched.

And then the Pattaya government passed laws making it illegal to raise livestock within city limits. The pigs, the chickens, the goats, everything had to go. It was a sad day for all.

Chapter 22

In 1986, Father Ray was given a twenty-year lease on a shophouse in Central Pattaya, with an option for a second twenty years, the cost to be one Thai baht per year, the gift of a man who only asked in return that the priest say Mass for him in the chapel on the premises once a year.

This was no ordinary chapel. There were two non-Catholics buried in the building near the altar and a Volvo car was preserved "in state" in another room. Father Ray accepted the man's kind offer, although he said at the time that he had no immediate plans for the property. That changed when Father Ray met a woman named Aurora Lee Sribuapun, a teacher of the blind who was herself blind.

Aurora was sighted when she was born into a Chinese family in Bangkok and she became blind at age five due to malnutrition and eye disease. Her left eye was removed when she was six and replaced with a glass substitute. In 1939, when she was seven years old, a relative suggested that she stay with an American woman who ran a school for the blind in Bangkok. She became the American's godchild. When she was nineteen, Aurora was sent to the Overbrook School for the Blind in Philadelphia, Pennsylvania, in the United States, becoming fluent in English and returning to teach at the Bangkok School for the Blind, one of the nation's first. She continued her education at the same time, earning a bachelor's degree at a Thai university, then returned to the United States, where she got a master's degree from Boston College in 1982.

Aurora's Thai husband was a massage therapist, also blind, and working in Bangkok. One of his clients was an Australian who sold medicine to Father Ray and in the years following, as Aurora continued to teach the blind in the Thai capital, she took three sighted children of blind parents to the Pattaya Orphanage because the parents---who were her students---believed they couldn't care for their children properly.

She remembered saying each time she went to Pattaya, "Father, you are the shepherd and here are more lambs."

By 1986, Aurora had been promoted from teacher to principal of a school for blind adults in Bangkok and when she asked Father Ray to refer any prospective students, he said he wanted to start classes for children in Pattaya. There were no schools for the sightless in the area, he said. Would she be interested?

"Father, do you really trust me as a woman, blind...?" she asked.

"If I don't trust you, why do I ask you?"

At the time, most of the blind in Thailand lacked any formal education, as is still true today. Many were kept at home, over-protected, allowed to do house chores but little else. The government offered its disabled citizens no benefits, nor was there any system to welcome them into society at large. Ostracism and abuse were commonplace. Some were taken to village fairs and put on the streets to beg. In this way, they became income earners for their families, all the more reason not to let them go.

Others, as adults, sold government lottery tickets on city streets---a government sop to the blind people---finding their way along the broken sidewalks and unprotected streets with their canes, or they became massage therapists. There was a common belief that the blind gave the "best" traditional Thai massage---a system of deep tissue, pressure point stimulation and manipulation of muscles and joints that was famous worldwide---but they still earned around the minimum wage, at best four U.S. dollars a day, a day that might last ten or twelve hours. Many others became fortunetellers or made flower garlands that children would sell at roadway intersections.

This, of course, was for those who weren't physically off-putting. If a child was multi-disabled, as many of the blind were, perhaps with other physical defects or perhaps physically impaired, it was assumed that what he or she could expect from life would be even less. Some had grotesque physical deformities. Some couldn't talk, only scream.

Even beggars had to look presentable.

The Redemptorist School for the Blind opened in May 1987 with seven children, aged four to twelve. The curriculum in some ways was the same as for sighted people, but the lessons were adapted to their loss and needs. Instead of drawing, the children were taught to mold with clay, and an abacus, an ancient Chinese device for making arithmetic calculations, consisting of a frame set with rod on which beads were moved, was used rather than a pencil and paper.

Perhaps even more important, the children were taught personal care. Before being turned over to Father Ray, almost all were dependent on others taking care of virtually everything. Many didn't even know how to bathe or brush their teeth. One young girl didn't know how to chew; she'd been given liquid foods all her life because her parents didn't think she could master chopsticks, a spoon, or a fork.

Father Ray, by direction from and through the determination of Aurora, who had done it for herself, wanted as many of the children as possible to be able to cope, to become self-sufficient, to know how to survive in the world on their own, to cook and perform household chores. How to walk the streets unaided and shop. How to live as normal a life as was possible.

Aurora said Father Ray gave her total autonomy, gave her the freedom to run the school as if it were her own. She said she never shared her day-to-day problems with Father Ray, such as where to find good teachers, how to get permissions from the government to operate a school and so on.

Some of the parents presented other problems. Some came and took their children back, said they missed their help around the house. And some students quit school and went home just to make their parents happy. Aurora handled such tasks alone.

"He gave me the opportunity," she said of Father Ray, "and so I went to him only when I really needed him."

Many of Thailand's blind children had known no freedom at all. They had been cooped up in their homes and villages and now, under Aurora's ministry, they were introduced to a multitude of liberties. As important, they learned the simple things---for example, how to pour water into a glass: just put your thumb over the lip while tipping the liquid into the vessel slowly and when you feel the water touch your thumb, stop pouring.

They learned how to live in a group, communally. They experienced social interaction with sightless peers, many of them for the first time; in the small villages, most disabled children lived totally alone and thought there were no others who shared their predicament, frustrations, and fear. At the Redemptorist School for the Blind, they learned differently. Sadly, there were many with the same loss.

Chang was seven when he arrived at the school in 1987, born blind to parents who worked as laborers on Bangkok construction sites; in his case history, no reason was given for his handicap. Paan, aged nine when she was enrolled, was completely blind, her father deceased, her mother aged and supported by her sighted children. Ahm's father was a plantation laborer and her mother, who worked in a commercial laundry, had German measles (rubella) when she was pregnant, so the daughter was born able only to differentiate light from dark. Ped enrolled in the school at five years of age, unable to bathe and dress himself; his father was a day worker when he could find work, his mother bought cheap organ meat from the slaughterhouse in Bangkok and grilled it and sold it on the street.

Pak was eight, arriving in 1990, also from a broken home. "We feel she has ability, but she is a very cautious girl and takes to things slowly. There has been progress in her studies and personal care," her case history said. "She is good in all kinds of games and sports. Her mother and father were divorced after a bitter fight which the girl remembers." The same year, Nam, just four, joined the school, blind since birth, apparently the result of a venereal disease acquired from his divorced parents, a policeman and a worker in a garment factory. They didn't ever come to visit him.

Tik, a five-year-old girl, was born prematurely and placed in an incubator that was said to have supplied too much oxygen, damaging her sight; she was able to perceive light but couldn't distinguish objects. Pon arrived with her twin sister Pan, both of them born prematurely, placed in a defective incubator and kept in it for two months; once again, too much oxygen was blamed for blinding two children who were sighted when they were born. "The parents love the two children and visit them almost every week, bringing them presents and candies," read the children's case history. "Now we see some progress in both. They still cannot bathe and dress themselves, but we are gradually making progress on these things."

(Over the years, and not only in Thailand, much blindness was blamed on exposure to high levels of oxygen in incubators. It was called retro-lental fibroplasia, which means behind-the-lens scarring. It is now believed that, although high levels of oxygen can exacerbate the problem, it is really the low birth weight and the prematurity that cause the disorder. This is called retinopathy of prematurity.)

In the photographs that accompany the children's case histories, their handicap is clear. In some, the smiles are grand, but in all the eyes are closed or milky white or in some other way not "right," signposts to a kind of difference that would mark them forever, irreversibly.

In the years ahead, their accomplishments would, as was true with the deaf and disabled, astonish them.

Today, there are nine registered blind schools in Thailand, but until the 1950s there were none, and during the first four years that Father Ray operated his school, it was, technically, an illegal operation. Unregistered. "It took that long to work through the bureaucracy," Aurora said.

In 1990, Father Ray wrote, "When the blind school started about three years ago, I never thought we would have to worry about the building for years to come. In actuality, the building we are using and the land it is on is not ours. We are using it and giving only a token rent because of the kindness of a Thai Chinese family in Bangkok. The head teacher [Aurora] has informed me that the building is not big enough for the number of children we have. Since the number will grow each year, it is urgent that we begin to build a new school as soon as possible. The land we are presently using is very small, and the only way to add on to the building would be to take away the small playground. Of course, then the children would have no place to play…"

In 1991, it all turned around. The school was officially accredited by a Thai government that now started providing annual grants, the sums based on the total number of students. That amounted to one million baht (U.S. $40,000 by the current exchange rate) the first year, about forty percent of which was dedicated to the care of the kids, the rest to help pay the teachers. And then ground was broken and construction was started on a big, new school. There were between thirty and forty students in classes now. When the new structures were ready, enrollment could increase four times.

Chapter 23

Commander Peter McGregory, a U.S. Navy chaplain known as Father Pete, wrote to his old friend in 1992 with an idea for rustling up funds. All Father Ray needed to do, he suggested, was to send some information about the Orphanage's activities to some of Father Pete's friends, people he thought would respond to a well-meaning pitch. Father Ray did not take his friend's advice and instead replied with a letter explaining why he not only wouldn't but also couldn't. The words revealed much about the depth of Father Ray's faith and what he perceived as his purpose in life.

"Basically, I am a shy fellow," he wrote. "It seems like I am not, but I truly am. I hate to go after anyone with the purpose of getting money. I know that is what I am supposed to do since I am running an orphanage, plus a free deaf school, blind school, handicap school, old people's home, street kid project and prostitute project. But I don't. Again…why?

"Because!

"I look at my work not with the eyes of a fund-raiser. I am a priest, and a fairly good one. I believe that The Big Boss Upstairs has a duty to me, which He dutifully fulfills. (Sometimes a bit slow and sometimes in an indirect way, but He does always come through.) For that, I thank Him…as I am sure He expects me to. It's His job to knock people over the head and get them to help me. My job is to do my work…and do it well…and witness Christ in the eyes of others. In other words, I take care of people's eyes. The Big Boss Upstairs takes care of their brains.

"Since I began this work thirty years ago, I have never had a fund-raising event, nor sent out envelopes for donations. Again, why?

"Because!

"For the reasons stated above and in THIS particular case, one more reason.

"People do want to help the poor, but they don't know who to give it to so that it will be spent for the purpose it is given. They do not want to give it to some monster organization that eats up their donation in administration or useless projects. But they really have no way of knowing who is real and who is not real. So if I make an appeal for funds, I am just one more of those charity groups in the big pot of charity groups. But I am not like them...so I don't want to be like them.

"Another reason. People who are wealthy are constantly pestered by all kinds of charities to give money. When they do give a donation, there is no real feeling of joy in their hearts because they know they are taking a chance that most of their donation will not go to the kid or the leper or the refugee. But because they are basically good people, they feel they should do something for the world, so they send it anyway. I do not wish to be classified among that group. I want donations from people who know me...who know what I am doing...and approve totally what I am doing.

"What am I doing?

"I am not giving temporary help to the poor. I am giving permanent help to them for their future. I have about a hundred handicapped students graduating each year who are getting the first job of their life. It is a job they could never have gotten without my school. I am taking care of orphans and giving them lots of love and the best education possible for their abilities. They will enter the world equal to anyone else, if not better. I am taking deaf and blind kids and teaching them how to read and write sign language or Braille. I am teaching them how to read, which is one of the greatest things in the world. I am showing prostitutes that they have dignity and should respect themselves. I hope to have them think about that and the value of life. I could go on and on. But I won't. I am probably one of the few people in the world who actually receives donations (though they may be small) from the very people I am helping.

"Having just reread the above paragraph, I apologize for the sermon.

"I guess it all boils down to my faith in God. It is sometimes strong and sometimes weak. I am human like anyone else. But I am consistent in depending on it.

"So far it's worked! You came here…and now you have just sent me a donation of $500 from your parish. Thanks very much. The Big Boss Upstairs did it again!!

"I never wrote a letter like this before…"

But it wasn't the only letter that included his thoughts about fund-raising. "It is not my policy to dog people for more funds," he wrote someone else. "If you were to read my letters that I send out, I never ask people directly for money unless they specifically ask me how they can help. I know other organizations do continually go after people requesting money by having fund drives and continual mailings. To tell you the truth, that has always aggravated me. I don't like the idea of continually badgering people to send more money. It is not that I don't need the money…but it is that I think if people want to give, they will give. If they believe in what I am doing, they will help.

"I, too, have read these advertisements in magazines and newspapers from various organizations who say you can sponsor a child for U.S. $5 or $10 a month. If you do this, you get their picture and you get a letter from the child, etc., etc. I will tell you truthfully there is no country in the world where you can support a child for $5 or $10 a month. Even those organizations which say they can support a child for $15 a month or more…I really have to wonder how much is lost in administration. As far as I'm concerned, I have hardly any administration. The little administration I have is less than the half of one percent of my expenses…and almost half of that one percent is used for postage in answering letters."

This is not to say Father Ray didn't make it easy to contribute, once a relationship was established. When people whom he knew, who, usually, had visited the orphanage, asked him how they might help, the priest sent a wish list, enumerating specific needs for what were now becoming called "projects." In his regular newsletters, he told his sponsors and donors about new activities and plans, often citing the lack of funds to cover immediate and future needs. He never directly solicited funds; every one of his benefactors interviewed for this book said, "He never asked me for any money ." (Or words to that effect.) But he made clear that as the numbers of people in his care increased, and as new projects and programs were introduced, his need went up as well.

It was also obvious that while one reason for taking those in his charge to perform in Pattaya hotels and aboard cruise ships calling at Laem Chabang port was to build the kids' confidence---and to introduce the able-bodied world to people they would otherwise likely never meet---another was because appreciative audiences tended to make donations.

No remarks about contributions were made in introducing the shows. No brochures with sign-up forms were distributed. No hat was ever passed. But when the orphans sang Christmas carols and the deaf kids signed "Silent Night" and when the wheelchair-bound students of the vocational school performed a choreographed sort of dance, people watching automatically reached for their wallets and pocketbooks.

There was a movie released in 1989 called Field of Dreams, in which Kevin Costner heard a "voice" telling him if he builds a baseball field in the middle of his Iowa cornfield, it will bring the immortal Shoeless Joe Jackson and other baseball legends back from the dead. The refrain through the movie, the "voice" that Costner heard, was, "Build it and they will come." And, sure enough, at the end of the movie, the cars bringing people to the cornfield ballpark were lined up to the horizon.

It was the same thing with Father Ray. He built his organization and with his avowed faith in The Boss Upstairs, they came.

"Every year on Christmas Eve, the little Buddhist orphans sing Christian Christmas carols in restaurants and hotels," the priest wrote in one of his end-of-the-year newsletters. "We once entered a restaurant that had very few customers, in fact, just one table of six people. So thirty orphans made a circle around the table and started singing 'Silent Night,' 'Joy to the World,' etc. The people were very nice and clapped after every song. As we were leaving they even gave a nice donation for the Orphanage. The owner of the restaurant told us the table broke out in great laughter after we were gone. When he asked his guests what was so funny, they answered, 'We're Jewish.' "

The Cunard cruise ship company called at the port frequently, giving its passengers a chance to visit Bangkok. Father Ray had made friends with the cruise line management over the years and always took a troupe of his kids and disabled young adults aboard to perform. Every time, the captain himself made a cash contribution, along with a large selection of toiletries, and, after making a small speech about the priest's good works, the captain's crew took up a collection.

Similarly, when the Queen Elizabeth 2 (QE2) on its annual round-the-world tours stopped at Laem Chabang, south of Bangkok and just half an hour from Pattaya, Father Ray and his kids again went aboard as guests of the captain.

Once, among the passengers there was a married couple from Europe. They were on a round-the-world tour to celebrate the husband's retirement. They sat quietly and seemed to enjoy the traditional Thai songs and dances performed by the orphans and the wheelchair dance by the disabled. Likely, no one noticed when the man slipped away, returning following a visit to his cabin. At the end of the performance, he introduced himself to Father Ray and gave him an envelope, saying, "Here's something for your kids." The priest thanked the man and slipped it into his pocket. When he got back to the Orphanage, he opened the envelope and found U.S. $10,000 in cash.

When they returned home, the couple sent an e-mail message, offering further help. The e-mail was misplaced and went unanswered. They next sent an inquiry by fax and it, too, was lost. Finally, the man's secretary called and she re-sent the original message, asking what Father Ray needed. A wish list was

E-mailed in response, suggesting Christmas presents for the orphans, a motorcycle for a teacher, pajamas for the deaf children, and a new bus. (The man had watched Father Ray and others push the existing bus to get it started that day at the port.) The man said he had hoped a bus would be on the list and said he would pay for it and for everything else as well.

Chapter 24

In the largest and the smallest of ways, Father Ray seemed unable to say no. Whatever the need he encountered, if there was any way possible to fill it, he did, or at least tried, and he never turned anyone away.

He was still working from the old military trailer when a homeless man wandered onto the Orphanage grounds. He was filthy and smelled and told Father Ray he was hungry. The priest welcomed the man, fed him, and provided clean clothing. The man was then taken to a clinic for a medical examination, where it was discovered that he had a venereal disease. It was recalled how unsettled everyone was when Father Ray informed them that the man would remain a guest of the Orphanage until he was well again.

On the other side of the welcome mat one day stood a young Canadian who had been coming to Thailand for many years, often as an amateur anthropologist, assembling collections of Southeast Asian art and artifacts that he sold to museums around the world. Now he was working on his first novel. "Back in 1983 when I was halfway through writing the book on Koh Samet, computers were making their debut in Thailand," he said, "and I decided it would be more efficient to learn how to write on one. So I moved to Pattaya and, learning Father Ray ran a computer school, went to see him about renting an Apple using WordStar. He wanted to see my writing first. After leaving the manuscript with him a couple of days, I returned and he said, 'This is good stuff. You're a writer. Look, writers don't have any money, so I'm going to rent you a computer to use here in the school and when you get your book published, pay us then. How's that sound?' And that's what we did. When my first royalty check arrived, I sent him the Canadian $750 I owed. And that's why, although I made a lot of religions into Bad Guys in the book, the Catholic Church…is left out of that."

Somnuk Pao-ngon witnessed countless scenes like this. She was from Chon Buri and studying hotel management on the weekends when, in 1992, she met Betty Roy and was introduced to Father Ray. Soon after that, she took over the desk outside the priest's office, usually putting in twelve-hour days, from six to six, because she felt uneasy about denying him her Saturdays, when she was in class.

"His style was not that of a businessman," Somnuk said, "he was a father. I wanted him to be my boss, not my father. But he never complained about what I did or didn't do. I didn't like the children running around like monkeys and I had to learn to accept it. It was hard for me to accept the 'open style' when, during the weekends, I was learning the opposite, the 'business style'."

She remembered it taking two years before her job definition became clear to her, as she filed and answered the phone and welcomed visitors. In the end, she remained five years, showing him her grades at the end of each semester. She had a Grade Point Average of 3.6, she said, and he was very pleased. "He wanted people to study, to learn," she said, "and he gave praise when they studied.

"His door was always open. I never knew if the people who came were here to get or give. I didn't know if they were asking for help or giving him money; it was difficult to judge, so I let them all see him. Which was what he wanted, anyway.

"He came into the office wearing T-shirts with holes in them. He never paid any attention to how he looked. The T-shirts were very old; he never spent any money on himself. I wanted him to tell people how hard it was to get money, but he didn't, he just gave.

"I thought he went overboard in giving presents to the kids at Christmas. I was from a poor family and thought he went too far and gave too much. He said he just wanted to give the children the best.

"The staff was well paid, so we did everything we could to deserve it. I was being paid 15,000 baht a month"---about U.S. $375, still a generous salary for a fresh university graduate in Thailand--- "and I was buying a house. And he gave raises every year.

"I was worried about his not spending money more cautiously. Father trusted people and he never investigated ways to save money. People would take advantage. Father would never talk about not spending, or trying to save money. It was impossible to teach him this.

"I expected people to have a good heart when they came here, but not all were that way. Too many took advantage. I didn't tell him this; I figured he wanted to give anyway. This kind of information is very sensitive. I didn't want to give him any more headache problems. It was one of the reasons I left the Orphanage.

"Father never expected anything of anyone, he just accepted what came. He never said no, he never refused. He'd say, 'Give him five hundred baht, a thousand baht.' He had a drawer full of money."

Chapter 25

Father Ray opened his home for street kids reluctantly.

Make that: very reluctantly. He had not asked advice from his friend Father Joe Maier, who operated shelters in Bangkok for homeless children from the city's meanest streets. If he had, his fellow Redemptorist would have told him that after a youngster lived on his or her own on the streets for a period of time, that person became an "animal," in the sense that a cat or a dog becomes feral when existing in a wild state.

To survive, Father Joe believed, these children adopted codes and behaviors outside any that were regarded by the population at large as socially, legally, or morally acceptable. And because there was no legal framework that would compel the children to remain in the shelter, they were free to leave any time they wished. Father Joe would have told Father Ray to expect a high drop-out rate and to be prepared for problems unlike any he'd experienced at the Orphanage.

Father Ray already knew this, or at the very least he sensed it. Over the years, he had tried to integrate a few street kids into the general population at the Orphanage, but admitted that they "really do not 'fit' since they are extremely street-wise and devious." What that meant was that even at an early age, sex and drugs were as common as violence and theft. And where orphans desired and clung to the ideal of family, street kids rejected it, suspicious of all authority on a good day, totally rejecting it on most days.

UNICEF, the United Nations organization that focuses on help for children, defined "street children" in two basic ways: (1) Children who work on the streets, but live with their families and (2) Children who live on the streets, fend for themselves, and have no contact with their families." Father Ray expanded that definition. "For us," he said, "the term 'street children' also includes children who are found working in inappropriate places or children from dysfunctional families [who] frequently 'progress' to becoming street children."

Pattaya was now a small city, with a population of some fifty thousand. In the years following America's war in Vietnam, it became one of Thailand's most popular destinations for sex tourists, drawing up to a million visitors a year, most of them from Europe, with Germany and Scandinavia leading the pack. Russia would join the mix in the 1990s, flying by charter planes into the U-tapao airfield, which had been turned over to the Thai military at the end of the war.

"The place is lit up like Hollywood Boulevard at night," said the Lonely Planet guidebook of that period. "Travelers will find Pattaya lacking in culture a well as in good taste, since the whole place seems designed to attract the worst kind of Western tourist."

The local government and Tourist Authority of Thailand tried selling the city as a family resort, emphasizing the fine accommodation and water sports, calling Pattaya "Thailand's Riviera," but such claims and comparisons made residents laugh or snort with derision. The truth was that three transvestite palaces offered glossy drag queen shows, giving the community a reputation as being a sort of open air Boys-R-Us, and South Pattaya Beach was one of the world's top destinations for pedophiles where young boys openly plied their trade. And hundreds, perhaps thousands of businesses, weren't interested in becoming a family resort.

Moreover, the beach was filthy, the sidewalks and streets were a mess, the sea off the beach was as black as India ink from years of sewage being piped by hotels directly into it (the city did not have a wastewater treatment plant until the 1990s), and there were so many bars and karaoke lounges and massage parlors and other sex venues that one of Asia's leading experts on human trafficking described the city as "the world's number one whore zone." The Lonely Planet guidebook called the place "the Garden of Earthly Delights, in the most Boschean sense," a reference to both the fifteenth-century Arabian erotic classic, *The Perfumed Garden* and the Dutch painter of the same period, Hieronymous Bosch, whose great triptych "The Garden of Earthly Delights" was, like most of his work, focused on themes of sin and divine retribution.

In January 1991, Father Ray wrote, "Here in Pattaya, the situation of the street kids is not too good. We estimate there are about four hundred of them. Some have run away from home, some have been kicked out of their homes by relatives and don't know what it is to have a bed and clean clothes. I start this project with much trepidation, but also with confidence that we can do something for them. The Big Boss Upstairs will be expected to do his share. So in your prayers, give Him a little reminder."

Many of the street kids came to Pattaya from distant provinces---in much the same way others migrated to Bangkok, Chiang Mai, and Phuket---believing money could be made from rich, gullible foreigners. For most, this promise was not fulfilled and the kids lived mainly on what they could beg or steal and a day's sustenance might be no more than some packaged dry noodles that cost five baht (twenty U.S. cents). Typically, they lived in small packs in abandoned buildings, creating loosely organized bands or gangs with other kids like themselves. These were patriarchal groups---the nominal leaders were always male---that did not espouse or give love, only a flimsy sort of loyalty to each other and authority to the strongest. And the ages ranged from toddlers to teens, the consequence of entire families of kids running away together.

Many, both males and females, had been in jail. Up until recently, seven-year-olds were treated by the law in Thailand as adults when it came to crime and punishment. Most had been physically or sexually abused at home---a leading cause of their becoming runaways---and many were now being exploited behind the padlocked doors of sweatshops and brothels. Sex was indulged openly. The drug of choice was glue that sold for six baht, the small tube opened inside a plastic bag that was held up to the face and inhaled. For all these kids, life on the street, with its freedom of movement and choice, minus adult authority, seemed an attractive alternative to what had become before.

Although the Thai government acknowledged its duty to protect children who were victims of exploitation and abuse, it lacked the resources---and, some said, motivation---to provide proper care for rapidly increasing numbers of neglected children. So it was left, mainly, to the NGOs, non-governmental organizations like Father Ray's. Thus it was in most developing nations.

Some told Father Ray to reconsider, if for no other reason because of the added drain on a cash flow already severely drained. More than ten years passed from the time he accepted the first orphan in 1971, and when he opened the school for the deaf in 1982. Since then, he had started schools for the disabled in 1986 and for the blind in 1987. Now, just four years later, he was going to launch another major project? He was already responsible for the feeding and sheltering and teaching of more than two hundred children and young adults, not to mention paying a growing staff. It was suggested that he might be biting off more than even he could chew.

Father Ray ignored the nay-sayers and once he made his decision to start a shelter, he went at it like an innovative, and daring, showman. Believing he would need some sort of bait to attract his elusive and highly suspicious target audience, he acquired an ice-cream cart and then patrolled the back streets, giving the ice cream away. Another day, he pushed a hot dog cart. Like a fisherman, he was "chumming" the waters.

The carts were equipped with bells, heralding the priest's approach. Over a period of four or five weeks, he had between forty and fifty children regularly greeting him, or, at least, willing to get close enough to take the free food. Getting them into a shelter in a shop house that was offered to him was another matter. Free meals, new clothing, medical care, showers, and a safe place to sleep were offered, but the children remained wary. Grown-ups had lied to them and abused them all their young lives. Why should they believe this adult?

Father Ray decided to use same chumming ploy at the shelter. "I think I am the only priest in the world who has opened a key club for Heaven," he wrote. "Let me explain. The building is four stories high, and the fourth floor is 'Heaven.' You have to have the key to get in, and you acquire a key with good deportment and hygiene. In Heaven there are video games, a color TV, a refrigerator filled with fruit and cool drinks, soft chairs, even candy and cookies. The idea is to be good and you will get the key to Heaven. (It's what we're all supposed to do anyway!) If you do not have a key to Heaven, you will have fruit, TV games, etc., also, but only at specific times. Those who have merited Heaven can go there any time they want and enjoy the Elysian bliss of a free canteen. I don't mean to give The Boss Upstairs any competition," he added, "since the kernel of the idea came from the way He runs things Himself!"

It was an ordinary shophouse near what is now the Carrefour market on Pattaya Central Road, not far from the Redemptorist Center and the Orphanage grounds. The amenities were basic: electric fans and cold water showers, meals served cafeteria style. This would be home for the street kids for the next six years.

It was not a quick success. In two years, the shelter still housed fewer than twenty kids and the drop-out rate was discouraging, just as Father Joe would have predicted if he'd been consulted. At the Orphanage, if the children weren't adopted they tended to remain through their teenage years and, for some, eventually, through young adulthood. At the Redemptorist Street Kids Home, the lure of open sex and drugs, the freedom of movement, and the absence of conventional rules proved for many to be more enticing than nutritious meals, cold sodas, and video games. A ticket to "Heaven" was nice, but the familiar anarchy of the street was more enticing.

The peculiar security that accompanied what most of the mainstream, or straight, world called misfortune and worse was only a few steps away, always beckoning. Once the children's bellies were full and they had new (or at least clean) clothing, and had slept off their amphetamine binges, the rawness of rules wore thin and a majority of them walked out, knowing they could always come back if they wanted. Just as they could always leave as they wished. Thus, many stayed untamed "animals," disengaged from the adults who wished to change their lives, like cats, willing to purr so long as they were stroked and fed, but never ready to give up their independence.

Father Ray noted in his Christmas letter in 1992 that the work with the street kids was "the smallest project I have, but it is the most difficult." Father Ray never wrote in his newsletters about the specifics of what made it the "most difficult." Who could, after all, comprehend? So, as best he could, the priest always put a happy face on the situation.

In 1993, a program was started to make the local people more aware of the street children. "Once a week, we have a little party and invite a handful of local business people. We give a slide presentation showing how the street children live and then give some talks. But the best part of the evening is when one of the street kids gets up and tells what it was like when he or she was on the street. You can hear a pin drop as the child tells how he or she had to go into the sex trade in order to eat. Each time I hear one of the kids tell their story my throat chokes up. Believe it or not, we have recently picked up a three-year-old with newly contracted venereal disease. Sometimes I sit at my desk and wonder if this is all a bad dream."

Often, he thought about quitting: close the shelter and the hell with it.

Chapter 26

Denis Gervais grew up in Louiseville, 100 kilometers north of Montreal, Canada, a native French speaker who didn't learn English until after he'd graduated from university at age nineteen and went to work for IBM as a Systems Engineer. (He remembers today that after taking a 14-week computer course in English, his technical vocabulary was good, but he still couldn't make small talk at a party.) An aunt was a nun at an orphanage in Montreal, where he attended primary school. From age twelve to fifteen, Denis studied at a seminary. When he started with IBM in 1966, he coached baseball for small kids on behalf of a Jesuit priest he describes as "similar to Father Ray, a visionary, a builder, a doer, very charismatic," a man who went from organizing sports programs for slum children to chairing the Olympic Games in 1976 when they were held in the same Canadian city. So perhaps Denis was, himself, programmed for what lay ahead.

At IBM, after learning English and sixteen computer languages along with the IBM product line, Denis was moved to Toronto to work in the IBM Laboratory on the development of online banking. From 1982 to 1985 he traveled, by his own estimate, seventy percent of the time: to Europe at least once a month, and to Australia, the Far East, and South America.

When he first visited Thailand, in 1983, during a seven-week-long journey, he remembered being in the air eighty-two hours and traveling a total of one-hundred and sixty-eight hours, including time in ground transportation, which, he said, was equal to one week of the seven. (When Denis reminisced, it often sounded as if he had become one with a computer; asked for a date to fit an anecdote, he gave it, along with the time of day and a weather report.) During that time, he said, he was introduced to golf, becoming almost addicted, eventually playing some of the courses in Pattaya.

On his sixth visit to Thailand, in 1991, he noticed the Orphanage sign on the highway and when the golf course he wanted to play that day was closed for a Navy tournament, he decided to visit. Father Ray took him on a tour and at the end of it, Denis said he'd sponsor one of the children and promised to return the next year and organize some sports programs.

In the first week of a ten-week vacation in 1992, Denis played golf three times. He then went to see Father Ray, who was puzzling over a computer book. The priest said he thought he needed a database which would make sense out of a donor list that was as disorganized as his desk. Denis was given a computer. He sat down and wrote a program and never played golf again on that holiday.

Denis was tall and spare, scholarly and soft-spoken, given to think about things slowly, rationally. When he returned to Montreal, Denis thought about going back to be a full-time volunteer at the Orphanage. He decided he would and put his house on the market, asked for early retirement from IBM, and caught the first flight to Thailand.

The first thing he did was look at the Orphanage's accounting system. He was appalled. It was not like Father Ray's desk: it was worse. The opportunities for skimming cash were not just obvious, but, as he put it, "tremendous." He said it took a full year before he even found all the bank accounts.

The good news was that after Denis wrote a new program and fed all the data into it, he discovered that every baht was accounted for. So clean was the operation, he recalled years later, that every bill was paid when it was received, even when it would have been wiser to hold onto the cash for the allowed thirty to ninety days before the due date.

Until his early retirement kicked in, Denis worked part-time for IBM in Thailand, while living as an unsalaried volunteer at the Orphanage. In the years following, as the sponsorship program grew, he saw a need for a new computer system to keep it managed efficiently. When the Orphanage had a hundred sponsors, at least five people called every month to say they hadn't heard anything about "their kid" recently. Denis created a program that made sure a new photograph of the child and an updated report went to every sponsor at least once every six months. The child wrote thank-you notes for gifts received, thus putting him or her closer to the sponsor. Visits were encouraged, and tracked. (By 2004, there were more than 3,500 sponsors in the United Kingdom alone, and it was rare that anyone wrote to say they felt ignored.)

Denis decided to tie up some loose strings in his life, left dangling from his childhood. There had been many early clues leading to what came next---the teenaged years in a seminary, the aunt who was a nun, the Jesuit priest who organized sports for slum kids---so it was no surprise in 1999 when he asked to join the Brotherhood of Redemptorists and then moved into a small room next to Father Ray in the Pattaya Community. He lived in this fashion for a year as a postulant, following that for a year in Montreal as a novice, then returned to Pattaya and his old desk. As a Redemptorist Brother, he couldn't say Mass, hear Confession or administer the other sacraments. At the same time, he took a priest's vows of poverty, chastity, and obedience, thus earning a place on what he called "the list of approved representatives of God." He quickly added that "everyone was on the same list. You can bless people, too. The difference is I'm a member of the Congregation and although I still do the same work as before I took the vows, I do it with a new light as a result of the spiritual training and close contact with the Redemptorists."

In 2004, Brother Denis Gervais was in the same office, still working as a volunteer.

*

"One day you will work for me for free."

Father Ray said this to another successful businessman in 1996. Alun Jones, a native of South London, was a man who marketed pharmaceuticals, who came to Pattaya on Christmas holiday. After the Orphanage children sang carols while he and his wife ate dinner in their hotel's dining room, he introduced himself to the portly priest accompanying the kids. Father Ray invited Alun and Sally Jones to come to his Christmas Eve Midnight Mass, drawing a map that led to St. Nikolaus Church. They did so and the next day, they visited the Orphanage and that's when Father Ray predicted the man's future.

(Father Ray's skill at prognostication was mentioned numerous times during interviews conducted for this book and while one person scoffed and said that sort of arrogance wasn't in character, others said it fit perfectly the priest's teasing sense of humor.)

They stayed in touch while Alun and his Sally were living and working on Bali and when the situation turned violent on the nearby island of Timor, British citizens were urged to leave Indonesia. The Joneses caught the last flight to Singapore, where Sally suggested they continue on to Thailand and visit the Orphanage. Two years had passed since their first meeting with Father Ray and when they entered his cluttered office in 1998, he reportedly rumbled in his always welcoming yet matter-of-fact voice, "Ah, you've come to work!"

For the next six months, Alun made himself useful in any way he could devise as he became acquainted with the organization and staff. He and his wife then returned to England, but stayed in touch.

The way Alun remembered it, two years later, in July 2000, Father Ray called him in the middle of the night and asked him if he would "dedicate" his life to working for him and the children. Alun talked it over with his wife and next day he paid off his lease. One month after that, in August 2000, they were in Pattaya, where Alun was told his main job would be to coordinate with the Pattaya Orphanage Trust in London.

Chapter 27

Riccardo Carini was born to Italian parents in England in 1930. Learning Italian and English from birth, to which he added fluent French, he and his brother ran a "confirming house" in London, a specialist export business that required Riccardo to travel much of the world while playing a role in developing economic growth in the U.K. from the 1960s through the 1980s.

He met Father Ray in 1982 when "a friend and I decided we would go to visit this sleepy fishing village outside Bangkok after each of us had fulfilled our business commitments---he in Japan, I in Bangkok---and we would have ten days in this restful place. Within an hour of arriving, I realized that I had made a dreadful mistake and when he finally arrived from Tokyo, he, too, was rather disgusted by what Pattaya had to offer. Trying to find something suitable to do, I picked up the equivalent of *What's On* and I was given four things that perhaps the visitor to Pattaya might like to do, the one more boring than the other, until I saw the last one, suggesting a visit to the local Orphanage, and that's what I did and that's where the story begins."

After meeting Father Ray, who took him and his friend on the usual tour, Riccardo returned to London and just before Christmas the same year, with members of his family and close friends, he established the Pattaya Orphanage Trust. It was an organization that in time would become one of the United Kingdom's top five hundred fund-raising charities, deliver to Father Ray as much as U.S. $1.2 million a year---a sum that in 2003 represented seventy percent of the Orphanage's revenue flow---and earn the son of Italian immigrants the honor of

Knight Commander bestowed by the Vatican. Initially, the Trust advertised in religious---mainly Roman Catholic---periodicals, for many years sending only modest sums to Thailand. But from 1994 onwards, the contributions accelerated rapidly. That was when Andrew Scadding, who had been a consultant to the organization, joined the board of trustees and installed a computer system that made operations more efficient. Andrew started in fund-raising as a volunteer at sixteen for the Yorkshire Association for the Disabled. During and following university at Cambridge, he continued to work with the physically disabled found-ing trustee of Africa Now, a small development charity, before becoming a trustee at the Pattaya Orphanage Trust. Riccardo retired in 1999---retaining a position as Chairman---and Andrew became Chief Executive.

The Trust in many ways reflected the Orphanage's fund-raising techniques. Four times a year it produced a slick, full-color newsletter, featuring one of the major projects in each issue. (Father Ray's own newsletter remained a black-and-white, typed personal letter to the end.) It developed an Internet web site with a news page that was updated weekly and a monthly e-newsletter that "keeps a growing number of supporters abreast of developments." And it aggressively sought financial support from trusts set up by numerous businesses and celebrities.

It also scored a major money-producing coup when, quoting Andrew, a "very dedicated and capable woman called Jo Boucher, who worked for the Trust up until 2000, made a highly detailed and very effective application to the National Lottery for support for the Job Placement Agency at the Vocational School. Our success was due in part, obviously, the school having a very good case to put, but in a very large part it was Jo's hard work and dedication which resulted in that case being understood and accepted." At the time, the U.K. government was charged with dedicating part of its lottery earnings to charities in what it regarded as the world's poorest nations. Thus, for five years, gambling losses incurred in the U.K. supported the disabled in a country that most of those punters likely had never heard of.

"The U.K. government has now decreed that Thailand is no longer a Third World country," said Andrew in 2004, "so we are no longer eligible for support either from the government or from the National Lottery: the government is concentrating its aid on the poorest countries and the National Lottery has had its income severely restricted, partly by falling ticket sales and partly by the government diverting some of its income to different channels."

Another short-lived windfall came when Baron Riccardo was successful in obtaining a grant from the European Union for US$250,000, a sum that paid for four of the five floors of the School for Deaf Children. "This was in the heady days when the E.U. had money to spend on helping those less fortunate," said Andrew. "Today the only money it spends in Thailand is a pittance devoted to Burmese refugees on the border."

Baron Riccardo additionally played a role in getting a smaller but similar organization going in France, Les Amis de L'Orphelinat de Pattaya (Friends of the Pattaya Orphanage).

Most impressive was the Trust's list of 15,000 individual donors and sponsors which Andrew called "a very ordinary collection of very generous people. I can tell you one story that makes me feel humble. One of our donors is a man who has to manage on a very small income from the state. He sponsors two children, which costs him what I guess is a substantial percentage of his monthly income. A couple of years ago, I wrote to him to invite him to allow us to put his name on our Roll of Honor, on a wall at the Orphanage. His response was simple and typical: he said he would prefer not to have his name on show, it was sufficient honor for him to be able to help."

The Trust also organized events on Father Ray's rare visits, usually arranging to have him speak at the Westminster Cathedral. "Father Ray was a great preacher," said Andrew, "and it was through his homilies that his supporters here could glimpse a little of the faith which had taken him to Thailand and into the service of the children of Pattaya."

One event turned slightly sour, however. That was in 2002 on Father Ray's last appearance in London, when he told the story of two infants in his baby room, both of whom suffered from Down syndrome, a chromosomal disorder that results in mental retardation and physical abnormalities. They were in adjacent cots and bonded in some way that no one understood, but all could readily see. When one died, the other expired shortly afterward.

Father Ray told the story to illustrate how the mentally challenged could nonetheless feel deep and real love. The problem was that he called the children "Mongols"---the disorder also was known as "mongolism" and in Father Ray's youth, its victims often were called "Mongolian idiots"---and instead of speaking of the "mentally challenged" or "retarded," he used the word "morons," a word that brought to mind a type of humor from the period when he came of age in America that were tagged "moron jokes."

"The problem we had," said Andrew, "was that for the only time ever, Father Ray was addressing the parish Mass in the Cathedral Nave and usually we had our Mass for the Trust in a side chapel. Amongst the congregation were parents of a Down syndrome child, who took deep offense to Father Ray's lack of political correctness and complained to the Cathedral authorities, who wrote an extremely pompous letter.

"Of course, Father Ray's vocabulary---and to some extent some of his preconceptions---were those of America in the Fifties, not effete London in the third millennium. Political correctness is not much of an issue in Thailand, and was irrelevant to Father Ray, who was busy doing God's work, not talking about it."

Chapter 28

"The most important news so far this year has been sad news for me," Father Ray wrote in summer 1990. "Mother Superior (that loving maternal and instinctively understanding woman of whom you have often heard me speak) is being changed. She has been elected as a consultor to the 'Big' Mother Superior, so she must live in the mother house which is about four hours away from here. She now has some peace and time for contemplation without this nasty old priest bothering her with bubble gum or fantastically wonderful new ideas and projects for the kids.

"We had a farewell dinner for her in a local Chinese restaurant and there were tears in many eyes, including my own. We have had a great time together, which she fondly mentioned in her speech. Actually, we were a good team (she was the better part) and I will truly miss her very much.

"Now for the surprising news…the new Mother Superior is the blood sister of the old Mother Superior!!! I have not gotten to know her very well yet; however I am certain her departing sister will clue her in on 'everything'! This much I know…if the name of the New Mother Superior is [still] said incorrectly by changing a vowel, her name means SHARK!! Be prepared for future adventures of Jaws, the new Mother Superior."

Sister Nomchit Aripak had served---struggled? ---with Father Ray for nine years. When she arrived in 1981, there were eighty orphans and when she left there were one hundred and twenty. During the same period, the Orphanage---the single word was now used to encompass all the projects---had experienced its greatest growth, including the start-up of the schools for the deaf, the blind, and the physically disabled. For the next six years, it was Sister Chamlam Aripak's turn.

"The new Mother Superior (Sister Shark) has started some of the old tricks the previous Mother Superior tried to pull on me," Father Ray soon reported. "However, I am well prepared for the onslaught. I will give this word of advice to one and all. NEVER volunteer to drive nuns about in your car. They only want to go a few miles to a certain store; but when you get there, you are only a few more miles away to another certain store. ('We might as well go to this other place, since we are so close already!!') Soon you are a good hour and a half way from home and you have spent four or five hours waiting in the car. After the fifth store, I decided to play a little trick on Her Highness. After she got out of the car, I changed the place in the parking lot where I had originally parked. I had devilish delight in watching Her Illustrious Majesty stomp up to where she thought the car was. Then further splendid pleasure in watching her in my rear view mirror, as she began looking for the car. She did not talk to me the whole way back to the Orphanage, for which I was immensely grateful. It is little pleasures like that which help make my life meaningful."

Another year passed and Father Ray wrote, "Mother Superiors are tough cookies, and Mother Shark is certainly no exception. As most of you know, Mother Shark's opinion of her 'cross in life' (me!) is that I am just a bigger boy than the rest of the orphans, but not yet fully mature for my age. (She cannot mean physically, so she must mean mentally!) One of my pursuits in life is to make her life happy. A few odd tricks now and then (like the time I faked a heart attack while I was driving her to town) should make our life together joyous and more like 'family.'

"I like to 'surprise' her with little acts of love and appreciation…but sometimes she surprises me! The other day, we had a party and I had her on the stage. I was presenting her with a garland of flowers in appreciation for all her hard work. When I gave it to her, I jokingly said, 'Don't I get a kiss?' The kids fell completely silent because they never heard me say that to her before. Then, she puckered up her lips and landed a wet little kiss on my cheek. I have never been kissed by a Mother Superior before! She had me speechless and she knew it. A sly 'shark-like' smile went over her face and my face turned red. The kids went wild with hooting and clapping. She won this time, but next time she won't. I think it's time to get a fake epileptic seizure during morning prayers."

There is no record of such a 'seizure,' but the pranks didn't stop. For Christmas one year, after two plastic toilet seats had broken in the rest room used by the nuns, Father Ray gave Sister Chalam Aripak a sturdy wooden seat. The next year he gave her a talking mirror that said, "Naughty girl, go wash your face!" and on another Christmas there were two pairs of slippers, one "that keeps saying, 'Ouch!' every other step, the other a pair that when you walk, they randomly give (to put it as delicately as possible) the sound of gas escaping from the human frame. I forgot to say that both sets of slippers have blinking lights on the toes. Merry Christmas, dear Mother Shark!"

(Father Ray's secretary, Betty Roy, said she convinced him not to give one gift he picked out, the figure of a woman with a big stomach that opened in front, where it was expected a woman would keep her jewelry. "It was," Betty said, "really gross.")

When a new building was under construction, she frequently sought the priest's advice, "asking about what color tiles, what kind of toilets, what light fixtures should we have and where should they be. I told her that where the toilets are located the walls should be painted brown...and where the urinals are, the walls should be a suitable yellow. It took her a while to visualize this and realize I was joking. All she could say was, 'Father Ray, can't you ever be serious?' (What did I do wrong? It might look good!)"

It must be said that Sister Chalam tried to give as good as she got. One year, her Christmas gift to him was an alarm clock that shouted, "Three...Two... One...GET UP!" Another Christmas, she gave him a plastic pig that oinked and walked with a wiggle and on the next, he said he received "a fat man doll, which had a cable coming out of it. At the end of the cable was a rubber bulb. When the bulb is squeezed, the man quickly lowers his pants and pulls them up again. Mother Shark was in uncontrollable laugher as I squeezed the bulb over and over again. There was no mention of who the fat man was supposed to represent, nor was there any explanation of why such a gift was given me. By this time, Mother Shark was in hysterics, practically in convulsions on the floor."

Another time, she enlisted the help of some of the children, getting them to "tell me that my shoes need shining, there is a hole in my shirt, or the sandwich I made last week is still in the refrigerator. The kids in their innocence do not realize they are being used by Mother Shark to do her dirty deeds. I try to live a quiet, celibate life, but having Mother Shark around is like being married without the fun."

And then there was the time that Sister told the children to clean out the Mitsubishi pickup truck that had been converted into a station wagon, the vehicle that Father Ray used for years to haul everything from elephant dung to school kids and nuns around. "My car is somewhat like my desk, IT IS NOT TO BE TOUCHED!" Father Ray later said. "It took me days to find most of my stuff again. Most of it had been thrown away. The kids knew they should not have cooperated in the act. 'She made us do it,' they said. Of course, I let the kids off the hook, but not Mother Shark! Retaliation was in order. A blow for bachelorhood was needed…the Boss Upstairs must have sent one of His best idea generating angels down to my side. The kids helped me trap a small live bat and we put it in her office. It took her two days to find out it was there. I did not hear the scream, but the kids said it was very loud. Thank you, Lord."

Chapter 29

Suporntum Mongkolsawadi was born in Nong Khai, in northeastern Thailand near the Laos border, with legs that didn't work. His parents took him to a number of hospitals and doctors. At age six or seven he was operated on and then fitted with braces and given crutches. But, he remembered, "The pain was terrible. I stayed with my grandmother and she took off the braces. The doctor suggested a wheelchair."

When he reached school age, Suporntum moved on his own to Nonthaburi, the urbanized province to the north of Bangkok, to attend what was then Thailand's only school for the physically disabled . He remained there for six years, boarding during the week, going home on the weekends, and getting around in a conventional wheelchair or, on the street, in a three-wheeled chair that was propelled by a hand-operated lever attached to the equivalent of a bicycle chain. It wasn't unusual, Suporntum said, to travel as many as twenty kilometers a day, activity that, along with the effort exerted in his wheelchair, gave him extraordinary strength in his arms, shoulders, and chest. This was typical for those who had lost the use of their legs. After finishing his secondary education, by which time his family had moved to Nonthaburi, he attended an evening school for one semester and then, in 1986, he was accepted as a student at Father Ray's school in Pattaya. Initially he took the three-month course in electronics repair (of toasters, fans, radios, television and the like). Then he enrolled in the two-year computer science course that was begun in 1987.

Suporntum remembered the school as being "unstable at first," as teachers came and went. Most were from the military, as there were no local universities at the time. Instruction was limited to weekends with homework assigned for the rest of the week. There were about fifty or sixty pupils, perhaps thirty-five of them studying electronics repair, the rest enrolled in the more difficult computer course. He said the computer class drop-out rate was high; in his class of twenty-seven, only thirteen graduated.

Classes were held in a two-story building erected on the Redemptorist Center grounds specifically for the school's use. There were ramps leading into the building and between floors. The elevator was large enough to accommodate several wheelchairs at once. Equipment used for instruction or practice repair was either bought at discount or provided without cost by IBM.

"Students came from all over," said Suporntum. "One year, more than sixty provinces [of seventy-six] were represented. It wasn't easy for them. Some exceptions were made, but most had to get themselves to Pattaya to be interviewed and take an entrance exam. The attitude of the disabled people themselves and their families was another problem. Many families were overly protective, they'd say, 'Stay home, we'll take care of you.' So, many stayed, but some others actually 'escaped' from their homes to come here.

"We did a lot of promotion in the beginning so people would know about us. We sent letters to hospitals, foundations, radio stations, and TV. Local welfare offices were contacted. We also had a sports program and that gave us a high visibility."

An athletic program made sense and although Father Ray was surprised a few years later when the students asked to have a swimming pool constructed, he supported the program from the start. Much of the motivation behind the vocational school---perhaps all of it, after all---was aimed at creating self-respect and determination in those who had none, and what better way than to give the disabled young people a way to beat their disability than through competition that was physical? From 1988, not only were the disabled students learning how to fix broken appliances and design circuit boards, they played wheelchair tennis and basketball.

"Everyone has heard about the Olympic Games in Korea this year," Father Ray wrote in his Christmas newsletter that same year, "but not many know of the Special Olympics, the…PARALYMPICS. It was held in Seoul in October. I am proud to say that one of our students at the School for the Disabled was chosen by the royal Thai government to represent Thailand. He competed in three different wheelchair races. His story is something out of 'Believe It or Not.' Two years ago, he applied and was accepted as a student in computer science. Up to that time, he had never studied computers and he did not speak English, but he immediately showed signs of being what we call a 'natural' on the computer. Now he is somewhat of a computer genius. He graduates just before Christmas and is the first student we have asked to stay on to become a teacher. It will be the first job of his life. His English is also very good now, and needless to say we are very proud of how this young man's life has been changed."

The new teacher who went to the Paralympics, of course, was Suporntum. His mother died in 1988 and he said he considered leaving the school then, but stayed on when Father Ray refused to allow it, offering the teaching job and assigning him, for a start, the young students in the computer class. Two years after that, he was promoted, becoming head of the computer department and five years after that, in 1995, he became the vocational school's headmaster.

Suporntum may have been an exceptional student and graduate, but he was not the exception to the rule. When asked for the names of some other students who might be called "success stories," he laughed and said, "How many do you want? A hundred?"

One of them was Duangdoaw Yothasri, called Nok, the Thai word for "bird." She was from a small Catholic village in the Northeast not far from where Father Ray had supervised the construction of a medical clinic when he was stationed there in the 1960s, long before Nok was born. At that time, Father Ray met the man who became Nok's father and when the priest started the vocational school, he was one of many the priest asked to spread the word. Three months later, the man's daughter, then eighteen, was in a motorcycle accident and lost her right leg from the knee. Nok began computer classes in 1990 and---only Hollywood would try to get away with this many coincidences---her teacher was Suporntum. And that wasn't the end of it.

For two years following graduation, Nok worked at a hotel in Pattaya, and for three years after that in Bangkok, returning to Pattaya in 1996 to become the vocational school's first woman instructor.

A year later, she and Suporntum were married by Father Ray and Father Pat Morrissy.

Nor were Suporntum and Nok alone. Sompong Rattanasang---called Henry by Father Ray and, in time, by everyone else---was born in 1963 in Saraburi, about a hundred kilometers north of Bangkok. His mother sold noodles in front of their house and his father labored on construction projects, paid by the day when he could find work. When Henry, one of four children, was three years old, he was playing in a canal and by the time he reached home he felt "feverish." A few days later, the diagnosis was polio.

Henry's legs stopped growing and although he learned to walk with the use of braces, his gait was uneven and the pain was great. His parents couldn't afford a wheelchair and even if he'd had one, he remembers that his province---no different from all the others, really---was not supportive of the disabled and it would have been impossible to navigate the wheelchair comfortably and safely. Nonetheless, he went to school, getting around as best he could, usually on homemade crutches or on his hands and knees.

After taking a one-year correspondence course in electronics repair, to get some experience he started taking in broken TV sets and other electric appliances while continuing to live at home. Nonetheless, when he applied for a job with a big company that did the same work, he was turned away because he was handicapped. For the next six years he worked in a small shop for a friend, "fixing video, camera, anything I can do," being paid the equivalent of U.S. $20 a month, plus food and shelter.

His parents were separated by now and for another two years he lived with his mother and siblings, visiting an agency that had been helpful when he was young. There, he was told about Father Ray's vocational school and soon after that, an older sister took him to Pattaya for an interview and exam. He was accepted and while his family urged him to stick to electronics repair, he was determined to learn about computers. By now he was twenty-eight and study habits were difficult to resume, but he finished the two-year course, using a second-hand wheelchair that had been donated by a Japanese charity. For the next three years, he taught at the vocational school, one hour in the morning, one hour in the afternoon.

In 1993, he was asked if he'd like to work with Denis Gervais in the Orphanage offices. Henry had learned English as a child, but had lost the facility, and now had to relearn it. This made it difficult to work with Denis, but he was now being paid ten times what he'd made in the small shop: the equivalent of U.S. $200 a month, greater than the monthly per capita income. He lived in a room on the Orphanage grounds, flanked by English speakers, and he soon regained his lost facility.

The pressure of the new job was intense. Often he worked twenty-four hours a day and he considered quitting, but during his second year in Father Ray's computer course, he had met Wanrunee Samnaksakul. He sought her advice. Wanrunee was from Chaiyaphum, once again in the poor Northeast, and was the daughter of a schoolteacher. She, too, contracted polio at age three, but her crippling disease was believed to be the result of a doctor's having given her an injection of outdated medication---another commonplace in undeveloped countries, where many of the disabled are the victims of poorly-trained physicians and expired or counterfeit pharmaceuticals.

She attended secondary school in Nonthaburi, the same Bangkok suburb where Suporntum had attended classes for the disabled. She continued her studies, finishing two years at a technical college before hearing about Father Ray. She was twenty-one when she started computer classes and met Henry, and graduated in one year. After working in Bangkok for a while, she returned to Pattaya to operate a small electronics repair shop and to work for two years in a computer school. Success remained elusive.

Henry was still working for Denis Gervais, creating programs for accounting and sponsorship, keeping the orphan case files up to date, and teaching computer skills to the older children and to adults at the vocational school. And…moonlighting in Wanrunee's various enterprises when she needed him. By now, they were sharing a room, secretly, because they were told that such behavior was not acceptable outside marriage.

Henry was replaced in the Orphanage office by another graduate of the vocational school and for a time he ran a small electronics repair shop in Pattaya, where he taught others how to fix broken TVs and so on. He was offered a job teaching full-time at the vocational school and told Father Ray he didn't want to teach. Asked what he did want to do, he said he wanted to work for Father Ray. He was given a computer, a desk and work to keep him busy. Henry also was a talented tennis player, competing in many countries in the games for disabled people, including the Olympic Games in Atlanta in the United States in 1996. And by 2003, he was in an administrative position at the Orphanage, with five others working under him.

Wanrunee also worked at the Orphanage, for five years, as both a receptionist and as a teacher of the pre-school children, and, finally, the same year Henry got his most recent promotion, she decided to become an entrepreneur. She opened a stall in a hypermarket that engraved photographs on stainless steel medallions that could be worn around a loved one's neck or used as a key chain. It was so successful that she leased a second stall less than six months later…and just a short while after that, she opened a beauty parlor…staffing all of her enterprises with people she knew she could trust---Orphanage and vocational school graduates.

That's four success stories. Suporntum said he was "still ready to provide a list of another 100."

Chapter 30

Father Ray made running characters of the two "Sisters Shark," using them in his newsletters, as in his life, for comedy relief. He did it again with the young orphan named Pheung. Father Ray called him The Orphanage's Holy Terror.

Pheung and his brother Lang were left in the priest's care in 1995 by their seventy-one-year-old grandfather, who had been taking care of the boys, but felt he was too old and poor to give the youngsters any advantages or see to their education. Their mother was dead and the father reportedly had a serious drug problem.

Pheung's case history said the father showed "no responsibility for the boys or anything else," telling the grandfather that he could give the boys to anyone who might take them. The father had remarried and the stepmother, who worked in a bank in Bangkok, refused to have anything to do with the boys. It wasn't an unusual story. Just another tale of abandonment. Thus, Pheung became what is called a "throwaway." Perhaps that makes it all the more wonderful that he became so loved by Father Ray, so esteemed that in the priest's newsletters he became one of the most endearing characters.

Pheung was five years old when he arrived at the Orphanage, delivered from Nong Khai, the same northeastern province bordering the Mekong River where Father Ray had served some of his early years in Thailand. An entry in the case history at age six takes note of the boy's missing front teeth and "huge smile." He was further described as "a very bright child who can always find some trouble to get into. His grades are average and he says that he doesn't like school. It seems as if his main problem is he just isn't getting enough stimulation and is bored. After school he loves to play at anything and everything. He likes to watch cartoons, Popeye being his favorite. Red is his favorite color and fruit his favorite food. Right now, like most small Thai boys, he wants to be a soldier when he grows up."

In his initial appearance in a newsletter the same year, when he was first given his unofficial name, the boy's manipulative charm was evident. "He has the face of a Dead End Kid," Father Ray reported. "He says things that are far above what is expected from a child his age. To top it off, he is a holy terror. The other day he came swaggering into my office, arms on hips. He made a sweeping motion with one arm and said, 'Why don't you keep this office clean?'

"I put my hands on my hips and asked, 'Why do you care?'

"Then the little devil ran up to my chair and gave me a big hug around the stomach (as far as he could reach anyway). After he had snuggled himself against my stomach, he said, 'Because I love you.' How do you handle a situation like that without producing a wee tear?"

The same year, Father Ray said Pheung's face resembled James Cagney's and when he smiled his gap-toothed smile, "you cannot stop from laughing. He comes into my office almost every day and crawls under my desk. He calls it Father Ray's house. He is also famous for breaking things. This morning he broke my reading glasses. Yesterday he broke my coffee cup. (Tomorrow I think I will break his neck!!) So it is only natural to ask, 'Why do I let him in my office?' It's simple, he is just plain lovable. He's a little monster, but a nice little monster."

In the years that followed, the incidents accumulated like jokes in a book. One time, The Holy Terror failed at learning how to blow bubbles with bubble gum and in the process spat the gum into Father Ray's coffee. Another time, he asked to watch television in Father Ray's office and when he left, Father Ray noticed the remote control no longer worked because Pheung had taken the batteries to operate one of his toys; it wasn't stealing, he was only borrowing, he explained when he returned the batteries, quite dead, at the end of the day.

"You have to admit that it is not exactly the same thing as 'stealing.' We will let The Boss Upstairs judge this one. I have a suspicion He will bust out laughing."

Pheung later brought a smelly stray puppy into Father Ray's office, asking if he could keep him. When the boy was told he had to wash the dog first, he took the animal to one of the Orphanage volunteers and said, 'This is Father Ray's dog and he wants you to give it a bath.' "

The dog was about seven weeks old and not yet housebroken. Father Ray reported later, "This morning Pheung took the puppy into the bathroom and held the poor thing over the toilet. He kept telling it to do its business, but the poor puppy just wanted to lick the boy's hands. Finally, the boy gave up and put the puppy down on the floor. You guessed it, that's where the frightened dog decided to do its thing. The boy quickly picked the puppy up and held it over the toilet again. In doing so, the startled, frightened, confused animal showered the washbasin, the outside of the toilet, the wall and a roll of toilet paper with his territorial watermark. Does anyone else have things like this happen to him?"

Again, from his case history, March 1998: "Pheung doesn't like to pay attention in school, nor does he like to do his homework. The result is his grades are below average. His work is untidy and he is still having trouble making the beautiful characters of the Thai alphabet. He would much rather be playing during class time. His teacher says that she must constantly keep him busy or he will fall asleep!"

He was described as lazy. He didn't do his homework and, his teacher said "he is really the brightest in telling lies; she has to be very careful with him. Pheung is a real 'people person' and is already known by all the teachers in the school. On the positive side, he seems to enjoy helping others and so he frequently is found helping a teacher or a fellow student. It is unlikely that he will be found helping a girl, though, because he is at the stage where he prefers to tease them."

Pheung was twelve in 2001 and noticeably short for his age, but he was considered healthy and strong, as demonstrated by his interest in sports. He was an avid football player and in the last newsletter written by Father Ray, in August 2003, it was reported that of the forty or so residents of the Orphanage who were taught the Korean martial art tae kwon do on the weekends, Pheung was chosen by the instructor as the student who showed some extraordinary talent.

"After several weeks in intense training," Father Ray wrote, "Pheung was entered into his first ever competition where, after beating six other fighters, he returned home with a gold medal."

Chapter 31

It was January 1991, the same month that final plans were completed to begin construction of the new blind school on land contributed by the Pattaya Cemetery Association, the same organization started by the Swiss businessman, Walter Meyer, who provided the land for the St. Nikolaus Church. The school's headmistress, Aurora Lee Sribuapun, sent Father Ray a note asking if the blind kids "could come and 'see' the movies with the orphans," the priest later recalled. "I was a little nonplussed at this request and went to see the head teacher [Aurora]. She explained to me that she has often gone to a movie theater to see a movie, even though she is blind.

"'We hear the sound and can imagine what is happening,' she said. So the blind kids came and 'saw' the movies. Our little orphans couldn't do enough for them. Suddenly the blind kids were being offered free food, cold drinks, and narrations of what was happening on the screen. It made my heart feel wonderful to see the spirit of kindness and goodness displayed by my kids. Maybe we are raising them right after all!"

By now, there were nearly fifty children in the School for the Blind and all were learning Braille, the system of writing for the blind named for the French deviser that used combinations of raised dots on paper that were "read" with the blind's trained fingertips.

"I hope to open up new careers for them," Father Ray wrote in one of his newsletters, "and I am wracking my brain to figure out what they will be. The Boss Upstairs had better start throwing something my way."

Construction of the new buildings limped along for more than a year, as Father Ray scrambled to find the funds for their completion. Much of the money came from Denmark, a plaque going up on a wall that surrounded the property, thanking "the people of Denmark," the Ronde Rotary Club in Copenhagen and Captain Vagn Christensen---a pilot for SAS who, like many others was taken on a tour by Father Ray and returned home to start raising money. More money had to come from somewhere else. But where?

It would not be the last time that Father Ray started a project with no idea how he would pay for it. Nor the last time that The Boss Upstairs seemed to answer his prayers.

In the Summer 1992 newsletter, Father Ray wrote, "on the 14th of May, the Thai Navy came to the old blind school. They did not come to visit the children. The blind children were not yet back from their long school holiday. They came to help move all the desks, beds, tables and other furniture from the old School for the Blind to the new school. A thousand feelings were squeezing my heart. Those feelings were a mixture of sadness and happiness. It felt funny seeing all the stuff I had worked so hard to get for the school disinterestedly being taken out and loaded into trucks. Nostalgia set in.

"I remembered the day when the blind school was first opened. We had only six students. (Now we have over fifty.) We started with two years of kindergarten and now we have that and five more higher grades. I never thought those first pioneer blind children would enter the fifth grade in a different building. I watched the refrigerator and stove being moved to the Navy truck and I remembered buying both of them and being so proud of our kitchen when we got them working. As the building slowly emptied, I felt a hollowness in my heart. Then I got in my car and drove to the new school.

"A different feeling came over me as I stood in front of that new building. Many things began to pass through my head. Long after you and I are with God, this building will still be educating young blind children. I remembered as a child my aunt telling me she had gone to visit the National Cathedral in Washington,

D.C. She added nonchalantly that she used to contribute a little bit to its construction each year and that was the reason she went to see it. Now, of course, this cathedral costs millions of dollars and I am sure my aunt's little yearly contributions were in the $5 to $10 range…but the point is SHE DID HELP BUILD IT!

"She is dead now and the cathedral lives on. With that story in mind, I began to think about the many people, like yourself, who have helped me build this new school. I prayed that at least some of you could one day come and see the blind children learning how to read, write, and take care of themselves in this building. Suddenly a big truck pulled alongside of me. Some of the sailors began unloading the refrigerator and stove. They brought it into the kitchen and I followed. When they were in place, I had the pleasure of plugging in the refrigerator and hooking up the gas to the stove. Then I found a place to sit and thank The Boss Upstairs for friends like yourself."

Ple arrived in 1991, another premature baby whose twin sister died at birth and who, like too many others, had lost her sight when placed in a defective incubator. Ple was a special case. Both parents worked in a factory near Bangkok and Ple was raised by her grandmother. When she was six years old, the grandfather died and Grandma went to work in the fields. After his death, according to Ple's case file, her grandmother thought it necessary to tie up the little blind girl with a chain inside their bamboo house during the day. The intention wasn't malicious; once she had left the house for the fields, Grandma feared Ple might fall off the porch or have some other accident. Some of the neighbors didn't understand and went to the newspapers, charging the grandmother with cruelty. Ple was taken to a children's foundation, which in turn asked Father Ray to care for her. She was not only blind, but also seriously retarded. When she arrived at the school, at age six, she had the mentality of a two-year-old and could speak only simple words: eat, go, water, etc.

Mac, enrolling at age seven, was a victim of German measles, a child of casual laborers who found work occasionally, competing for low-paying jobs with an estimated two million other poor workers in Bangkok. An early note in his case file said, "Mac is in Kindergarten 2 and is a rather slow, quiet child … [he enjoys] holding people's hands or just sitting near people. He likes to dance, especially if anyone will dance with him."

Sawan and Serm were twins, two more victims of a faulty incubator, who were taken to the school when they were nineteen months old; neither walked yet, nor talked, and both tended to sleep all day, remaining awake all night.

Convention was suspended in the Redemptorist School for the Blind. Just as was true in the School for the Deaf and the school for the physically disabled, and for that matter in the Orphanage, the human mean was suspended or set aside and what the majority of the world's population took for granted was denied; "normalcy" embraced new meaning. It was like Alice on the far side of the looking glass, frustrating and frustrated at every turn.

Visitors to the School for the Blind---including twenty or more Danes on an excursion led by Vagn Christensen every year---watched as the children walked slowly in twos and threes, holding hands. Some walked alone, feeling their way with their feet, knowing the school's grounds from long experience, so moving with relative confidence, but never at a run, as they circumnavigated the oval driveway in the school courtyard. Others sat motionless in the open concrete assembly area, some face down as if asleep or rocking, caught in what are called "blindisms," associated with so many of the sightless everywhere: picture Ray Charles and Stevie Wonder rocking gently, metronomically as they sit at their keyboards.

Some of the younger children, attracted by the foreign voices, approached with arms outstretched, hugging the visitors and climbing them as if they were trees or climbing frames, showing openly what could be interpreted as a hunger born of isolation and loneliness. One small boy hunched his tiny body against the waist of one of the adults, clinging with his spindly legs and arms as if he never wanted to touch the ground again.

A loud buzzer sounded and with assistance from some of the teachers, the children lined up according to uniform---those in blue and white in one file, those wearing green shirts in another, and so on---the color combinations designating grades. This took about ten minutes as several broke ranks and wandered away aimlessly, to be retrieved by patient staff. Slowly, the youngsters settled themselves and became quiet. Another buzzer sounded and off they went in snaking columns, one child's hand on the shoulder of the child in front, knowing how many steps it was to their designated classrooms.

Chapter 32

Audrey Williams lived in a four-bedroom chalet in England, her life one of ease, devoted to rearing two daughters and the calm of suburban life, when suddenly her fifty-eight-year-old husband, a financial director, suffered a massive heart attack.

"When George died, I realized I could sit around moaning about what I had lost or be positive about the future," she later said. "I saw an advert for the Pattaya Orphanage in Thailand and decided to sponsor three of the children there. One day, I suddenly felt how easy it was to sign a check and send it off and how little that really means to a child.

"All children need to feel they're special to someone, that they're more than just a person to be fed and clothed. I knew I should be doing more. I suppose you could describe it as a calling of sorts. I wrote to the Orphanage, asking if I could work there as a volunteer for three months and, to my great surprise, they said yes. I bought myself a ticket, packed up the house, went to Thailand at the end of 1997, and never looked back!"

Seven years later, Audrey was still there, working as an unpaid volunteer, serving as the organization's 'Special Guest Master', a sort of tour guide for visitors, a ready assistant to anyone who needed a friendly hand or voice, someone who lived on the Orphanage grounds and found time to change diapers in the baby room and bake pies for Father Ray.

In the years before his death, she also became one of his trusted confidantes, sharing with him a concern for the children. She was in her fifties;

the priest, more than a decade ahead of her in years, was what she came to regard as an older brother. She also shot straight from the hip, telling the Father Ray precisely what she thought, even when it was critical of his behavior or belief.

Audrey was not a Catholic, but she considered herself a Christian, and once when Father Ray said he loved the children, she challenged him. He said he did. His love for the orphans and the homeless and the disabled was genuine. She asked him, "Then why don't you love yourself? You must love yourself before you can truly love others."

It was Audrey's way of issuing a warning. Father Ray still wasn't taking care of himself. He didn't exercise, he ate and drank too much, and he smoked incessantly. The way Audrey recalled it, Father Ray harrumphed and grumped, the way he did whenever she took him to task. Audrey quoted the Commandments: "Love thy neighbor as thyself." Then she gave him a look and exited his office.

She said she believed her big brother appreciated honesty. He wanted his staff to state their feelings fully and openly. Otherwise, they weren't doing their jobs.

Successful non-government organizations---what commonly are called NGOs---often depend on outsiders like Audrey for their support, and without it, most would sink. Father Ray's stitched-together organization was no exception---relying on financial and in kind contributions from individuals, corporations, trusts, and so on, but also on volunteers. Most did not remain for as long as she did, but their service was as essential as it was irreplaceable. And their unpaid presence was part of what kept the overhead costs below what they would be otherwise. When Audrey was looking into sponsoring orphans, she said she was appalled by how much of the financial contributions went to salaries and office overhead elsewhere, while the Pattaya Orphanage had one of the lowest ratios worldwide.

A majority of the unpaid workers at the Orphanage came from Europe. Consider, for example, Derek Franklin, who lived his first nineteen years in Wales, then worked as a waiter at Harrods in London and as a cook in Australia.

Next, he trained back in the U.K. as a pediatric nurse and, deciding he wanted to work with children abroad, he first heard about the Orphanage when he saw Audrey interviewed on a British television show in 2000. He wrote, got a visa, planned to stay six months, remained a year, and in 2002 at Father Ray's invitation, he joined the staff and moved into a room over the Orphanage offices. Now he was being paid for his service as the point man and manager of the youthful volunteers who queued for the chance to work for free.

As the Orphanage's Volunteer Coordinator, to each applicant he sent a copy of a handbook describing the organization, making it clear that although Father Ray was a Roman Catholic priest, he did not "try to convert those in his care." The would-be volunteer also was told what was expected:

"For full-time volunteers, we do ask for a commitment of six months. This may seem like a long time, but all our volunteers are surprised how fast the time flies. The work the full-time volunteers do is very varied. The volunteers get to experience working in all the projects. At the Orphanage, the volunteers spend a lot of time in our baby rooms. At any one time, we have around fifty babies and small children under the age of three. The Thai caregivers [on staff] do an excellent job and they really appreciate the help that the volunteers give them with feeding, bathing, and changing diapers. But most important is the time the volunteers spend hugging and playing with the babies.

"Also at the Orphanage we have several physically and mentally disabled female residents. The volunteers spend a lot of time with these girls, taking them on daily walks, helping them do their exercises, taking them swimming or for a special treat to Pizza Hut or McDonalds."

A requirement was English fluency, because all full-time workers were expected to help the children practice their English, which was taught in most Thai public schools---usually poorly, due to awkwardly assembled textbooks and instructors who were not fluent themselves. There also were three English courses at the vocational school; the electronic students were taught Basic English three days a week, while the computer science students had an hour of English every day. Full-time teachers taught three or four classes per day and were "expected to be well prepared for classes."

Other duties included visiting the old people in the stateless home, the blind and the deaf and the street kids.

Short-term volunteers---many of them serving during their own school holidays---"do not start any new work projects as we feel that if a volunteer is here for only a few weeks, then by the time the children get into a routine and get to know the volunteer, it is time for the volunteers to leave. So, many of our short-term volunteers help us in the baby room."

The work schedule ran from 8:30 to 5:00, Monday through Friday, 9:00 to 5:00 Saturdays, with every fourth weekend being designated as an "extended" one, starting at Friday noon, although "we do expect volunteers to be available to work at short notice, if it is for the benefit of the children or students in our care, and most weekends we do expect one volunteer to be available to show visitors around."

Single and double rooms were provided on the Orphanage or Redemptorist Center grounds, along with meals, provided on a schedule by staff cooks or prepared by the volunteers themselves, many of whom didn't want Thai food all the time and purchased Western makings at a nearby supermarket. Rooms were "basic," with ceiling fans and cold water showers. There also was a common room with air conditioning, TV, and video and stereo systems. All volunteers were provided with bicycles to get around town and to the other projects.

"One of the most difficult aspects of being here in Thailand is not the hot weather, the different culture, or the language barrier," Derek warned in his handbook. "It is having to live in a house with ten other people you do not know. It can be difficult at times, but most people learn to be tolerant of others."

Volunteers were expected to pay their own air fares, medical insurance as well as bring their own bedding and towels.

In applying, candidates were asked for a statement "explaining why you wish to become a volunteer...your CV/resume...three references, which will be checked…a tape of your spoken English…photographs…and a preferred start date." They also were told that there would be a "police criminal record check."

"With over seven hundred orphans, blind, deaf, physically disabled and elderly in our care, we have to be sure that we have the right people working for us," Derek wrote. "We therefore have to check all references to make sure that they are genuine. It is not that we do not trust anyone, it is just that there are many people in this world who would wish to harm our children."

Once applicants were approved, they were told the rules. There was a dress code: long-sleeved or short-sleeved shirts, full-length trousers and skirts---"no showing off the shoulders and the knees." No mini-skirts, no earrings on the men, only conventional earrings on the women, and "no nose-rings/studs or tongue piercings."

Smoking and consumption of alcohol were forbidden in the work place. There were weekly meetings with the coordinator and all adhered to the "Child Protection Policy" that was distributed to all new arrivals.

It was clear; this was not summer camp or a typical Thailand holiday. Yet, there were many more applicants than positions. Many came back again and again. Others were told to reapply when there were too many candidates for the number of openings.

Usually there were about forty who made a three- to six-month commitment, with a fluctuating number staying three to six weeks. In December 2003, the international mix was typical, Derek said, with volunteers from the U.K., France, Australia, Belgium, Ireland, Canada, Japan, and Denmark. (Over the years, the largest number consistently came from Denmark.) The average age was early twenties, although the Pattaya International Ladies Club, whose members were middle-aged, also volunteered regularly.

As was true for adoptions, few of volunteers were Thai. Derek told one story that didn't go a long way toward explaining why, but it did reveal why one young Thai male didn't stay more than a few days.

"Scandinavians are known for their freedom," he said, "and one day this young man found himself seated between two busty Danish women wearing only their bras and knickers. He was so embarrassed, he packed up his kit and he left. We now discourage that sort of thing, even when it's confined to quarters."

"Without volunteers, the Orphanage would go on," Derek said, "but a lot of little things would suffer. Old people would be alone. The blind kids wouldn't get to the beach. And the babies would go with less cuddling."

Chapter 33

In the Christian religion, Lent traditionally was a season of fasting and penitence, lasting the forty weekdays from Ash Wednesday to Easter. In the wake of the reforms set in motion by Vatican II conference in the early 1960s, Catholics shifted the emphasis from "giving something up" during Lent to doing something positive for other people, such as volunteering in a soup kitchen every day. For older Catholics, the Lenten season remained a time of austerity and was dedicated, in part, to halting what was perceived by the penitent as a bad habit and offering the sacrifice up to God.

Father Ray had two such habits and for much of his adult life, he waged war with them. He was substantially overweight and he smoked cigarettes. And Lent often was when he tried to atone, to lose weight and give up tobacco.

"I have decided to give up cigarettes for Lent," he wrote a friend, "and on this the second day I feel like taking an M-16 to everyone who gives me the slightest problem. However, in my own calm way, I only shout them out of my office."

Another year, he wrote in a newsletter, "There is an ancient custom of 'giving' something up for Lent. Being loyal to traditional values, I have given up the dreadful weed called tobacco. It was not an easy decision to make. I softened it by promising to get off the habit for the six weeks of Lent. After Lent, we shall see what happens."

He then went off on a tangent. "Actually," he wrote, "tobacco has its name by accident. The Indians of the West Indies smoke it through a tube. The tube was called tobacco. The Spaniards mistakenly then called the plant by the name of the tube. Hence, the poor plant has gone all these years without its rightful name, which now has been long forgotten. That is probably why fate has dogged its trail with misery and brown lung. It has lead a cursed history stuck with the name of an insignificant hollow tube. Lent is not all that long; you can do it, Brennan!!!"

Just as he knew arcane trivia about his nicotine addiction, he also knew how to play the Lenten game. When he boasted that he'd got all the way through the season without smoking, but then returned to his two- and three-pack-a-day habit, a friend asked why if he could quit for forty days, couldn't he stay off the stuff? Ray revealed his secret. Most people thought giving up something for Lent meant that from Ash Wednesday straight through Easter, you went without.

Not true, said Father Ray. Lent was the forty weekdays that went from February to March, from Ash Wednesday to Easter. That left one day a week and, Father Ray told his friend that meant he could smoke on Sundays. Like a lawyer who'd found an uncrossed "t" in a contract, Father Ray had found a loophole, releasing him from his self-administered sentence on a technicality.

Still, he did try. "He got down to ten a day," said his secretary, Toy. "He tried to use a filter. He'd put away his ashtray, so it wouldn't remind him. He tried the [nicotine] patch. A friend once bought $200 worth! Nicoderm. And he gave most of them away."

About dieting, he was far more serious. Photographs show him only slightly pudgy as an altar boy and as a youngster in his military school uniform, as if he hadn't yet lost his baby fat, and by the time he was ordained, the new Father was tall and lean.

But then as his sister recalled, when he went home after his father died, he put on fifty pounds in eight weeks, and for the remainder of his life he never lost it, frequently adding to it.

He wasn't self-conscious about his bulk. In fact, in many ways he reveled in it. Although he may not have liked it when one of the Mothers Shark called him "White Elephant" and one of the blind children, running her sensitive fingers over his face so she could "see" him, said he was the size of a water buffalo, he was genuinely amused when the kids rubbed his belly for luck before a test. He also sometimes played a game with the younger ones. They'd line up opposite him and a few steps away from where he stood, then run toward him, throwing themselves into the air and punching him in his soft gut with their heads, as both he and the children laughed with genuine delight. Still, he knew that all that weight was a threat.

"For those of you who know me personally, you will be delighted to hear I am trying to lose some weight," he wrote in a letter whose message would be repeated many times. "What convinced me that this was necessary? I saw some pictures of myself, taken by the kids. That was enough!!! I went to a scale (an item I usually try to avoid) and had myself weighed. I was astonished when I read one hundred and seventeen kilograms. That's two hundred and fifty-seven pounds!! I bought myself a pair of running shoes and am determined to get myself in shape again. What amazes me…I already feel better."

So what happened? He gained rather than lost, had gone up to one hundred and twenty-five kilograms (two hundred and seventy-five pounds). Inevitably this happened when he went on one of his mandated home leaves, when he gorged on the rich cheeses and desserts that were hard to impossible to find in Thailand and, he confessed, he grew bored. On one leave, he said when he returned; he actually got a job as a Good Humor Man and took the wagon full of sweets through his old neighborhood. The job lasted only a day, he added, because what ice cream he didn't eat himself, he gave away to children he met.

The result of such behavior was evident after a television documentary crew visited. When Father Ray viewed the film, he saw a "big fat priest waddling around the Orphanage instead of walking. The diet began soon after that, and I am pleased to inform you that although I am still very much overweight, I am not waddling anymore and have lost forty pounds or eighteen kilos. My goal is a total weight shedding of seventy-five pounds, or thirty-four kilos. Now, I must admit I have new incentives for this weight loss …read on…

"Incentive 1: An English friend of mine has offered me ten pounds sterling [about U.S. $15] for every pound I take off. However, the dirty skunk set a condition. I had to lose at least thirty-five pounds or the deal was off.

"Incentive 2: An American friend of mine, saying he won't be outdone by an Englishman, has offered me $20 for every pound I take off and again I had to lose at least thirty-five pounds or the deal was off. However, this stinker put an even heavier condition on the wager. The official weigh-in day will be five days before Christmas. These two masochistic friends of mine tried to hide their sadism under the cloak of helping me live longer for the sake of the kids!! Anyone for giving me incentives to stop smoking?? (I am accepting bids of no less than $10 a day!) However, I must draw the line somewhere, so I hereby announce that I will accept no bribes (no matter how juicy you make the deal) to stop my beer. That is sacred and not negotiable!! Amen."

Year after year, the reports continued in the same manner and if he made light of the effort to change, it was clear that he did try, often dropping as much as twenty-three kilos (fifty pounds) in a couple of months. In his office in the Orphanage, herbal weight-loss "cures" were lined up on a shelf near bottles of after-shave and hair tonic, and among the holy texts were books on dieting.

For weeks, he'd almost starve himself. But then his love of beer and ice cream---both consumed by the pint and rarely one pint at a time---and gargantuan meals won out, supplemented by friends who came back from abroad, at his request, with delicacies he enjoyed: fat cylinders of gorgonzola (Italy's most famous blue-veined cheese), cases of Baileys Irish Cream, and butterscotch liqueur.

"I started a diet about six weeks ago and I am desperately trying to keep at it," he wrote a friend. "So far, twenty pounds have been shed. Believe it or not, my goal is to lose fifty more pounds. I am not in a hurry…but I am serious about it. It seems to me I was serious about another diet a few years ago that went kaput! I won't let it happen again. (Say a wee prayer for me to persevere!)"

In 1999, he wrote, "If you promise not to laugh, I will tell you something. I am on a diet again. (You promised you would not laugh.) The Great Brennan Diet began a few months ago. I was visiting someone in the hospital and eyed a reliable hospital scale. I asked the nurse if I could weigh myself and she agreed to help me. As the numbers on that scale began to whiz by, I consoled myself thinking it would stop at about 220 pounds (one hundred kilos). To my astonishment, the scale stopped at two hundred and seventy-five pounds (one hundred and twenty-five kilos). I was shocked. Even the little Thai nurse made a gasping sound. So as I lumbered out of the hospital, I realized the moment of truth had come…I needed to lose the blubber. I am proud to say that I have lost twenty-five pounds (11.36 kilos). I intend to lose fifty more pounds (22.73 kilos). Please do not send me any candy. The flesh is weak."

Toy said, "He tried acupuncture to improve his circulation. He tried breathing pure oxygen. He went on a diet of soup and vegetables. He tried just about everything, but he never stopped smoking and he lost tons but always gained tons back, and he usually ended up heavier than when he started."

He even tried scare tactics, when an American doctor living in Thailand, Richard Williams, showed him the videotape of his most recent angioplasty, a surgical procedure often performed when a poor diet and smoking led to cardiovascular disease.

Father Ray continued to eat and drink and smoke.

Chapter 34

In his continuing effort to do something for the street kids, Father Ray soldiered on. In summer 1994, he used the word "plodding" to describe his work. "It is the most difficult of all the projects, although it has the least number of children in it," he wrote. "The children are loveable, but street-wise. Since we cannot force a child to stay with us…they often just take off one day never to return. They become homesick for the street and its dark unknowns."

The sad stories were as worrying as those the priest heard for years at the Orphanage, with the added fillip that the children not only lived without parents and love---as had most of his orphans---they also were small guerilla warriors, self-trained for survival in a hostile environment, untrusting of all authority, including Father Ray's.

One boy, Kai, abandoned by his parents when they separated, sought help from government's public welfare offices. He was put in a school and never contacted again. He had no lunch money the whole school year and no home to sleep in, or any money to continue his studies at the end of the term. So he went on the street, getting leftover food from the Buddhist monks at a temple. The police were looking for him when he arrived at Father Ray's door.

Another boy, Doh, had lived for a time with a distant relative who told the boy he had no parents. The children of the mysterious "relative" attended school, but this boy was kept home to take care of the water buffaloes. After a while, the physical beatings he was given impelled him to run away.

"They give all kinds of reasons why they ran away from home," Father Ray wrote. "But the real reason they ran away was because they felt they were not loved. Love is so important in raising a kid. It gives the child security and feeling of 'belonging.' For the street kids, any love shown them from outside their family, namely from us, was nice but not what they really want. What they really want is their parents' love. Nothing else fills the bill. We are just nice outsiders, but not their family."

Dao was five and a half years old when he and his brother, Man, a year younger, arrived, father's whereabouts unknown, mother remarried, both kids left with a grandmother who was arrested on drug charges and a grandfather who was a "world-class drunk" (quoting from the home's case history), and both found by one of Father Ray's outreach workers "wandering about the slum."

Rak was seven and her twin sisters, Fin and Faan, were four when mom went to work in Pattaya's "entertainment industry."

Father Ray had come to expect many of the orphans to be young---newborns, after all, were commonplace---but it came as a shock to him to find so many small children actually living on the street. How in the world did they fend for themselves? It was no wonder they arrived so frail and usually diseased.

"Some are so young and so little, you just want to hug them to death," the priest wrote. "It's hard to believe they were even able to make the decision to run away from home. But they did, and they fended for themselves on the street, begging or stealing food, according to circumstances. You might be a bit surprised when I tell you they are still stealing…but in a different way. They now steal all of our hearts away every day."

Father Ray stayed the course, like the classic children's book titled *The Little Engine That Could*. It was about a small train that encountered a very high hill. It was a hill so steep and the summit seemed so far away, the engine doubted its ability to reach the top. As the train began its climb, the engine huffed and puffed, "I think I can, I think I can, I think I can…"

It would still be a while before Father Ray got to the part of the story characterized by the jubilant engine's cry: "I knew I could, I knew I could, I knew I could…"

"We have to make friends with street children and get their confidence," he wrote in another newsletter. "We might just talk with them over a long period of time, show kindness to them, or even invite a child to have lunch with us at the home. It takes a lot of time for us to get a child's trust and into our home. Why? Because the children must come of their own free will. With the police, it's different. They just arrest them on the spot and the kids are taken away to a detention center. During the last six months, the police have conducted twenty-seven sweeps of the streets. They arrested four-hundred and eleven street children, of which two-hundred and sixty-six were Thai children and one-hundred and forty-five were Cambodian children. The police are doing their job and they are not to blame. The parents and relatives of these children are the culprits. I feel they are they ones who should be put in detention centers. But you can see what a tough job we have."

There were elevations of mood as well as disappointment and distress, of course, and from the former, Father Ray sought and found sustenance. One group of kids decided to raise hundreds of quails for their eggs, consuming some themselves while taking the rest to school to sell. (Father Ray insisted that all street children of school age attend classes in the neighborhood schools.) Demonstrating their talents as entrepreneurs-cum-scam artists, they offered a deal to their classmates: buy ten eggs in the course of one week and get an eleventh egg free.

In another letter, Father Ray told the story of a boy who decided to ride his bicycle all the way to Bangkok---at least two-and-a-half hours away by car, so who knows how long on a bike---in horrendous traffic and at great risk, because he "wanted to look for a friend of his who is also 'on the street.' He wanted to bring the kid back to our home! Unfortunately, he failed to find the friend, but he did get back safely."

Father remembered a Christmas when one of the street kids gave him a foot-high Christian church made from paper and cardboard, with a cross made with a pencil stuck inside the stem to keep it upright. "The child who made it is a Buddhist," Father Ray wrote in his year-end letter. "He has been on the street since he was eleven years old. He is now sixteen. When he gave it to me, he said it is a gift from his heart for the help we have given him to start a new life. Then he reached for my hands and before I could pull them back, he kissed them. That turned on the tear machine for both of us. I hugged him and told him I loved him. He said he loved me, too."

In a sort of postscript, Father Ray revealed the source of his strength, the motivation for his easy acceptance of the Redemptorist pledge to do good for the poor. He did good because it made him feel good to live up to that pact.

"That little episode alone made all my work for the last year well worth every drop of sweat and every strand of gray hair. It is a powerful feeling to 'know' you have really helped someone. Your help in my work has helped that young person and many other children change their lives. How pleased God must be with you and me for 'our' sacrifice and work."

Chapter 35

Every year in late spring, the United States holds joint military exercises in Thailand with the military of several countries. Thailand is the locale and always a participant because of its role as a key ally in the region, dating back to the war in Vietnam.

Cobra Gold was one of the largest exercises involving U.S. forces in the Pacific Command. It debuted in 1981 and usually involved at least five thousand and up to fifteen thousand U.S. fighting men and women, and was designed---in the words of the U.S. Embassy---"to ensure regional peace and strengthen the ability of the Royal Thai armed forces to defend Thailand or respond to regional contingencies."

What the media usually reported when the military arrived in Thailand for the exercise, many of them on ships anchored within sight of Pattaya's beach, was the rush ashore by the soldiers and sailors on R&R (Rest and Recuperation). The media spotlight was on the men, many of whom recreated a scene straight out of the 1960s and early 1970s, as thousands of young Thai women poured into the city from sex markets in Bangkok and elsewhere, filling Pattaya's bars and massage parlors to overflowing to meet the sudden wave of testosterone and American dollars. Inevitably there were ugly incidents, including fights, rampant public drunkenness, and, one year, charges of group rape.

What wasn't much reported was the good that Cobra Gold delivered, what the United States called the Cobra Gold Community Relations Projects, a mandated part of the exercise aimed at building goodwill at the local level.

Father Ray was one of many who benefited, as truckloads of food and goods arrived at the Orphanage gates, along with volunteers. One year, Navy engineers installed a huge concrete water catchment tank. Another time, they designed and built a football pitch, the first on the Orphanage grounds. Toys were distributed, courtesy of the Marine Corps' Toys for Tots program. Uncounted numbers donated leftover or unwanted packaged military meals, what once were called C or K rations and now were called Meals Ready to Eat, or MRE's; the children at the Orphanage called them "Mamee."

"The kids in the Orphanage look forward to their coming," wrote Father Pat Morrissy in a 1995 newsletter when Father Ray was on a home leave. "The chaplain always brings a group of the 'boys' to the Orphanage for a cookout featuring hamburgers, hot dogs, and pork and beans. People everywhere are 'into' fast foods and our orphans are no exception. You wouldn't believe how many burgers and dogs a young boy can put away until you see some of our lads go at it.

"The kids take so naturally to these American fellows, and vice versa. Many of the sailors have children of their own, and just coming and playing with our kids, holding the small ones in their arms, eases some of the sorrow they experience at being separated from their own children. Often the negative effects the Navy has on the resort are featured in the news items. Their visit to the Orphanage is proof that there are at least some positive and good effects."

In May 2002, the human side of the joint military exercise burst onto the nation's front pages and evening television news as never it had before. That was when Matthew Scott, a young orphan adopted from the Pattaya Orphanage in 1982 when his name was Khalom Priyakoot---now twenty-four years old and a corporal in the U.S. Marines---decided to find his natural mother.

"I went to the Orphanage in Pattaya," he said, "because my [adoptive] parents told me I was raised there. My unit's chaplain and Father Ray at the Orphanage knew each other well, so they helped me out."

However disheveled and disorganized Father Ray may have appeared in terms of his wardrobe and office work space, with the help of an efficient staff, he prided himself on keeping meticulous records. So the next day the young Corporal Scott was given a copy of his birth certificate and, after joining others from Cobra Gold in visiting the babies in the same building where he himself had spent his first four years, he returned to his military base to request further help.

Captain Sompop Suvitayalangka, naval aviation director at Sattahip, said he didn't pay much attention when he heard the young man's story through subordinates, but after meeting him and sensing his sincerity, as well as observing his Thai looks (despite his foreign name and the fact he no longer could speak the language), he asked the country's numerous military-operated radio stations to help.

"Normally it would be an impossible job to find the real mother, even if a person had all the time in the world," Father Ray wrote in his next newsletter. "Amazingly, and against all odds, they succeeded! The mother and son were joined in a tearful, but joyous, mother and son monumental kiss and 'bear hug'…amid the applause of his new friends in the Thai military."

The marine's mother was located in just three days, found working as a day laborer in Bangkok. A birthmark on the marine's neck helped his mother to recognize him when they met at U-tapao.

"She told me how sorry she was about putting me in the Orphanage. I understand that. So we worked out the karma. I wasn't mad," he said.

Chapter 36

"Pat was bounced around by uncaring adults for a long time, starting when he was only fifteen days old. He was finally taken to an orphanage in Ubon Ratchatani, in northeastern Thailand. His father refused to accept him as his own and the mother, with four others to look after, could not take care of him.

"When Pat was four years old, a Thai couple unofficially adopted him and he lived with them for three years. For some unknown reason, he was then sent to live with a relative of the adoptive mother, with whom he stayed for only a year. After that, Pat was returned to the Ubon orphanage.

"Shortly after that, however, the adoptive mother showed up at the orphanage and asked to have Pat back. The orphanage would not agree since it was their opinion that Pat was not receiving the loving care they felt he needed. At that point, the 'adoptive' mother asked to have him for a few days' visit. The orphanage agreed to this, hoping that perhaps something could be worked out for the good of the child.

"When the woman did not return with the child as promised, it was found she had put Pat into another orphanage. They returned him to the Ubon orphanage, but when Ubon closed they asked us to take Pat. Pat is a very good-looking boy who does above average work in school. He has a good character, is helpful and tidy, and full of confidence. He has the makings of a great person," Pat's case history reported.

Born in 1979 in Yasothon, another province in the poverty-stricken Northeast, Pat came to Pattaya in 1990. As a youngster, his favorite subject was science, his favorite color white. He collected stamps and by the time he was sixteen, his favorite subject was geography, a natural outgrowth of that hobby, though he still said he wanted to be a doctor, or perhaps a lawyer, when he grew up. He was a "room leader," responsible for seeing that the younger boys did their cleaning chores in the morning before going to school.

At sixteen, with three years to go before finishing high school---late by Western standards, but common where there is little education when young---he and Tho, another boy from the Orphanage, spent eight months with Tom Vincent in the United States in a new Orphanage program designed to encourage English fluency as well as a sense of worldly sophistication. Pat remembered the experience with delight, as he and Tho traveled with Tom to Florida and Washington, D.C., and he enjoyed bodysurfing in the waves in Hawaii, but he also recalled the English lessons as "very difficult for me. I had to use sign language, except when we visited the Thai restaurants." He continued his English lessons when returning to Thailand and classes in a Catholic high school in Sri Racha.

Repeatedly, Pat was recognized for his good grades and leadership capabilities. When a group of supporters from Denmark came to visit, Pat, representing all of the residents of the Orphanage, gave the welcome speech in Danish. Graduating from high school with a 3.56 grade average (out of a possible 4.0) and after winning twenty awards or certificates for outstanding academic and religious attainments, he applied for a place at Assumption University, Thailand's first Catholic university, then regarded as the country's leading business training institute, where virtually all classes were taught in English and textbooks were from the U.K., U.S., and Australia. He placed second in the entrance exams.

Pat was not alone.

Pachanee Nanthaniran was another. She was from Udon Thani, born in 1972, when the big U.S. airfield in the northeastern province began to shut down operations and curtail the bombing runs over the Ho Chi Minh Trail. She was one of four children and five years of age when their father "left us." At age ten, her mother "was very ill and she thought that she could not support me anymore." A doctor sent the mother to a Catholic nun who had worked at the Pattaya Orphanage. Pachanee's mother said it was the ten-year-old's choice.

"I traveled to Pattaya by train," she wrote in 2004 in a small autobiographical sketch. She volunteered to write it when, after being asked to be interviewed about Father Ray, she discovered she couldn't, not without bursting into tears. "I still remember everything on that day since that was my first time to leave my family and traveled without my parents. I cried all night till the train arrived in Bangkok. I was very confused whether my decision was right or not. I missed my mother and my family so much.

"I arrived the Orphanage in the afternoon and Mother Superior asked me to wait for Father Ray until 7:00 p.m. The first time I met Father Ray, a very giant farang. [Thai for foreigner, usually reserved for Caucasians.] I'd never seen any farang in my life before, except on TV. I still remember the first words he asked me, 'Are you Chinese? Are you a good student?' By this he meant you must get a very good grade. And from that day I became his daughter."

She, too, earned a bachelor's degree from Assumption University, the first of Father Ray's orphans to earn a university degree. She worked for two years after graduation as a secretary at the university's computer center and then as a secretary to the finance and accounting officer of a company at the port in Laem Chabang, near Pattaya.

"In the future," she wrote, "I would like to have my own business, just a small one which I am good at, e.g., clothes, book shop, jewelry, or cosmetics."

"I think I have a better chance in my life, my career or even my future as today it's only because of Father Ray. He gives me a great chance to have opportunities like others, without him and his support I will never have a good future as now. Besides of a great chance to have a good education, he gives me love, warm as other families have. I can tell you that I had never felt of myself of being an orphan at all because I do sure know that he loved me even more than my real father does.

"Many of the orphans, particularly older ones, knew Father Ray was very sick in his last days. Some visited him in the hospital almost every day. We expected the worst, but prayed it would not happen. When I learned he had passed away, I was heartbroken as then I felt I was an orphan. But, I know Father Ray's love is with me and I will continue to do my best from his teaching to make him proud."

Sometimes entire families of children came. Yai arrived at the orphanage in 1983 when she was thirteen years old, accompanied by her sister Ning, twelve, and their twin half-brothers, Tho and Lek, not yet three years old. They were from Nakhon Sawan, a bustling trade center on the Chao Phraya River several hours' drive north of Bangkok with a population that was largely Chinese. The father of Yai and Ning abandoned his wife and children not long after Ning was born. The mother remarried and had the twins. Again, a husband deserted her and the kids. The mother did the best she could, making sweets during the day and selling them from a pushcart in the evening.

Yai's file at the Orphanage noted, "Because of the strain of hard work, even in rain and bad weather, she became very ill and finally died in January 1983. Since the children had no family, they were taken in by neighbors who soon decided they did not want them anymore as they had children of their own. They contacted us and requested that we take the children. When they arrived here, Yai and Ning had completed only two years of schooling. They had missed long stretches of their education because they needed to stay home to take care of the twins while the mother was out working."

They were asked if they were interested in continuing their schooling. [They, in fact, had no choice; all orphans of school age went to school, but Father Ray wanted some feedback on whether the idea appealed or not.] Although they started late, both girls did well academically and Yai learned to play the saxophone and a kind of Thai violin, while Ning had a wonderful singing voice. Both attended classes at Assumption University, and after two years, Ning transferred to Bangkok University; both earned degrees. The two girls also were participants in and the beneficiaries of the Orphanage's foreign home study program---Yai going to the United States, where she lived with Father Ray's sister Sharron and her husband in Texas, Ning to the midlands of England, where she lived for six months with a retired couple who later moved to Pattaya.

While in America, Yai met a Cambodian-born American man; in June 2000, she brought him to Pattaya and married him. Father Ray himself was in the United States at the time, undergoing medical testing and treatment, so the ceremony for the first "graduate" of the Orphanage to be married was performed by the local bishop. Father Ray wrote:

"Dear Beloved Daughter of Mine, Yai:

"Today will be a great day for you and the beginning of a new part of your life. I am sad that I will not be the priest at your marriage. However, I WILL BE THERE IN SPIRIT. It is a great honor to be married by a bishop and I am glad you have that honor. I remember the day you and your family arrived at the Orphanage. You were a little girl then, but were obviously the one that your sister and brothers looked up to with respect. Since that time, you have grown into a woman and I have watched that change over the years. I know you will be a good wife and a good mother. I have tried to give you and your family a good life and I feel that I have succeeded in that respect. But the joy you have given me over the years was worth any sacrifice I may have made for you. And now you are prepared to go to a different country, with a new husband and a new life. I pray that God showers you with His grace and gives you an abundance of happiness in your new life.

"I don't think it is possible for any man to love you as much as I love you. You are my loving daughter, and will always be that to me for the rest of my life. It may seem strange for a man who is not your 'blood' father to say such a thing, but it is true.

"After your marriage ceremony, when you put your flowers on the Shrine of

Our Mother of Perpetual Help, you will be doing the same thing as I did as a young seminarian. I did not put flowers at her shrine; I put my life there and put it in HER hands. Pray to Her when you put your flowers at Her shrine. Tell Her that Her son Raymond wants Her to become your mother and guide you in your new life. I will be there in spirit to help you do that.

"I don't know how to say it any better, so I will say it again.

"I LOVE YOU, I LOVE YOU, I LOVE YOU.

"Pray for me. Your Loving Father, Raymond Brennan."

Yai responded: "I love you, too, Paw Ray, and you will be an angel in my heart now and forever. I will pray for you. Your Loving Daughter, Yai."

Yai and her husband, who was in the U.S. Army, continued to live in America.

Following her graduation from Bangkok University, Ning, Yai's sister, went to work in communications and public relations at the Royal Cliff Resort, only a few kilometers from the Orphanage. There, she met and married a computer graphics programmer. In 2004, they had a year-old daughter and were building a house in Samut Prakan, near the highway connecting Bangkok with Chon Buri and Pattaya.

Ning continued to visit the Orphanage and Father Ray in the same way that children visited their families and "home" everywhere else in the world. By the late 1990s, there were many young adults who had gone on to start families of their own. Many still lived in Thailand, while others, who were adopted, returned to Pattaya from abroad.

No one at the Orphanage has forgotten one young man who came back with his wife and their baby child. He wanted Father Ray to bless the infant and as the now elderly priest took the child into his arms, the man fell to his knees, grabbed Father Ray around the knees and wept, crying, "Father, father, father…"

Chapter 37

Six mornings a week, shortly before 8 a.m., the students of the Redemptorist Vocational School for the Disabled gathered on the outdoor basketball court, across from the administration, dormitories, and classroom buildings.

One of the first to appear was a one-legged man with a crutch. He took a position in the center of the court and as others arrived, he amused himself by keeping a woven takraw ball aloft, using his only leg to do so, leaning on his crutch as he executed a jerky yet graceful hop and a skip and a kick, and then another one.

A one-armed man came down the driveway next, pushing a wheelchair. In it was a woman without legs.

They were followed by a man with one leg much shorter than his other, lurching forward and sideways by turns. His books were tucked under an arm.

Emerging from the dormitory building in twos and threes and in larger groups, the students limped and hobbled and dragged game legs, or in their wheelchairs did morning "wheelies," throwing front wheels into the air while balancing on the rear ones.

More students sat quietly at concrete tables nearby beneath leafy trees, some holding a book in place with an elbow where one arm ended and turning the pages with the remaining hand. Chatting and gossiping, waiting for the assembly to begin.

All wore school uniforms, burgundy shirts and black slacks or skirts.

A bell rang at 7:50 and everyone wheeled or hobbled into ranks, facing the flagpole and the rows of their teachers, who were standing or in wheelchairs of their own just outside the basketball court. (In 2004, twenty-five of the twenty-eight instructors at the school were disabled.) The flag was raised and everyone sang the King's Anthem (Thai national anthem), the way Thais everywhere began and ended every day, at 8 a.m. and 6 p.m. The singing was followed by prayer, everyone putting their hands together as if in prayer, the traditional sign of Thai respect and greeting called a wai---that is, if they had two hands and both hands functioned. Otherwise, just one hand or arm sufficed.

This was followed by the Teacher of the Day coming forward on wheels or crutches with announcements and a brief talk designed to be inspirational, including a brief discussion of the "word of the week," regarded as a part of the school's instruction. Words like "diligence" and "flexibility."

At 8:05, everyone exited the basketball court and crossed the driveway to begin classes, climbing stairs if they could, wheeling their chairs into the outsized elevator or using the ramps that connected all the floors. It was a big building, more utilitarian than attractive. On the upper floors were separate dormitories for those in wheelchairs and those students who could, in some fashion, walk. There were single beds for the chair disabled; double bunks for the others, pushed close together like the cribs in the Orphanage baby room because enrollment always exceeded capacity.

On the lower floors there was a library, and classrooms had wide aisles between desks covered by computers and electronic gear in various states of assembly. There was a big, airy cafeteria (with the smell of cooking fish). On the flat roof clothes were washed by hand and there were lines for drying the clothes in the sun.

The pace was measured. As Sister Pavinee Pichaisrisawadi, the school's director, put it, "Working at the Redemptorist Vocational School for the Disabled is always challenging for me. In the past, I liked to work fast but now I must slow down and learn how to accept things as they are."

The disabled students moved matter-of-factly, yet it was enough to move anyone with all four limbs to tears. Father Ray wept openly when he handed out the diplomas to his graduates as they came forward on squeaking wheels and clicking prosthetic devices.

He also shot straight from the hip when he saw something that he didn't like, and at the vocational school, sometimes he was annoyed. He rarely preached and almost never lectured, but in his comments to the students, usually at graduation, no matter how proud he was as they collected their certificates, he was not reluctant to give them some stern advice. One year, the word of the day was "consideration."

"I went to visit a company that had accepted one of our graduates as an employee," he said. "We were having a nice conversation when he casually mentioned that he has no handicapped people working for him anymore. I was surprised and asked what happened to the graduate we had sent him. His answer was, 'He quit.'

"I asked him if he wanted more graduates after the next graduation. His answer was, 'No.' I felt ashamed to hear his reason for not wanting more of our students. 'I can't run a business with new employees who quit their job before they even work here one full year.'

"After a little investigation, I found that it is not an uncommon thing that our graduates leave the job we get for them. Some after only a few months. It does not take a lot of brains to realize that graduates doing that will eventually make it hard for us to find employment for future graduates. I even feel the school might think about making graduates promise to stay in the job (obtained for them by the school) for at least one full year.

"It is possible that after a student graduates from the school and begins work, a better opportunity or a better paying job is offered them. In such a case, there is an internationally recognized method of quitting a job, which should be followed. Namely, a notice called 'termination of employment' is made by the employee. It is simply a letter telling the employer that you intend to leave his company. You do not have to say why you are leaving, but you must give the employer enough time to find a replacement. Therefore, the usual practice is to give four to six weeks advance notice before you leave the company. The businessman I mentioned above did not receive any notice of termination from our graduate. If he had, perhaps he would have been willing to hire one more of our students.

"Perhaps that student might have been you."

In addressing his disabled students another time, for Father Ray the word of the day was "gratitude."

Surely, most of the graduates were grateful and they were not hesitant to show it. "It's very interesting," said Ron Small, the school's first dean, "that from our first class of twelve students, the school has found its current dean, at least three very capable current instructors and managers, and all of the remainder of that initial class constantly return to either assist, provide donations and material, or otherwise assist the current program."

However, not everyone behaved in this fashion and Father Ray took them to task for that.

"Our school has a fantastic reputation here in Thailand," he said, opening without any clue as to what was to follow. "We deserve that excellent reputation because we are the best! There is no vocational school for the handicapped better than ours.

"We are good in everything except one thing," he went on, getting down to the nitty-gritty. "We do not show enough gratitude to the school for all it has done to change your life. The school gave you free education, free food, free uniforms, free water and electricity, free parties…and some of you even got free trips abroad because of our school. The school obtained a job for you after graduation. The school has been 'giving' to you all the time.

"The sad thing about all this is that few graduates ever think of repaying the school for what it has done for them. Even if a student after graduating from our school could only afford to send one baht a month to help the school…it would be a sign that the ex-student was grateful to the school.

"There are many graduates earning good salaries. A salary they could never have received if they had not attended our school.

"Our school is not a government school run by taxpayers' money. It is a private school. The school has to seek its own money, by begging, so that you could learn a profession and support yourselves and your family.

"Think about where you would be now, and what you would be doing, if you were not a student in this school. Think about what your future would be, if you had not attended our school.

"I say these words to you because I feel you need to think about these things. You talk about equal rights with all Thai citizens, and you talk about fairness. I think our school has a right to see your gratitude. I think it is only fair that you try to pay back to the school, at least some of the expenses used to feed and educate you. Even if you can afford to send only a small amount of money to the school each month. What counts the most is not the money (although it will certainly help). What counts the most is that we see you are grateful for what we have done for you."

Father Ray closed this message almost harshly, quoting an Asian saying: "It is better to be bitten by a cobra every day for one-hundred years than to have an ungrateful child."

Chapter 38

Father Ray continued to reject many of the traditional ways to raise money. He did not hold fund-raising events: benefit concerts or golf tournaments or testimonial dinners or shows that charged admission. He did not ask for donations through the mail and except in the earliest years, he did not place contribution boxes in public places. He did not make luncheon and dinner speeches before civic organizations and afterwards pass a hat. He did not sell T-shirts and coffee mugs and baseball caps. Or candles and other arts and crafts fashioned by the kids.

The last was most important. Some of the blind children may have been taught how to make artificial flowers, others how to give a therapeutic massage, but learning how to read and write Braille and become self-sufficient while living alone were far more important. It was for the same reason that he decided to teach the physically disabled electronic repair and computer science, rather than how to gold-plate orchids for the tourist trade.

He saw nothing inherently wrong with the poor and disabled making and selling flower garlands at roadway intersections. Nor did he openly criticize the government's lottery program that hired the disabled to sell tickets on the street each month. (Privately, he said he thought there were many better ways to assist.) He did not wish to elicit sympathy from those who were not orphans or in some fashion disabled, but to gain respect for those who were.

He also scorned public recognition for his efforts. Occasionally he agreed to be interviewed by the media and he was pleased when a documentary made in

Pattaya by television station WTTW in Chicago, "Christmas with Father Ray," was rerun every December in his hometown. Donations always arrived in the weeks following, but what was important to Father Ray was that he was getting the message out; he wasn't asking for money, he was talking about the miracle of his kids. He didn't consider this solicitation. It was an acknowledgement of what children and young adults could accomplish against the worst odds. It was applause not for him, but them.

He was uncomfortable when he was praised for his work. He called the flattering and respectful 1983 article about him in the *Reader's Digest* "crap." This was typical. It wasn't his doing. It was the work of The Boss Upstairs. He really believed that.

However, in 1993 a sleek, photographic book was produced called *Thoughts from the Pattaya Orphanage* and nine years later, in 2002, came a sequel, *More Thoughts from the Pattaya Orphanage*. Both were 160-page, hardcover compilations of photographs taken at the Orphanage and in Father Ray's schools, each black-and-white picture facing a page that contained an inspirational quote approved by Father Ray, and both were sold as fund-raising items.

Products. A word that was, until then, anathema.

Some of the quotations in the books were anonymous, but most were by figures well-known, and all were in the public domain, thus required no permission and came at no cost. Winston Churchill's exhortation to the British during World War Two, "Never give in. Never give in. Never give in," was illustrated by a picture of a student at the Vocational School who had no arms or legs. A line from Stevie Wonder---"Just because a man lacks the use of his eyes doesn't mean he lacks vision"---faced a photograph of a blind boy playing a harmonica. A tiny child asleep lent poignancy to Henry David Thoreau's "Dreams are the touchstones of our character." Five children gathered around Father Ray, two of them rubbing his belly for luck illuminated a comment by actor Woody Harrrelson: "A grown-up is a child with layers on." Two small children wearing Santa Claus hats seemed to be thinking what Robert Louis Stevenson wrote: "A friend is a gift you give yourself." A photo of children in a classroom, language books before them, was fitted to Mahatma Gandhi's advice to "Live as if you were to die tomorrow. Learn as if you were to live forever."

- "Life is either a daring adventure or nothing." Helen Keller
- "Some men see things and say, 'Why?' I dream things and say, 'Why not?' " Robert F. Kennedy
- "The mind is everything. What you think, you become." Lord Buddha
- "Make the other person feel important." Dale Carnegie
- "The lowest ebb is the turn of the tide." Henry Wadsworth Longfellow
- "O Lord, thou givest us everything at the price of an effort." Leonardo da Vinci
- "Never look down on anybody unless you are helping him up." Jesse Jackson
- "Until you try, you don't know what you can't do." Henry James

To the cynic, the lines may have sounded saccharine, even syrupy…the sort of sentiment expected on a Hallmark greeting card or at the bottom of the page in last month's *Reader's Digest*. Yet, many illuminated Father Ray's willingness to go out on a limb---"because that's where the fruit is," as Mark Twain said on another page---to step away from the road well traveled.

The books urged readers to do the same.

The idea for the books was that of Patrick McGeown, an Australian who worked for an advertising agency in Bangkok. Patrick said, "I'd read about Father Ray in a magazine, but I'd never met him. The *Bangkok Post* ran a competition inviting all the ad agencies to submit an environmental ad. Each ad would be given a full page in the paper and the public would judge the winner. Our topic was litter reduction and because I was the English copywriter, I was asked to create it. I thought about it and felt this topic needed a hands-on approach. We decided to clean up a bit of dirty Jomtien Beach (just south of Pattaya) and show the before and after shots. We asked Father Brennan would he let his kids do the cleaning. 'Sure,' he said, so the ad showed fifty-five of the kids as well. The ad won the competition and thousands of posters were made in English and Thai. I brought the posters down to the Orphanage and presented them to Father."

In the priest's office he met Paul Knights, a young British photographer who had come to Thailand to develop his portfolio. A friend of his mother's said her civic group sent regular contributions to an orphanage in Thailand and Paul wrote, asking if he could visit. Father Ray said yes, of course, and after completing an introductory ten-week course in the Thai language, the photographer set forth, meeting Father Ray and moving into an unoccupied room in the Stateless Old People's Home. The priest also made available a space in his onetime office, the trailer at U-tapao that was still on the property. Paul turned it into a darkroom.

Paul was in the priest's office when Patrick arrived, coincidentally showing him some of his pictures. "I happened to notice these magnificent black-and-white photos," Patrick said, "I asked what they were going to do with them. 'Possibly a brochure,' Father replied. I suggested a book. They just stared at me. Paul got excited. It took about fifteen minutes of convincing and Father said, 'if you can do it, do it.' So I raised the money to print it, Paul took more photos and I dug up some quotations and then did the typesetting. It was a labor of love."

Finally, Pat came to the priest and said, "Father, we are ready to print."

"How many will you print?"

"Two thousand copies."

"Two thousand copies! I'll be selling bloody books for the rest of my life."

"Father, you do what you do best---you pray that they will sell---and let me worry about the selling side."

Patrick McGeown also was involved in the second book, but now there was a new photographer.

Sean Godsell was born of Irish parents in London in 1956, one of seven children. He worked as a carpenter and then studied photography in

Cambridgeshire for four years in the mid-1990s, going to Thailand in 2000. While planning the trip, he found the Pattaya Orphanage while surfing the Internet and decided to ask Father Ray if he could take some pictures.

"I wanted to chronicle people in need," Sean said. When he arrived, Father Ray was in the United States, so Sean talked to Denis Gervais, and then Alun Jones took him on a tour. He remembered that when they walked into the baby room, he thought, "Wow! That's amazing! All the joy that was radiating through the whole place. I said I wanted to help and they asked me to do a follow-up of the original book of photographs."

When he returned to the U.K. soon afterwards, Sean called Paul Knights on the Isle of Wight, then visited him. A few months later, Sean returned to Thailand with his cameras, intending to remain for a year, moving into a room above the Orphanage offices. When he arrived, again Father Ray was not there.

Eventually, Sean did meet the man he came to think of as a "gentle giant." When Father Ray saw some of the photographs, he encouraged Sean to continue, said a second book was a good idea. In the months that followed, Sean served as the Orphanage's unofficial photographer, taking pictures of the babies for the adoption program, whatever was needed, and sometimes helped teach English at the blind school. And as he developed his photographs, he showed them to Father Ray, who urged him to exhibit them.

"We talked about being Irish and both loving photography," Sean recalled. "He gave me so much encouragement. He said the first book brought him so much joy."

Sean stayed in Pattaya for six months longer than planned. That meant a year and a half without pay, so he returned to England to regroup and work again as a carpenter. *More Thoughts from the Pattaya Orphanage* was published just before Sean left Thailand in 2002, although he would return many times as a visitor.

By 2004, more than 15,000 copies of the books were sold, most of them in Thailand, where a book that sells 3,000 copies is regarded as a best-seller.

Chapter 39

One of the older men in the home for the stateless, Father Ray's shelter for the aged ex-prisoners from the immigration jail, was making his own home brew with rice and sugar that he had taken from the kitchen where his meals were prepared. "The final product looks like water with a few drops of milk in it," Father Ray reported to his mailing list. "It is a potent brew, indeed. It is really a horrible tasting drink…and for that I am thankful. No one takes too much of it.

"One of the women, sixty-nine years old, has 'romantic inclinations' for one of the younger men, sixty-one," he went on. "She makes him little sweets and gets very angry if he offers them to anyone else. He, fortunately or unfortunately, is not the least bit interested. As a matter of fact, he doesn't give her a second look. One time I heard him tell her, 'Leave me alone.' She thought she would punish him for making the remark, so she did not talk to him for several days. He could not have been happier."

Father Ray continued to find reward in what was his smallest venture. By 1991, he told his readers, Jimmy was on the wagon, or said he was, which meant he didn't drink when he didn't have any money left from the small weekly allowance provided by the Orphanage. Of course, Jimmy insisted he was still "off the booze" when someone bought him a drink, because he wasn't paying for it. Where was the logic in that? Take your need for that back to the West. In Thailand, looking for logic was the quickest way to confusion.

Two years later, Jimmy, then eighty-nine, was in a wheelchair. He'd had a couple of strokes and was being pushed around by one of the Orphanage volunteers. "He told me that he only wants young girls to wheel him around," Father Ray wrote, "---not the male volunteers. I told him he was a dirty old man. He looked at me, smiled and said, 'THAT'S RIGHT!' Jimmy is probably not long for this world, and I am sure Heaven will not be the same after he gets there."

Meanwhile, the man who stayed in his room for ten years, refusing everything except food---to everyone's surprise---emerged and rejoined his peers for meals in front of the TV set. No one made a big fuss. Some didn't even notice.

One year on Christmas Day, Father Ray joined his elderly charges for a seafood meal with wine. One of the old men, who was partially blind, decided to give a speech. "He went on for about ten minutes...then he decided to sing a Latin Christmas carol. He is a Buddhist, so I was amazed that he knew the song, especially that he knew it in Latin. Then I found out that as a child he went to a Catholic school. He is now nearly eighty-three years old and he never forgot 'Adeste Fidelis.' For that, everyone got an extra round or two of wine.

"The old people received their presents, too. Most of the gifts were useful things. They like candy and soft cookies or cake. So everyone got their own little private supply. However, I could see them eye-balling the half-gallon of wine that I brought. We had a nice toast in honor of the Holy Season and sang some carols. As the wine sunk lower and lower in the bottle, the singing became more and more joyous. God bless all of them."

In another newsletter, he said, "We have a lovely old lady at our home for the stateless aged. She is slowly going downhill. In her prime, she was a bundle of fun and energy. Now she falls asleep as you talk to her. The few old people we have left are all feeble in some way. We give them a loving and dignified life, as we watch them slowly taking short little steps toward their Creator. Most of them need help in bathing and other personal needs. Some are blind or almost blind, others can hardly walk."

The number of residents was dwindling. There were no more old people in Bangkok's immigration jail, or so Father Ray was told, and sadly but inevitably, those living at the Redemptorist Center were, one by one, going to Father Ray's

Big Boss Upstairs. For those who remained, little changed. Easy-to-chew meals were served. Those who could were taken for walks by the volunteers and those who couldn't sat under the trees and talked quietly or merely sank into their memories. They took naps. Occasionally, they argued about what to watch on television.

The children were not asked to take
Christian education, but Christmas was
always the most anticipated day of the
year, when Father Ray dressed up like
Santa Claus and gave a bag full of
presents to each of his kids; one year, he
arrived in a hot air-balloon

Father Ray believed it was always best for a child to have
two loving parents, but when they weren't there, he told a
visitor---not immodestly, but cheerfully, gratefully---that he
thought his kids probably were happier than most

Buddhists in Asia touch the Happy
Buddha's belly for good luck and
Father Ray's was a reasonable
facsimile when the children wanted
help in school tests

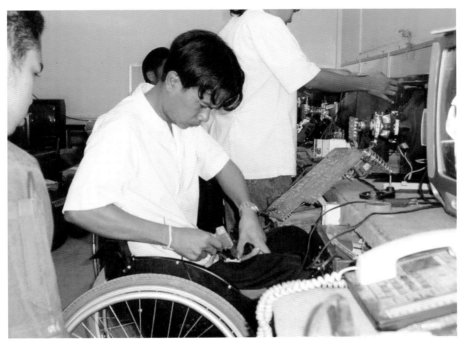

As many as two hundred young men and women every year attend the Redemptorist Vocational School for the Disabled, learning electronics repair and computer skills, living in a dormitory setting, and participating in a full schedule of recreation and sports

Father Ray believed physical activity was a
necessary match for education and
rehabilitation; a basketball court and a
swimming pool are on the school grounds
and many of the students and faculty
regularly win medals in contests held
around the world

"The children are a year older," Father Ray
wrote in one of his regular newsletters, "and I
am a year younger." In all those letters, he
said, "God bless you...and keep me and the kids
in your prayers to The Boss Upstairs."

(Top) Every year, dozens of the older children join in Pattaya's beach cleanup campaign

(Left) Baron Ricardo Carrini, founder of the Pattaya Orphanage Trust in the UK

(Right) Father Ray's office manager---some say she was the one who actually ran the place---Radchada (Toy) Chomjinda, listens to her constituents

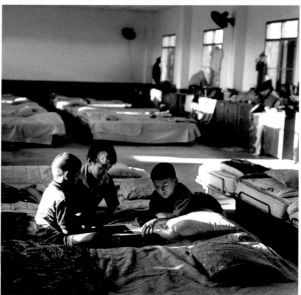

(Top) The building to the left was dedicated in 2002 to house the young girls, the building center background was dedicated in 2004 for the young boys at the home for street kids

(Bottom) Young children at the Orphanage study in their dormitory

(Above) The blind lead the
blind in a walk around the
Redemptorist School for
the Blind property, the first
in line being the oldest and
most familiar with the path

(Right) Aurora Lee
Sribuapun, founder and
principal of the School for
the Blind, herself blind
since childhood, comforts
two of her young students

(Above) The opening of the School for the Blind was presided
over by HRH Princess Maha Chakri Sirindhorn, a great honor

(Below) HRH Princess Maha Chakri Sirindhorn presenting her
father His Majesty Bhumibol Adulyadej's award for academic
excellence in high school to Somkid (Pat) Wongsrikaew

(Left) Father Ray and Father Morrissy officiated at the wedding on May 9, 1997 of Duangdoaw (Nok) Yothasri and Suporntum Mongkolsawadi, who met when he was her teacher at the Redemptorist Vocational School for the Disabled

(Below) Father Ray was never prouder than when Pachinee Nantaniran became the first of his youngsters to graduate from university on June 17, 1998

(Above) The door was always open to
Father Ray's office for his kids

(Below) Father Ray with teacher at the
School for the Deaf for over 20 years,
Srikanya Boonserm, as the kids show
the "sign" for "I love you"

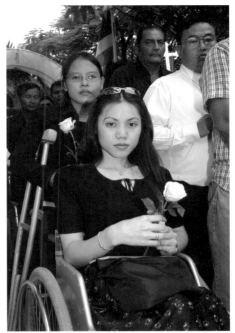

Ceremonies accompanying Father Ray's funeral included parades and processions, even a band, but all in a spirit of love and respect

Father Ray was taken from Bangkok to
Pattaya in a traditional Thai coffin with
gold trim and later transferred to a coffin
that bore his name; for two days, children,
co-workers, friends, and supporters came
to pay final respects and to pray

(Above) Father Philip Banchong Chaiyara
(left) was joined by the children and
students, lining the long driveway, waiting
for Father Ray's coffin to be taken into the
Orphanage

(Below) Representatives of His Majesty the
King attended the funeral, bringing some
Royal Soil to be used in the burial

A photograph of Father Ray with
twins, Wepa-wee and Wepa-da,
(above) that was the inspiration
for a statue designed by Professor
Prawat Raksiam and cast by
MonzArt Bronze Bennyline Co.
was unveiled at the Orphanage
100 days after his death (opposite)

The twins in 2003 (right) posing
near their home in Italy

Chapter 40

Men of the cloth---Catholic priests, Protestant pastors, preachers of almost every faith---are famous for telling jokes whenever they find themselves in a group of other men and Father Ray always had several handy, using them to open a casual conversation with friends, and sometimes to start a speech, or merely to lighten the day's burdens with laughter.

On a shelf in his office was a small book called *Jokes Priests Can Tell*, collected by Monsignor Arthur Tonne, who gave as his address a rural route in Kansas. Many of the jokes were credited to such publications as the *Catholic Digest* and *Catholic Workman* and *Capper's Weekly*, the latter a periodical whose point of view ran parallel to that of the *Reader's Digest*. Although many of the jokes were "religious," some even using the Pope as a foil, it wasn't likely that Father Ray used this book as the source of his humor. The humor wasn't bawdy enough. For example:

One of my parishioners came back from a pilgrimage that included Rome and a big public audience with the Holy Father. "Father, the Pope gave me his own special blessing. He was riding through the crowd in his Popemobile when he suddenly turned toward me, made a big sign of the cross and said real loud, 'God bless you.'

"I wonder why he would do that," I asked.

"I think, Father, it was because I had just given a big, loud sneeze."

Another from the book:

Father Murphy stopped in the fifth grade as they were practicing some of the hymns for Sunday Mass. He noticed that all the children were singing with enthusiasm except one little boy who sat at his desk, not making a sound. When asked why he was not singing along, the lad responded with a grin: "Well, Father, somebody has to listen."

No, Father Ray's sense of humor ranged wider and further, as did that of many other clergymen. Some were irreverent, even risqué, a ploy frequently used to put laymen at their ease. It was as if the clergymen were saying, "Even if I'm wearing a collar, and have taken an oath of chastity, that doesn't mean I'm not one of the guys." It wasn't true of all, of course, but many proved that they could smoke and drink and tell jokes with the best of them, and like Father Ray, they matched their temporal friends drink-for-drink and joke-for-joke. Swapping salty jokes was, as the saying goes, a "Man Thing" that went along with the alcohol and suited the male posturing that Father Ray frequently encountered in the business world.

Some of his humor Father Ray found on the Internet, recycling it among his friends. One E-mail that went out listed some of what were purported to be answers that kids gave for a Bible quiz:

- Jesus was born because Mary had an immaculate contraption.
- The miracle of the resurrection was that Jesus could move that big stone.
- Lot's wife was a pillar of salt by day, but a ball of fire by night.
- The seventh commandment is, "Thou shalt not admit adultery."
- The epistles were the wives of the apostles.
- Christians have only one spouse. This is called monotony.
- Solomon, one of David's sons, had 300 wives and 700 porcupines.
- Unleavened bread is bread made without any ingredients.

From another that went out from his computer:

The other day, I went to a local religious bookstore, where I saw a "HONK IF YOU LOVE JESUS" bumper sticker. I bought it and put it on my car. I'm really glad I did. What an uplifting experience that followed.

I was stopped at the light at a busy intersection, lost in thought, thinking about the Lord, and didn't even notice that the light had turned green. That bumper sticker really worked. I found lots of people who love Jesus.

Why, the guy behind me started honking like crazy. He must really love Jesus, because he leaned out of his car window and yelled, 'Jesus Christ!' as loud as he could. It was like a football game with him yelling, 'Go, Jesus, go!'

Everybody started honking then, so I leaned out of my window and waved and smiled at all those loving people. There must have been a man from Florida back there because I could hear him yelling something about a sunny beach and he was waving in a funny way, with only his middle finger in the air. I asked my kids what that meant. They just giggled and said it was a Hawaiian good luck sign, so I leaned out of my window and gave the good luck sign back to him.

A couple of people were so caught up in the joy of the moment that they got out of their cars and started toward me. I guess they wanted to pray, but then the light turned yellow and I stepped on the gas. And a good thing I did, because I was the only one to get across the intersection. I looked back as them standing there and gave them a big smile and held up the Hawaiian good luck sign as I praised the Lord for such wonderful folks.

Another that went out to close friends took another swipe at religion:

There were three good arguments that Jesus was Italian:
(1) He talked with his hands,
(2) He had wine with every meal, and
(3) He used olive oil.

But then there were three equally good arguments that Jesus was black:
(1) He called everyone "brother,"
(2) He liked Gospel, and
(3) He couldn't get a fair trial.

But then there were three equally good arguments that Jesus was Jewish:

(1) He went into his Father's business,

(2) He lived at home until he was thirty-three, and

(3) He was sure his Mother was a virgin and his mother was sure he was God.

But then there were three equally good arguments that Jesus was a Californian:

(1) He never cut his hair,

(2) He walked around barefoot all the time, and

(3) He started a new religion.

But then there were three equally good arguments that Jesus was Irish:

(1) He never got married,

(2) He was always telling stories, and

(3) He loved green pastures.

But the most compelling evidence of all---three arguments that Jesus was a woman:

(1) He fed a crowd at a moment's notice when there was no food,

(2) He kept trying to get a message across to a bunch of men who just didn't get it, and

(3) Even when He was dead, He had to get up because there was more work to do.

Other jokes and jibes were political. Father Ray had no love for recent American presidents and Bill Clinton and the George Bush---both One and Two---got regular attack.

Where did his jokes come from? Where does any joke teller's repertoire of humorous stories come from? Usually from other joke tellers. Once connected to the Internet, of course, people stopped telling jokes and started sending them, in volume, electronically. Father Ray was one such mass E-mailer, checking joke websites on his own and forwarding gags sent by friends. Many of which will not be retold here.

He offered no apology for what made him laugh. "God has to be a hell of a nice guy," the priest once said when being interviewed. "Otherwise, He wouldn't give us a sense of humor where we can laugh at wonderful things and we can laugh at dirty things. He must be a guy who wants us to have an appreciation of all kinds of things."

Chapter 41

In a way, it was very much like what had happened through history and around the world, where as sons and daughters came of age, they entered the family business.

In Asia, this is still more commonly practiced than in the many other places. In Thailand, and elsewhere in the region as "developing nation" status and "globalization" arrived, more and more children were demonstrating their independence, striking out on their own, finding careers in fields totally apart from and often alien to their past.

For many others, only the fashions and times had changed. They still were content to apprentice in the business operated by their parents, then take over when their elders died or retired. Doctor's sons still became doctors, the owners of a thousand kinds of shops and companies bequeathed their careers to their offspring; just as there were still generations of carmakers in Detroit named Ford, and the names of Hollywood sons and daughters who became stars themselves would fill several miles of marquees, in Thailand the decisions to follow mom and dad into the family business were as certain as the heat and the humidity. The lines of succession were clear.

So it was at the Pattaya Orphanage, where from the 1990s onwards many of those on staff, as secretaries and receptionists and even as key junior executives, were orphans who'd spent their early years in the baby room---either as infants themselves or as teenagers changing the diapers of their fellow orphans---and in the nearby dorms.

Phennipa "Phen" Rachakit was one of them. She was born in 1976 and raised in Trat province. She was an unwanted child and her parents divorced: mom's location unknown, dad a gambler. So she lived with her grandmother for a while, hundreds of miles away, near the Cambodian border, and at other times with aunts and uncles. Finally, the child's grandmother felt that this was not good for her, as she was being used more as a servant than treated as a family member. So the grandmother brought Phen to the Orphanage in 1986, when she was nine.

"It wasn't scary at the Orphanage," she remembered, "---not like it was scary outside. It was like home."

Her file at the Orphanage revealed her favorite subject in school was math, her favorite food fried rice, her favorite colors green and dark blue. She also loved sports, ranging from ping-pong to basketball, football and volleyball. In 1996, Father Ray sent her to England, where, as part of the Orphanage's learn-English-abroad program, she lived for a year with a couple who were teachers.

When Phen returned to Thailand, at twenty-two, Father Ray asked if she wanted to continue studies at a college or university. She said no, she wanted to work at the Orphanage. Father Ray convinced her to try another year at a technical college in Sri Racha. She agreed and began studying computers and accounting. She continued to live at the Orphanage, where, as was customary for older residents, she continued to help with the smaller children

For a time after that, she worked at the Redemptorist Center as a receptionist and then, for several months helped set up the accounting program and greet new customers at a small electronics and computer repair shop in Pattaya, funded by one of Father Ray's longtime supporters. By 2004, she was married to a mechanic, with whom she had a one-year-old child, and she was working at the Street Kids Home.

To Phen, Father Ray was "Big Daddy." "He gave me a new life," she said soon after the priest's death. She then burst into tears and said, "I cannot tell anything more."

Luksamapa Monyarid, called "Luke," was another "graduate" who didn't stray far from home. He was a late arrival. Born in 1970 in Rayong, a nearby coastal province with deserted beaches and large durian and pineapple farms, he came to the Orphanage when he was seventeen. His mother was Thai and his father was an American who had served in the U.S. Air Force at U-tapao, the base that sent planes to bomb Cambodia and Vietnam. Some time later, his father wrote him, transmitting vital information about his birth, but the letter was lost. An aunt raised him after that and it was her name on his birth certificate.

When Luke was seventeen, he was sent to the Pearl Buck Foundation, a charitable organization named for the famous novelist that helped mixed-race Asian children. The foundation, in turn, sent him to Father Ray. At that time, such children in Thailand, and in much of Asia, were shunned. In the 1990s, this would turn around and they were embraced as pop stars, topping the recording and movie charts, discovering success as models and television news presenters. But in 1987, Luke was pretty much on his own and although he finished secondary school and had started in high school, he was, in most ways, another child adrift.

Father Ray gave him a job at the Redemptorist Center, working in the dining room. After Luke completed his high school studies, the priest sent him to Singapore for six months to work on his English and then to Assumption Business Administration College in Bangkok. There, he earned straight A's and worked part-time as an assistant in the university laboratory, graduating with a Bachelor's degree in computer programming in 2002. He went on to get a master's degree in computer business and commerce.

Not long after that, Luke went back to work for Father Ray, setting up a Central Purchasing Department aimed at combining food and supplies acquisition for all of the organization's projects---the Orphanage, the School for the Deaf, the School for the Blind, the Vocational School for the Disabled, the Stateless Aged Home, and the Street Kids Home. The idea was to coordinate the needs of all and buy in bulk, even cut out the middle man in some cases by going directly to the farm, and thereby save money.

In 2003---thirty-three years old and single and still living at the Orphanage---Luke presided over a small warehouse constructed on the grounds of the Redemptorist Center, a few steps away from the Chapel and the center's swimming pool. Near the building's entrance was a long, narrow office with glass windows and air-conditioning, desks and computers arranged in rows. Adjacent to the office and taking up most of the rest of the high-ceilinged building was a space lined with shelves, where canned and dried foods were stacked in order.

There were small mountains of rice in fifty kilogram (one hundred and ten pound) bags and five-gallon tins of cooking oil. By 2004, rice consumption for all the projects was four hundred kilos, or eight-hundred and eighty pounds, per day---enough, when cooked, to fill the bed of a large pickup truck. Near the entrance of the warehouse were cartons of canned pineapple from Hawaii and corn from Oregon, contributed by the U.S. military during recent Cobra Gold exercises.

A third, long, narrow room closed off from the food was also lined with shelves. Here were kept the office supplies.

Luke said he had been in touch with his mother, who was living in America, but the contact was tenuous, he said; she hadn't visited him, nor had he been to the United States. There still was an aunt in Rayong, he said, but this---the Orphanage---was home.

Chapter 42

Radchada Chomjinda, better known by the common Thai nickname of Toy, arrived at Father Ray's door at a good time, when the Orphanage and other projects seemed to have settled into a satisfying routine and when she was at a crossroads in her life.

In 1996, there were four orphans in their final year of university studies. Six more were in temporary homes abroad to improve their English and learn more about the outside world by living in it; three were spending a year with sponsoring families in the United States, while two were in Scotland and one was in England, each of them for six months. Seventeen others started their first year of school that year. Using secondhand musical instruments that were either purchased or contributed, Father Ray had two bands in the Orphanage, one Western classical, the other traditional Thai...playing in a room only a few meters from Father Ray's office.

When a big, new department store opened in Pattaya that year, the manager asked if any of the older children wanted weekend jobs. "I knew the kids would jump at the chance," Father Ray wrote in his summer newsletter. "Every Saturday and Sunday, about ten of our kids can be seen collecting the shopping carts from the parking lots. They get about a dollar a day from the store, plus they also make a little extra money from tips when they help someone bring their shopping cart to their car."

There were ninety-five students in the School for the Blind, who were learning how to walk along the roadway outside the school wall without assistance. The deaf kids were learning to dance as their teachers kept the beat to music that went unheard by clapping their hands, the vibrations sent forth keeping them in step. Students at the vocational school won sixty medals at Thailand's national sporting day for disabled people---the blind kids won another nine---and two of the disabled students volunteered to teach the orphans computer science.

"I spoke to the two students afterwards and they told me how sorry they felt for the orphans," Father Ray wrote in his autumn letter. "One of them even had tears in her eyes. I thought it was quite amazing. This sorrow for the orphans was coming from a young lady who had only one arm and a young man with a shriveled leg."

Toy was told much of this when she came to the Orphanage for an interview. She told Father Ray that she was the fifth born of nine children. Her father worked for the Tobacco Monopoly in Bangkok (the government's cigarette factory) and her mom was a dressmaker in a baby shop. She herself had an impressive resume---having worked for fifteen years in Bangkok as a secretary for advertising and business firms, as well as for the Japanese Embassy, Finnish Embassy, Queen Sirikit Convention Center, and UNICEF. She told the priest that as a child she always had wanted to be rich, so she invested all her savings in a travel agency and stocks and bonds, but ended up losing everything.

An older sister, a nun who'd worked with Father Ray in a refugee camp during the period when Cambodians were fleeing the Vietnamese occupation, told Toy about the priest's work in Pattaya. He hired her on the spot and told her to work with Brother Denis Gervais on sponsorships. For the next three years she did that, learning just about everything there was to know about how the organization worked. The Pattaya Orphanage Trust in the U.K. by now had expanded its fund-raising activities enormously and the spin-off organization was in operation in France. More money was coming from Denmark, along with a growing number of adoptive parents and volunteers.

It was a time to rejoice and, as always, weep a little. In 1997, the collapse of the Thai economy made contributions in pounds and dollars and marks and kroner worth up to twice as much, and new construction was begun. A graduate of the vocational school, despite the lack of arms and legs, was teaching computer science in Bangkok. At the same time, Father Ray, tiring easily, turned over responsibility for the street kids, the blind, and the stateless to a new assistant, and then got pneumonia and broke his arm. His Santa Claus suit didn't fit that year, and he vowed again to lose weight.

In 1998, Father Ray took some of the older orphans deep-sea fishing (one boy caught a seven-foot sailfish), construction of a new building for the deaf was completed, the School for the Blind was rated highest nationwide. And in an attempt to make Pattaya the first disabled-accessible town in Thailand, Father Ray invited the provincial governor, the mayor, and other high officials to partici-pate in a special demonstration.

"After they all got to the vocational school," he wrote, "we put each of them in a wheelchair and took them downtown! Once there, they were 'released' on the streets to see what a difficult time a handicapped person has in Pattaya. You should have seen those guys trying to wheel themselves up over a curb. A wheel of one wheelchair got caught in a broken sidewalk. They were supposed to enter some restaurants that had a few stairs at the front door. It was hilarious."

Father Ray's new problem was a detached retina. No problem, he said; it could be fixed and there were children at the blind school who didn't have irises.

In 1999, a dozen orphans were studying at the university level, a new dining room and kitchen were opened on the Orphanage grounds, there were nine disabled graduates of the vocational school on the payroll (not counting those on the school's faculty), and the street kids were helping clear the land on a nine-acre parcel outside of town that would, in time, serve as their new home.

By now, Toy said her "crisis" of lost savings was long forgotten when, the same year, Father Ray's secretary resigned and she was offered the chair at the desk outside the priest's office. "Father Ray told me if you select the job you love, you will never have to work a day in your life," she said, "and I say today that no other job compares. I never leave the office before six o'clock, I never feel sorry, I never thought about how much I earn here as I did in my previous jobs."

Toy couldn't have weighed forty-five kilos (one hundred pounds) and with her big glasses and small, almost geisha-like steps, executed rapidly as she moved from place to place, it was easy to think she might be more movement than efficiency. That would have been a mistake. No one in the office had better control, not even Brother Denis, who after a career at IBM had a memory that seemed computerized. For the rest of Father Ray's life, Toy was his helpmate and gatekeeper.

Her desk looked only slightly tidier than her boss's, but she, too, knew where everything was on it. (But there were never---ever---any electronic toys that beeped.) She also knew where everything was in a row of filing cabinets to her left, and spun around on her wheeled chair whenever she had a moment to go to her computer and do what executive secretaries always do: keep a hundred balls in the air simultaneously, making sure everyone got an answer to whatever question was asked, while organizing Father Ray's life as much he might permit. Once, she said, she tidied up his desk, but only once. His anger rang in her ears for days afterward.

She fielded phone calls that were screened only superficially by the front desk. She welcomed visitors, both anticipated and unexpected, sending some in to see Father Ray if he was in, handing many off to Audrey Williams. She made uncounted phone calls every day, arranging airport pickups and meetings for Father Ray and others, while coordinating transportation for field trips for the kids, some going off for a day with longtime supporters and friends to the beach or to a crocodile farm or to the water park in Jomtien. Some of the older children went on longer trips, to Kanchanaburi or Hua Hin or Chiang Mai. She coordinated everything.

She sat in on meetings to choose who among the older children would go abroad; they had to be good in English already, she said. She talked almost daily with the heads of each project and, of course, bantered with the children, young and old, who customarily wandered into the offices after class.

She opened the mail, stapled the checks and money orders and---in a surprising number of cases---cash to the letters, told Father Ray about the correspondence she thought he'd want to see, helped him with his replies, and sent the rest to other staffers to process where appropriate.

Bills were sent to Brother Denis. Letters asking about adoption went to Suwanna Cheownawin, who had processed hundreds of applications since coming to the Orphanage in 1982 and still occupied an office in the original Orphanage building a few steps away. Sponsorship and donation letters went to someone else and after he left, to Tim Hague. Tim had worked in Bangkok for Father Joe Maier for many years and now helped keep the computer files up to date and supervised the writing of thank you letters and the sending of photographs (and later, when possible, videotapes) to the sponsors and donors. Letters from would-be volunteers were given to Derek Franklin. Media requests were generally given a lower priority, following Father Ray's direction to say thank you before saying please.

"Father Ray said the more you give, the more you get," Toy remembered, "and I feel I gain and gain and gain. I start every day with happiness."

Chapter 43

Right up to the end, the street kids were a cross to carry up Father Ray's own version of Calvary. His experience grew along with the numbers of kids, but it never got any easier.

In 1989, Father Ray was offered, a little more than seven acres of land several kilometers outside central Pattaya, a hog farm that was closing down. Although he had no immediate need for the property, he thought it was bargain priced at 2.9 million baht (US$116,000) and in one of his rare moments of financial stability, he bought it. Nine years later, he needed it. The population of his street kids' shelter in town was beyond capacity.

"We have over fifty kids and there is simply no room for any more," Father Ray wrote. "Although there are several hundred more kids on the street, we have stopped looking for them in the evenings, the reason being we have no space for them to eat and sleep. We will use the existing home plus the future building on the new property. That will allow us to take in at least fifty more."

The property seemed ideal in many ways. However reluctant he sometimes was to have anything to do with the problems connected to street children, Father Ray could see their numbers growing in Pattaya and the size of the new property guaranteed space for considerable expansion. It also occurred to him that if the home were distanced from the temptations of downtown Pattaya, situated several kilometers from the tourist areas---with no connecting public transportation---then perhaps his dropout rate might fall, while keeping the traffickers in drugs and sex from easy contact with the children.

The land's size further made the cultivation of fruit and vegetables possible and because the property was outside the city limits, if he chose to raise pigs and chickens again, he could. Neighbors in the sparsely populated area said there was plenty of water close to the surface. There were good schools less than a kilometer away. And, most unusually, and exotically, only a few hundred meters away was an elephant refuge and show grounds, reminding Father Ray of the time when elephants were his neighbors at the Orphanage and he used their poop to make methane gas.

Construction of the first building began in 1998. On the weekends, the older children were bussed to the property to help clear the land and enjoy the countryside. It was to be a two-story structure, with offices on one side downstairs, a kitchen on the other, and a large open-sided area in the middle for eating and, during rainy weather, play. Dormitories and lavatories and another open space were planned for the second level. Completion of the project was slow due to a lack of funds and it wasn't until Spring 2000 before some of the kids were moved.

"Try to imagine what a young boy or girl, about nine or ten years old, would be like if they were roaming the streets for a year," he wrote in that year's Christmas letter. "For that whole year, they were finding food for themselves, any way they could. They would be looking for clothes they could steal off clothes lines; they would be learning exactly the things you do not want a young child to know. They would be taught or forced by older street kids to do anything they were commanded. In most cases, we can turn them around and give them something they sorely miss far more important than clothes, food or water, real sincere love. In the past, they have been little thieves and have done all sorts of nasty things that shock even me. This year, they are going to sing Christmas carols on Christmas Eve at the hotels!"

There were sixty at first, seventy by the end of the caroling season, then aged five to sixteen, the youngest usually entering the shelter with older siblings.

By March 2001, a vegetable garden was in and one hundred and thirty fruit trees were planted. "They are still only seedlings a foot or so high, and even though I keep ordering them to grow faster, they refuse and listen only to Mother Nature instead of to Father Brennan," he wrote in his Easter letter. "Some day, we will have an abundance of fruit for the orphans, handicapped, blind, deaf, old people and of course the street kids, too. Our idea is for the kids to be able to sell their produce to the various projects. They have already started growing and selling vegetables on a small scale."

That was the good news. The bad news was that, again, the home's capacity was stretched and Father Ray had to limit occupancy in the new structure to boys---who represented three-quarters of the total---and leave the young girls back in town. Sexual segregation was imperative. As young as they were, few were sexual innocents. Many had been abused at home before becoming runaways and more were reluctant targets for Pattaya's numerous pedophiles, while still others had started sleeping together on their own; sex, like lying and stealing, had become a "normal" part of their lives. To reunite the children on the same property, yet keep them separated after lights out, Father Ray desperately needed a new building for the girls.

Much of the strength of the operation in the early years came from a young man named Supagon Noja, called Ja. He was the son of a rice and fruit farmer from northern Thailand. While still in high school, he had lived for a while with an Italian priest, helping him teach and farm with the Hmong and Akha hill tribes. Moving to Bangkok as a teenager, Ja worked as a waiter and in a food factory to pay for his university education, earning a bachelor's degree in business administration. Next, he worked for six months for Father Joe Maier's Human Development Center. By now, Father Ray's old friend Father Joe had founded and was operating more than two dozen slum kindergartens, and in a two-story building near the port was running the city's first HIV/AIDS hospice and a shelter for street kids. It was here that Ja got his first experience working with the "throwaways and runaways"---as Father Joe called them---

talking to them on the street, counseling the ones with drug problems, bringing as many as agreed back to the shelter.

In Pattaya on holiday in 1993, two years after Father Ray's first street shelter opened, Ja met the priest and soon after that began cruising Pattaya beach and the streets, talking to the kids. Unlike Father Ray, he had no ice-cream cart to use as bait, but already the priest's home was well known among the youngsters and it's fair to assume that word was that at the very least the Redemptorist Street Kids Home was good for a hot meal, a wash-up, clean clothing, medical care, and a safe place to sleep.

There was more than that, of course. The same regulations applied in the new location as at the old: no sex, no drugs, no violence, no theft, no lying, etc. While some of these rules were difficult to enforce, their existence alone imposed a structure that the youngsters weren't used to and many didn't like. And for all ages, attendance at school was mandatory.

"Up in the morning at 5:30," said Ja. "Six a.m., clean the house. Breakfast at 6:30. Seven, they get pocket money according to grade level to pay for school lunches, up to twenty baht each. Then it's off to school in our bus so we know they actually get there, some to temple school, others to the government school, again according to age. Return home at 4:30 or 4:45, to clean the grounds. Five o'clock, sports. Their choice: football, volleyball, whatever. Six o'clock, shower. Dinner at 6:30. Study from seven to eight."

While Father Ray planned a second building for the girls, he also wanted to build a high wall around the property to discourage after-dark departures. In the meantime, one out of every three stayed for a while and then returned to the streets.

Chapter 44

By 1993, there were more than seventy students in the school for blind children, a year later more than ninety.

"I am constantly surprised by what they can do," Father Ray wrote in his regular report to friends. "Even though they are blind, they make exquisite replicas of flowers. They use rice flour and coloring. The finished product is as good as anything you can find in a shop. They also make marvelous little purses out of leather that they sell to visitors. They can hardly make them fast enough for the demand. People do not buy their products out of pity; they buy them because it is a good product."

Father Ray was surprised by his sightless charges: "Believe it or not, they love television. Of course they are blind, but they like to listen to the television. They say it is much more exciting than the radio."

But he also was saddened and dismayed: "Unfortunately, some parents of the blind children seem to have little love for their child. Some never come to visit their child during the entire school year. Others do not bother to bring their child home at the end of the school year. We have to keep sending them letters to come. Some parents do not come…we have to take care of them until school opens again. Why they do that I don't know. Perhaps it is because they are ashamed of their child. If that is the reason, they should feel ashamed of themselves. With others, it could be poverty; they simply don't have the money for transportation or the finances to add an extra mouth to their tables.

"The faces of blind children can sometimes be disturbing," Father Ray went on. "We have one older boy who has no iris. His eyes are all bulged out and white, like someone cut a slice off a ping-pong ball and put it in his eye socket. He is a very good student. The gentleness and genuine goodness inside the blind children makes me love them dearly. They are the children of My Boss Upstairs…who since He is a Spirit, doesn't have an iris either."

With or without family support, at the school the children were embraced. Moo, was nine when he was enrolled and right away started to learn the Thai alphabet; he was one of the rare and lucky ones---his parents visited him regularly. Sakda, a seven-year-old, came to Father Ray because overcrowding and a long waiting list denied him entry to one of the state-operated schools. ("After a year of training in daily self-care," his case history reported, "very little progress has been made. He can barely attend to any of his daily needs except feeding and dressing himself with the help of a teacher. He is under close observation, but it appears highly unlikely that he will be able to enter primary school.")

Mew was another little boy, aged four when he was turned over to the school by an aunt, who needed similar instruction in basic life skills; a year after his arrival he was able to feed himself, but "still needs help in attending to other daily routine requirements and sanitary care." Lak, five, was mentally retarded and "very weak physically" and he, too, was "barely able to take care of any of his daily needs except feeding himself with help from a teacher" and it was believed that he would never be able to undertake primary education.

The harsh consequence of being handicapped colored every case study kept so meticulously by Father Ray's staff. Every year, and, later, every six months, every blind student (students in the School for the Deaf and the Vocational School and in the Orphanage, too) was evaluated and an update was entered into the computer files. Progress in blind school classes, in learning Braille in English and Thai, and math and all the rest, as well in mastering self-sufficiency, was noted and new photographs were taken. But the language was not always encouraging.

"An extremely active and restless boy, it seems difficult for him to sit or stand still," read one. Another noted, "She needs continuous help in attending to daily needs and entering a formal educational program in future is out of the question." "Communication between him and his teachers is proving to be difficult and demanding a great deal of patience ..." went still another.

The school principal, Aurora, painted a rather grim picture in 2003, when, she said, ninety percent of the blind in Thailand still had no education, despite the growing number of centers that were teaching some basic trades. She said new laws mandated that all handicapped individuals were entitled to an education, but teachers and the institutions themselves could not accommodate them. Half of Aurora's students were multiply handicapped---most of them mentally slow---and for them there were no other facilities anywhere in the country.

Not all was so distressing.

Some years ago, a blind adult in the United States wrote an autobiography called *If You Could See What I Can Hear.* This was a reference to the fact that when we are denied the use of one of our senses, or that sense is diminished in some way; one or more of the other senses accelerates in effectiveness to compensate. Thus, a blind person usually has better-than-average hearing, or, rather, hears what most of us don't even notice. (Just as a deaf person develops visual perception in ways most of the hearing population usually does not.) So it was at Father Ray's School for the Blind.

"When the various schools close for the summer, each school gives a little show," he wrote in 1997. "By far the best one this year was the show given by the School for the Blind. Their musical ability astounds me. Music for them is one of the great pleasures in life. They use something like a little keyboard with a tube attached, which they blow into. They also are expert in playing the ancient musical instruments of Siam. One particular instrument is made of bamboo with a handle the student holds and shakes. Each student holds just one, but each one is a different note. They play an entire song with each student knowing just when to shake their musical instrument. The sound is beautiful. The entire set of instruments is very inexpensive. The set we have was donated to us by a kind Thai lady. She herself is going blind and she knows the difference music can make in any person's life."

In music, the student Supaphon Ngern-Opas, nicknamed Apple, was something of a star. She learned to play the bamboo rattles described by Father Ray and the harmonica, flute, keyboard, and a little guitar, as well. She also had a soaring and singular voice.

Born in 1975 and a resident of the school since she was twelve, Apple always was one of the oldest students and by 2001, was on the school office staff, answering the telephone and assisting Aurora. (Telephone work had been an outlet for employment for the blind in years past, but most of those jobs dried up when the switchboard was replaced by recorded message machines.) She also helped teach the students to do what she did best, make music.

Just as the orphans performed in public, so, too, did the blind. There was a class in music and after lunch every day, the children were encouraged to sing and play musical instruments for half an hour. In time, a sort of choir was formed and they followed the trail blazed in Pattaya by the orphans, singing in hotels and in other public venues, as far away a Bangkok, as well as in the auditorium on the school's second level for special occasions and for foreign visitors.

Always, Apple was the star. In addition to songs she performed in Thai, both popular and traditional, she memorized many English language hits. Her favorite was "Amazing Grace," sung without instrumental backing. Joan Baez and Judy Collins and other Western singers who regarded the song as one of the most heart-wringing in their repertoires, might be humbled by Apple's rendition. And surely reduced to tears.

As Father Ray was whenever he visited the blind school. "Here I am into this letter and I have forgotten to thank you for the donation you sent," he wrote in Christmas 1997 "I really appreciate what you have done and can assure you the money will be used well. Part of your donation will be going towards improvement of the School for the Blind. The blind children did not receive many gifts this year, but luckily we had extra toys from the Orphanage. So they got all kinds of goodies.

"Although the great majority cannot see at all, some have partial vision. They have to put their gift very close to their face to see it. The other blind children put their hands all over the doll or plastic toy to 'feel' its shape. As I grow older, I pray that The Boss Upstairs never takes away my sight."

In 1998, the school "received a rating higher than any other school for the blind in Thailand. It is even a higher rating than the big government school for the blind in Bangkok."

A year later, Father Ray claimed another first, saying "we probably have the only school for the blind in the world that gives their students a monthly day for getting a massage. As a matter of fact, as I write this letter, the students are getting one right now. The headmistress of the school (who is blind) has a husband who is almost blind. He has a school for teaching blind people how to give the famous ancient Thai massage. He brings his students here every month to give them practice. Giving massages will be their means of self-support in the future."

The same year, he wrote about a young female student who asked him what the color red looked like. "How do you describe a color to a blind person? My answer was that colors are like ice cream, it's all ice cream, but there are many flavors. She accepted that (I think), but of course I really had not answered her question. It made me remember that as a fifth grade boy, I had entered a basket weaving class taught by a blind man. All us kids were in awe of him because he told us he had an ability to 'feel' color. He would go to the table with the reeds and give us the right color we requested. It mystified me that he could actually feel color. Later on I realized that he simply memorized the position of each bundle of reeds. But that was the door that led me, about thirty years later, to be interested in the blind.

"What a marvelous thing is color. God could have made the world in sepia or black and white. But in an act of Divine Frivolity, he decided to splash color everywhere, even in the heavens. Yet, He let some people lack the ability to see those colors. The eternal question human beings ask is, 'WHY?'

"I don't know. But because of the young girl like the one mentioned above, they have made me more aware of the beauty of creation. When blind people get to Heaven, I think God is going to give them a marvelous and spectacular color show extravaganza…just for them…alone. People like us will be jealous."

Chapter 45

One of the splendid ironies of modern American history was that the children and grandchildren of refugees from the Old World had the opportunity to return to the scenes of the poverty and repression of their elders. And so it was that when the newly ordained Father Ray was on his way to Thailand in 1961---accompanied by his sister, mother, and a classmate from the seminary, Fr. Philip Viraphong Wacharathit, one of the Redemptorists' first Thai priests---he stopped in Ireland, where he visited relatives and then kissed the Blarney Stone.

"Kiss the Blarney Stone and receive the gift of gab." That was the way the legend went and every year, thousands came to do it. By the time Father Ray visited Blarney Castle, built in 1446, it was included in every bus tour that went to southwest Ireland. If the thought of standing in queue to kiss a rock wall wasn't off-putting enough, it wasn't a simple thing to do. After climbing a steep, narrow staircase---so designed to give access to fifteenth-century attackers only one at a time---to kiss the stone you had to bend over backward and lower yourself down about two feet into a crevice at the top of the castle. All in Father Ray's party performed the feat, although, as his then seventeen-year-old sister Sharron recalled, her big brother didn't need to, he already had the "gift of Blarney."

"We also visited relatives in Ballybunion and I remember going to a farm somewhere near Dublin. We continued on and after touring quite a bit of Europe, Ray and Father Philip left us in Rome to continue their journey to Thailand. It was a very sad parting."

Such travel later became quite common for the priest. Though he spent most of his adult life in Thailand, by the time he was in his sixties, Father Ray was an experienced traveler, his office at the Orphanage silent and empty quite frequently, sometimes for months at a time. Too often in the end, it was to return to the United States for medical attention, but there also were pleasant home leaves and regular excursions to the capitals of Europe and Asia.

The trips "home" to the United States were the most numerous and even when they included time in clinics and hospitals, they also took him to Texas where both his brother and sister now lived. "It always amazed us how close we were considering the age differences," Sharron recalled. "Don, Ray, and I had several trips together. It was a good way to get him away from all the work he was doing. We would sit and reminisce about growing up and the stories from our past. These were special times for us as we really hadn't grown up together.

"My five daughters were constantly surprised by Uncle Ray. Ray was home for the birth of Nora and took care of Shannon and Megan while I was in the hospital. He was a wonderful storyteller and filled their imaginations with things from stories of the *Monkey King* to making Erin, the youngest, a queen. He crowned her with a paper crown which she still has twenty-five years later. Shannon, Megan, Nora and Erin all visited Ray in Thailand. Only our fourth-born, Amy, was not able to, but revered her uncle from reports brought by her sisters and his occasional visits home."

When he returned from his travels, Father Ray gave full reports to his friends at the Orphanage. Following one visit, he said he and his brother had shared a room and because of their differing views regarding neatness, it was agreed that there would be a "line" drawn down the middle of the room and each of the priests was to keep his own personal habits on the side designated as his own.

Whenever possible, Father Ray took care of business while traveling. Sometimes this involved no more than making a side trip to visit the one-time residents of the Orphanage and their new families. Twice, in Europe, where there were many adoptions, reunions were organized, giving the kids a chance to get reacquainted as well as see their former "father." The woman who had arranged so many of the adoptions during her long service at the Orphanage, Suwanna Cheownawin, and Father Ray's secretary, Toy Chomjinda, accompanied him to Denmark where they visited with thirty families in an event organized by the local adoptive center. Two years later, Toy went to Germany with Suwanna for what was an annual meeting of some twenty-five Thai orphans.

The priest always said he was amazed to see how big they were and, though pleased by their successful acceptance of their new country and culture---and, especially, of their new families---he couldn't help being somewhat saddened to realize that they no longer could speak Thai, or, in fact, remember much about Thailand or the Orphanage, because so many were so young when they left. Toy said of the German visit that "all the children spoke German and had German names. I called them by their Thai names and they didn't understand."

On one of his trips to the United States, Father Ray visited Denis Gervais, then taking the year for spiritual training to become a religious brother. On another, he visited his "daughter," Yai, and her husband. Frequently he made other journeys to Hong Kong, at first to buy software for his office computer system (before Thailand got up to speed in software marketing) and cheap toys for Christmas. Often he took Denis Gervais with him and they always had a meal with his friend Bill Mangelsen.

"Father Ray loved steak," Bill said, "and he always stayed for a few days, so I'd make reservations at Ruth's Chris Steak House, Morton's, or the San Francisco Steak House. He always wanted to buy the meal and I had to resort to tricks to be sure the bill came to me. It was a game we played."

Two of his greatest travel "highs" came when he met two of the most visible and remarkable religious figures of the twentieth-century.

Mother Teresa he met in the city where she based her worldwide organization of Sisters of Charity, Calcutta. She was not a Redemptorist, but her order tended the needs of the poorest of the poor and when Father Ray visited her in the late 1970s---there appears to be no record of the precise date---he posed for a photograph with the woman in her offices. Not long after that, the picture was on his office wall.

It was, he said in a newsletter in 2003, "the most valuable picture of myself that was ever taken. It's a picture of me standing next to Mother Teresa. It was taken many years ago while I was visiting her in Calcutta. I treasure it highly. I even had it copied in case something happened to the original. What a woman. I attended Mass with her every morning, and when she prayed I could feel in the air the power she generated. Anyway, I have asked her in prayer to put all my kids under her protection."

The Dalai Lama Father Ray met in 2000 when they found themselves in Copenhagen at the same time. "I no sooner entered the room where the Dalai Lama was, when he rose to greet me," the priest wrote. "We talked about many things and I was surprised that he knew so much about our work in Pattaya, for the orphans, the handicapped, street kids, blind and deaf children. At one point, he embraced me and said, 'You are my friend and my kind of priest. I want you to pray for me.' You can imagine how I was humbled in the presence of this great man."

They exchanged gifts---Father Ray gave him a copy of the first book of *Thoughts from the Pattaya Orphanage* and a small statue of the Orphanage statue, the bigger boy carrying a little boy on his back, and the Dalai Lama presented him with a holy shawl called a kadak---and then they posed for photographs, one showing the Dalai Lama with his arm around Father Ray.

That photograph went onto his office wall next to the one with Mother Teresa.

Chapter 46

"We have a new girl at the Orphanage," wrote Father Ray. "I took her out of a filthy dog cage in which she was locked by her mother. The poor little thing was in dirty rags, wet with tears and shaking when I broke open the lock and picked her up. She put her little arms around my neck and held on so tight that I felt she never wanted to touch the ground again, just to hang on to me forever.

"As I walked away with her in my arms, she kept looking back in fear that someone would make her return to the dog cage. When we were far enough away and she felt safe, she threw her wet head down on my chest and gave a terrible unearthly moan, such as I have never heard from a child before. It was so strange a sound that it frightened me. By the time we got to my car, she was asleep.

"I had to drive the car to the Orphanage with her still asleep around my neck, since she simply would not let go, even in her sobbing sleep! I will never forget the feeling of that young child giving me, a stranger, her full confidence and hope. I sincerely feel that if I have accomplished nothing else in my life except rescuing her, my mother's pain at my birth has now been rewarded…and my entire life is worth this one accomplishment.

She is clean, is bright-eyed and happy now.

"In cases like this, I often wonder if when she is older, will she remember that cage? I really hope that she does not."

Many who arrived at the Orphanage had a horror story that got them there. Some got past, or over them. Some did not.

They differed in detail, but shared a commonality: rejection and abandonment. They also shared the best efforts of the Orphanage.

Sometimes that wasn't enough. The trauma was just too great.

Dai was just four years old and riding on a bus with his parents in the southeastern province of Trat, near the Cambodian border, when it was halted by bandits. The passengers were robbed and then shot. Dai's mother apparently threw herself on top of her son. He was the only survivor of the massacre, found at the scene the next morning and taken to Father Ray by a Buddhist monk. Eight years later, he remained alone most of the time, stuck in his thoughts, responding to music sometimes, but little else.

Another child, Yossawat, was two months old when she arrived at the Orphanage, abandoned by her parents when they divorced. She was adopted by a German couple, but they said they could not take her with them as she refused to accept them. The adoption was cancelled, the first time that had happened.

"She is extremely careful in whom she places any trust," is the way the case study phrased it when she was twelve. "She prefers to be on her own most of the time. We doubt if she will ever give herself to anyone easily. We also feel that her poor performance in school is related to her experience of being abandoned by her parents, which also probably motivated her to reject the couple wanting to adopt her."

More than fifty of Father Ray's kids had gone to new homes in Western Europe, the United States, Australia, even Kenya and Trinidad. But because so few foreign adoptions were permitted by the Thai government each year, the incoming tide was greater than the one going out, and the Orphanage population grew.

Pet's parents separated when his mother was pregnant; she had a neighbor take Pet to Father Ray when he was eight days old. Mot was the sixth born and sickly, so his parents left him at a Catholic convent when he was two months old; for a year, he was in and out of the hospital before recovering and then was taken to Pattaya. Supra was born deaf and left at the Orphanage by his father after his mother died, was adopted at age four by a man who died when the boy was seventeen; Supra then was returned to the Orphanage. Nat's mother left the infant with a family whom she barely knew; Mom promised to pay them monthly, but the family never heard from her again.

Gai may or may not have been the child of a Thai woman and a foreign man; in any case, the Thai husband disclaimed paternity and the boy was taken to the Orphanage when he was five months old. Chaay was left with his grandmother and, when his mother never returned and Grandma found herself begging for milk, he was taken to an orphanage in northeastern Thailand, suffering from malnutrition and anemia; soon after that, he was brought to Father Ray. Sak's father was in jail and the little girl was with him---it was still a common practice for children under the age of three to stay with a parent in prison, though usually the prisoner was the mother; after seeing the father beat the girl, another prisoner convinced him to let Sak go to the Orphanage at Pattaya.

Roat was left with neighbors soon after he was born and his mother disappeared; when the boy was eight, his foster father died and the widow felt she was unable to give him adequate care. During the early months of pregnancy, Paan's mother and father separated; the mother went to work as a maid in Bangkok, where she was told she had to get rid of the boy or lose her job; she visited the Orphanage the first year, was never heard from after that. Tham and his sister Bim came from two blind parents who divorced and remarried others (both to blind spouses again), and no longer wished to care for them. King was slightly retarded and Gaa was unable to speak clearly.

They came from other orphanages when those institutions closed. They came from the streets. Some were accompanied by police. One child was found in a dumpster. Still another in another locked metal cage.

Students at the vocational school also had harrowing biographies. Daw was born with deformed legs but learned to walk on the pads of his knees, and although his arms were deformed as well, he was able to manipulate objects with his fingers. Air fell off a ladder when he was a year old and not taken for treatment, thus losing his ability to walk. Yai was injured playing football when he was twenty, was hospitalized for two years, and after several operations was able to use his arms but remained paralyzed from the waist down.

Tom was eighteen and working for a roofing material manufacturer when he fell onto a saw that cut off his right arm and was told by the doctor that he could have sewn the arm back on if he'd brought it with him, but it was a three-hour drive away; to this day, he dreams of running back and getting that arm. Em put himself through university while holding two jobs, gaining a degree in agriculture, and while surveying some land for his employer, stepped on a mine left over from a war and lost a leg.

It was shocking how many were crippled by polio, a consequence of outdated vaccines. Others were disabled by prescriptions of wrong medicine. Dozens and dozens more arrived with missing arms and legs, thanks to motorcycle accidents, a leading cause of death for Thailand's young.

And still they not only survived, they blossomed. Grew up. Went to school. Built incredibly successful young lives.

Kattareeya "Katt" was one of them. Katt's mother herself was disabled---one leg being shorter than the other---and was a dressmaker by trade, and her father was a motorcycle taxi driver. Katt came to the Orphanage from Bangkok when she was three.

At thirteen, in her first year at secondary school, her favorite subject was English and her favorite color pink. Katt excelled at Thai classical dancing and, when cruise ships came into the nearby port, she performed a classical Thai dance on board as part of the Orphanage's show. She said she wanted to be a nurse.

At sixteen, Katt was responsible for closing the building where she lived each night and for getting supplies for all the other girls. Her favorite subject was still English and in the school English test she scored 7th highest in the province. Now she said she wanted to be a tour guide or a secretary.

At nineteen, she was enrolled at Assumption University in the Arts and Business English program. She remained on campus on the outskirts of Bangkok most weekends, but returned to the Orphanage when she could to help the younger kids learn Thai classical dance.

At twenty-two, in her third year at ABAC, her grade point average was 3.15 (the highest being 4), and the next year it went to 3.55. Katt graduated in late 2003 with English as her major and soon afterward was employed by a Canadian company in Bangkok at a starting salary of 20,000 baht (US$500) per month, at least double the starting salary for most university graduates.

Ekkachai Janthorn was born in 1979 in Uthai Thani in Thailand's rural north, where his parents grew corn and sugar cane. When he was very young, he contracted polio and used a walking frame to get around until 1996, when he acquired a wheelchair from public welfare. After completing six years of primary school, Ek stayed home for a time before going to work in a center for disabled people near Bangkok. There, he made frames for clocks, earning 3,000 baht (US$75) per month, a minimum wage.

Ek had always been interested in electronics and when he heard about the Vocational School for the Disabled, he applied and was accepted. In a year, he completed the electronics repair course and also showed an interest in sports, winning a bronze medal in the fifty-meter backstroke competition in the National Sport Games for the Physically Disabled. He also completed several wheelchair marathons, in Songkhla, Pattaya, and Bangkok; traveled to Japan to compete in a relay race with four others from Thailand, placing eighth among the forty Asian teams; and participated in the Flora London Wheelchair Marathon in London in 2003.

Still, it was the small challenges he faced every day at home that gave him the greatest satisfaction. He was one of three graduates of the vocational school selected to operate a retail shop for electronic and computer repair in Pattaya and it was here that his physical prowess and grace were most evident. Customers could drive to the shop for service on their car radios or stereos and Ekkachai would wheel himself out to the curb, swing his body into the vehicle, remove the device for repair, fix it in the shop, and then reinstall it in the same swift fashion.

With identical facility, he moves himself around outside the shop. He has a three-wheel motorbike for the long trips, with a long handle for a gearshift similar to those on automobiles of the 1930s, which he shifts with his hands, his wheelchair mounted on the back. Once at his destination---a multi-level market, say---escalators are no more a challenge than an elevator. He merely rides his wheelchair onto it, grasps the moving hand rails and away he goes.

Unfortunately, Pattaya, like many other cities in Thailand that have installed "handicap ramps" at main street corners still hasn't done anything about making the sidewalks passable, leaving them impossibly blocked by telephone booths, utility poles, street vendors, stairways, and other obstructions. The ramps have served one group, however---the motorcyclists, who now use the sidewalks as if they were but another lane in the road.

Chapter 47

Father Ray had been in Thailand for nearly forty years, in Pattaya for almost thirty, when the Christian world began its third millennium, and if anyone doubted the value of his good works, the year 2000 put them away forever. In small ways and large, in private moments and very public ones, Father Ray was both praised and blessed.

This was the year when one of the children he raised from childhood, Yai Deekham, became the first to be married and another orphan, Pat Wongsrikaew, won the highest honor given to young Thai students by Thailand's king (photographs of both events went up on his office wall); when students at the vocational school won medals in an international competition in the Czech Republic for creating websites and for assembling personal computers; and when he was embraced---physically as well as spiritually---by the Dalai Lama.

By now, honors heaped on the Vocational School for the Disabled were a commonplace. Not only was every graduate still guaranteed a job, the trophies won for wheelchair tennis and basketball as well as for swimming and other sports were so numerous that no longer was there room in the glass cases that lined two walls in the largest room in the school's office building. Father Ray's school also continued to overwhelm all competition with other (able-bodied) vocational schools nationwide in computer skills.

This also was the year when, during his longest absence from Thailand, a period of seven months, he entered the world-famous Mayo Clinic in the United States for the most exhaustive series of tests of his life. The findings were not good. And then the year closed with the most serious surgery of his life.

The bad news began in April, when Father Ray stopped in Los Angeles to visit with J.T. Warring, an American insurance executive who'd first visited the Orphanage in 1988 and subsequently became a good friend. Although he was not a Catholic, J.T. said he was trying to arrange an audience for Father Ray with the Pope. According to his friend, Father Ray just shook his head. He was scheduled to meet the Dalai Lama the same month in Denmark and that was more than enough for him.

The meeting between Father Ray and the Dalai Lama was the notion of Bjorn Falkenbrink, a longtime supporter of the Orphanage who thought it would be interesting to put a Catholic priest who had worked in a Buddhist country for three decades together with what he called "the Pope for Buddhist people," who happened to be in Denmark at the time of Father's Ray's visit. Bjorn said the meeting which took three months to arrange was planned to last ten minutes, but after forty minutes the two men were "still chatting along, talking serious but also joking with each other." Photographs taken by Bjorn show this to be true.

J.T. said they were walking from Father Ray's motel to a restaurant for dinner when the priest stepped on some loose paving and fell, fracturing a leg. The priest was told to remain in the hospital but refused, even though, J.T. said, he was in such poor condition that he needed help checking himself out. For the next three weeks, much of the time spent visiting his brother and sister in Texas, Father Ray was confined to a wheelchair.

He had graduated to a walker and a cane by the time he went to Copenhagen as a guest of the Countess Irene Wedell. The Countess was one of the Orphanage's longtime supporters and had visited Pattaya several times, tending the babies along with volunteers from her country. Now she was opening her castle to the public to raise funds for Father Ray. Hans Christian Andersen, the famous children's storyteller, once wrote about the castle, so now thousands seized the rare opportunity to see it, the price of admission going to the Orphanage.

From Europe, the priest returned to the United States, where he checked himself into the Mayo Clinic, a charitable, not-for-profit organization renowned for its tests, opinions, and treatment of virtually everything medical. With three clinics and four hospitals in three states, it employed more than forty thousand physicians, scientists, nurses, and allied health workers and attracted half a million patients a year.

The patient from Pattaya went to the clinic in Rochester, Minnesota, for what would be the most complete physical examination of his life. Tests were conducted in July and the results were given to him the following month in a half-inch thick report that reflected the expertise of dozens of physicians and technicians, none of whom had much good to say or anything the priest either wanted or was surprised to hear.

For his coronary artery disease, impaired glucose tolerance, pedal edema (the swelling in his legs that drove him to the clinic in the first place), dyspnea (shortness of breath), and possible obstructive apnea (loss of breath entirely while sleeping), he was told in no uncertain terms to give up alcohol and cigarettes and go on a diet.

The phrases prescribing treatment of his ills formed a litany of resolve like those Father Ray made himself each year at the start of Lent. A "no added salt, low-fat, low-cholesterol diet" was recommended. Weight reduction was "encouraged." (The specialist who examined his low sugar tolerance went so far as to get very specific: "avoid cookies, candies, and bakery products.") For his smoking, a nicotine patch was suggested. Another doctor said, flatly, "Discontinue alcohol use." While still another urged a program of "aerobic exercise."

Predictably, Father Ray put a positive spin on the report, sending an E-mail to his friend Bill Mangelsen in Hong Kong that he had received "good news about my heart. It's in good condition, as a matter of fact, I was told it is good and strong. Just to make sure, they did an angiogram and I came out with flying colors. My shortness of breath is from overweight and smoking. My lungs are clear (thank God) and in general I am in pretty good health." This was not true, but as always, it wasn't so much denial as it was a desire not to worry his friends.

He did admit to two problems. "My eyes are not too good, but should improve when they remove the oil that was put in to hold the retina in place. They usually put a gas bubble in the eye, but because I had to fly to Europe, they used an oil solution instead. My feet still feel like I am walking on pads with rocks inside them, but they are working on that." Nothing the Mayo Clinic said was contestable. Father Ray knew that. But he also surely knew that the lifestyle change that was urged likely would never be made.

Likely it was also too late to turn the course of events around, and the big priest knew that, too. Despite his claim to have a "good and strong" heart, he did not. Nor was there any record of his having an angiogram at the Mayo Clinic. Although Mayo physicians did say his cholesterol count was well below 200, the line at which risk usually is drawn, he already had had an angioplasty in 1997 at the Bangkok Heart Institute. This was a common surgical procedure conducted to remove or reduce blockage in the coronary arteries, aimed at increasing blood flow to and from the heart and, perhaps, prevent a heart attack.

But then, soon after his return to Thailand from the United States, he was hospitalized for a quadruple "bypass" operation---open heart surgery performed because it was believed that, in his case, another angioplasty would be fruitless. Hundreds of thousands of these operations were performed every year in the United States alone and medical skills in Thailand were close to or equal those at "home," so there was no need or desire for Father Ray to go any farther than Pattaya International Hospital. So, there, in November 2000, less than a month before the priest's sixty-eighth birthday, doctors removed sections of some veins in his arms and after cutting them to the desired lengths, used them to form loops that, literally, bypassed the problem areas, by stitching them to the coronary arteries on either side of the blockages. The surgery was considered a success.

Chapter 48

"Ek was eleven years old when his mother abandoned him and his younger brother and sister. Their father, an alcoholic, was unable to support them, so the three kids spent their days and nights begging on the streets of Pattaya. They had never been to school…"

In this fashion began a "case study" for three of the residents of the Redemptorist Street Kids Home.

"Khem was born in prison. His mother, already pregnant, was sentenced for selling drugs. According to Thai law, a child born to a mother during imprisonment is allowed to stay with her until he/she is three years old, which Khem did. A friend of his mother in prison, having completed her own sentence, agreed to take care of Khem. A lesbian, she was known to little Khem as 'father' and worked in a bar, leaving little Khem to wander the streets. He was six when he was found by one of the outreach workers and the 'father' agreed that he should come to the shelter…"

As Father Ray's health failed, his projects prospered. It almost seemed that his waning strength in some eerie way fed the well-being of the Orphanage, schools, and homes. And no project was growing faster than the Street Kids Home…

By the time it marked its tenth anniversary in 2001, the program to aid children from the streets was a great success. The drop-out rate remained high---with as many as four out of ten leaving the shelter after a short period---but construction had begun on the second building, a three-story structure to house the girls (who were still in a temporary facility several miles away), as well as a library and computer classroom.

The police also were now cooperating more fully. Previously, they had made periodic sweeps of the streets, usually at the request of politicians, taking the children to holding centers. The police permitted Ja and other outreach workers from the home to visit those centers, but now, rather than detain the children at all, the government operated homes where the kids were kept until other places could be found for them. Many went to Father Ray, who had also by now appointed a new director of the home.

This was Samphan Akrapongpanich, born and raised in Bangkok, trained in accounting at Chulalongkorn University. He had worked for the Metropolitan Electricity Authority for twenty-seven years and knew Father Ray and the work of the Orphanage intimately, because the priest's secretary, Toy, was his wife. Six times, Father Ray had asked Samphan to come to work for him, and in 2000 Samphan took early retirement to become controller of the Orphanage.

A year later, Father Ray also asked him to take the director's chair at the Street Kids Home and to help with the organization's biggest financial challenge yet. As soon as the new building for the girls was completed, the priest said, he wanted to add still another structure that would become the new home for the boys. It would be five stories high, accommodate three hundred and twenty children, and cost nearly U.S. $800,000. When it was complete---and that was possible by 2004, the priest said---the boys would be moved. The original building would then house the computer classrooms, thereby freeing space in that building for more girls. The original structure also would be used to house new arrivals, so that the children could undergo a sort of "decompression" program before being integrated with the others.

"Father Ray said they needed time to adapt," said Samphan. "He'd had problems in the past. Some of the new kids were a bad influence. We wanted to have the time and space to teach them discipline, how to be social in an acceptable way."

Father Ray's dreams sounded good, as they always did, but not everyone supported the plan. Where, they wondered---as always---would the money come from? Father Ray insisted, said The Boss Upstairs would provide, and in 2002, construction began with no one having any idea how its completion might be financed.

Samphan admitted he had no previous experience that prepared him for the Street Kids Home, so he left the day-to-day operation to his staff of twenty. There were four outreach workers on the street, including Ja; thirteen in "operation" (maintenance, kitchen, office workers, and drivers); two more working on a new farm several miles away that was now being aimed at providing produce for all the projects (a plan hampered by the poor quality of the soil); and a final two working on the weekends, teaching some of the older children how to bake bread in one of the home's first skill programs.

Ja and his fellow social workers were at the core of the operation. Two were male, two were female; Ja was the oldest at thirty–three. They continued to talk to the children on the street, followed them to their homes (when they had any), talked to their families and offered to help. They also visited downtown Pattaya and this is where they encountered their greatest risk. There were bars and certain commercial "hang-out" sections of Pattaya where it was made clear that they were not welcome. There were some people who didn't want the kids taken off the street, because of their exploitable value. Pattaya was not a do-good town and do-gooders were not always appreciated. Three times in the first years of the new millennium, Father Ray's employees were shot at while cruising the streets and once someone put a bullet through a window of the Home's office. The pane of glass was not replaced, the hole left as a reminder of Father Ray's determination, a symbol of his accomplishment.

Meanwhile, the routine of changing lives---or trying to---continued. Samphan said, "Everyone has to help clean house, wash their own dishes and laundry. They get extra chores if they break the rules. We're harder on the boys than the girls. No TV. No football. We take away their fun and privileges. No extra money.

"The biggest problems are stealing and lying," he said, "and..." he paused, shyly adding, "love affair." He said that as the number of kids increased---in 2003, there were one hundred and twenty-six in residence, forty-four of them girls, ages ranging from five to eighteen---that problem increased as well.

"The older ones help the younger ones, show them how to brush their teeth, wash their hair. We don't assign that. There's no big sister, little sister, big brother, little brother. If we did that, maybe they wouldn't get along, so we let them work it out themselves and they usually do, just as if they were siblings in a real family."

Chapter 49

Like Reverend Martin Luther King, Jr., he had a dream, in fact many dreams. Unrealized dreams can be nightmares, too. And so it was for Father Ray. He was a man of huge appetites, as revealed by his falling health, but not all the hunger for more did him harm. He had accomplished so much, affecting, deeply, thousands of young lives. Yet, it never was enough.

In 2002, he wrote a friend that he was "thinking of starting a free meal a day to those hungry, no questions asked. Believe it or not, there are many here in Pattaya who are hungry. Even foreigners. I am getting prepared for it now and I expect to start the project in two months. The time slot for the meal will be between one and four p.m. We will also seek out old people living in squalor and bring them a hot meal, with a little bag of food for their evening meal. Pray that we can make it successful."

It never happened.

Nor was he able to start a home for the mentally disabled children. This was a dream that recurred for years, prompted in part by the presence of multi-disabled children at the blind school for whom, he said, he really could do little more than offer food, shelter, and love. More than once, he and members of his organization looked into it, but the need for skilled caretakers and medical staff made it beyond his reach.

On the other hand, the institutions he had begun had succeeded far *beyond* his dreams, and none more than the vocational school. Its influence and that of its graduates, on the state of the disabled people in Thailand was significant.

The state of the disabled people had improved in many ways, but there was so much more to do. Thailand was not yet a disabled-people-friendly country. There were now eight vocational schools operated by the government and three private ones, including Father Ray's. Still, under fifty percent of the graduates of government schools found jobs. Suporntum Mongkolsawadi, still headmaster of the Pattaya school, said, "The government says feed them, give them shelter, give them some education, it's better than nothing, then send them on their way and hope they can find work."

No one really knew the figures because no good surveys had been made, Suporntum said, but it was estimated that eight percent of the population were disabled in some way, either blind or deaf or challenged mentally or physically. There were sixty-six million people in Thailand, which meant nearly five million people were disabled…and of those, only two percent were in the labor force.

"Why?" he asked. "Attitude." He pointed to what happened to two attorneys qualified for appointment to the Constitution Court, the highest court in the land---qualified in every way, that is, except for their physical impairments. "They weren't even considered!" he said, "and no one even lied about why. They were physically disabled people, and thus ineligible."

Some new laws were on the books. In the first two years after medical and rehabilitation assistance was mandated in 2002, some 360,000 disabled people received help. (Though many of the wheelchairs, canes, hearing aids furnished to them were cheaply made and often defective.) More legislation required all public schools to accept disabled students, but the schools were not prepared for them, just as when wheelchair ramps were installed at many street corners in the larger metropolitan areas, the sidewalks themselves were so cluttered by utility poles, telephone booths, police boxes, stairs leading to pedestrian overpasses and to the Skytrain, and other impediments, not to mention the thousands of street vendors, and the sidewalks were so poorly maintained, it was impossible for anyone in a wheelchair to navigate. Consequently, the wheelchair users are rarely seen in public and then usually rolling along the curbs in the street, leaving the ramps for the use of motorcyclists who came to regard the sidewalks as another lane in the road.

In 2004, the Thai Health Promotion Foundation, through its Reduce the Risk of Accidents Network, announced plans to bring shock tactics into the nation's living rooms by using people who had been disabled as a result of drunken or other reckless driving, to tell television viewers of their terrible experiences and how their lives were ruined by what an editorial writer for the *Bangkok Post* called "a moment of madness."

"While this is aimed at stopping more people from becoming needlessly incapacitated," said the *Post*, "let us not forget the plight of those who are already suffering." There were just too many obstacles and even off the street, they found simple things like toilet entrances too narrow for a wheelchair to pass through. Multi-level floors presented another hazard. Public telephones were set too high for people using wheelchairs to reach. The list of dangers and inconveniences goes on and on.

All that said, Suporntum and Father Ray's efforts were making an impression and bringing about real change. That there were wheelchair ramps at all in Bangkok and Pattaya and elsewhere was a consequence of protests and demonstrations led by the school's students and staff.

In December 1999, another big step was taken, when offices in a building on the Redemptorist Center grounds was turned over to the newly created Job Placement Agency for Disabled, launched to help all disabled Thais---not just the graduates of Father Ray's school---find suitable jobs and contribute positively to the community. Initially, the agency---with Suporntum as its director---was sponsored by the National Lottery Charities Board in Britain with a grant of 418,000 pounds (about US$625,000) spread over five years.

"I went to Father Ray and asked him, 'How far can we go with this?' He said, he wanted to help all the disabled people in the world!"

Most impressive, of course, is the progress, and influence, experienced by the 1,500 graduates of the vocational school. Many now work for "name" international firms, such as Toshiba, Honda, Motorola, Telecom Asia (renamed True in 2004), and numerous top Thai companies, schools, and resort hotels, while twenty percent have opened their own repair shops in their home towns and villages. It is in the workplace, after all, where the disabled people, laboring side by side with the non-disabled, will change perceptions and attitudes.

Another positive impression has been made as growing numbers of Father Ray's students and teachers---in 2004, twenty-five of the twenty-eight instructors were disabled people, twenty-two of them graduates of the school--- compete in national and international games. "Father Ray always said determination was most necessary if the disabled people were to succeed," said Suporntum, "and he believed that sports could help develop the kind of confidence that made winning possible. We never had physical education teachers or professional coaches. We trained by ourselves, and we have competed in the Special Olympics every year since 1988 in Seoul, representing Thailand. The students choose what they want to do, wheelchair racing, one-legged high jump, one-armed javelin, swimming, wheelchair tennis, and so on, and most participate, training after classes for two, two-and-a-half hours, as many days of the week as one can."

Father Ray wrote in 2001, "Over a thousand handicapped youths participated in the Thailand Annual National Games for the Disabled. Every student in our vocational school went. For the first time, we did not come in first for gold medals. Every year, as far as I can remember, we always came in first. This year we came in second. However, we did win the most medals of any school. Our school performed a wheelchair dance for the opening ceremony. I am just an old 'softie,' so my eyes got watery and my throat tightened up. My admiration and love for those young disabled kids is indescribable."

Father Ray was especially pleased in one of the earliest national contests, when his pupils competed against wounded Thai military. The government provided them with brand new racing chairs---chairs designed especially for such competitions---and the vocational school had ten-year-old wheelchairs.

"We won by meters!" Father Ray exclaimed on television. "Meters!"

Another time when the cameras were rolling, he said, "Feed the hungry, clothe the naked, water the thirsty, heal the sick, shelter the homeless, blah blah blah blah blah. If you don't do something, you're a fake."

Chapter 50

As his health failed, Father Ray knew it was time to pass the torch. It was a good and efficient supportive team he had in place, yet it was, after all, so far as the image went, a one-man show. What to do?

One of the first tasks was to change the name of the legal entity. From the beginning, everything was in the name of the Redemptorist Fathers of Thailand, the formal name of the mission dating back to the 1950s. When Father Ray started the Orphanage, it "belonged" to the Redemptorists. The schools for the blind and the physically disabled and the center all had the word "Redemptorist" in their titles. But over time, as Father Ray's projects increased in number and size, this became somewhat awkward.

"Eventually, everything came to be called 'the Pattaya Orphanage,'" said Brother Denis Gervais. "That was the way the public thought of us. It hurt, because when people gave to the Orphanage, when we had five projects, we had to give it all to the Orphanage, cutting out the others. We needed a single entity, with the power to allocate general contributions as needed."

The name proposed was the Father Ray Foundation, but Father Ray rejected it, said he didn't want his name used.

"He resisted the idea vehemently," said Brother Denis. "We argued, said it was his name that was known and nobody would contribute to something called anything else."

For weeks, the discussion continued and, finally, the priest agreed to have his name used, and then he rejected it again and told Brother Denis and others in the office to find another name. Brother Denis said that after much arguing, finally, he agreed again, but said he didn't want or like it. A meeting was scheduled for November 2002 to make the name change final. "He backed out again," said Brother Denis, "but all of us ganged up on him and he went along."

Presiding at that meeting was Father Philip Banchong Chaiyara, then the Superior of all the Redemptorists in Thailand. He was younger than Father Ray but, effectively, his boss, as well as his choice as successor. There was another priest, a foreigner, who was said to want the job, but Father Ray was certain he wanted a Thai in his old chair and, in fact, Father Philip had moved into an office beside Father Ray's cluttered office a month before the meeting when it was decided, at last, to change legal "ownership" of all the projects to the new foundation's name.

Father Philip was in few ways like his predecessor. Where the priest from Chicago was ebullient, and his booming baritone voice and charisma, as massive as his height and bulk, commanded any room he entered, Father Philip was reserved, a man of modest height, weight, and demeanor.

Father Philip, the son of farmers who had raised cattle and water buffalo, was known to say, in private moments, that leading the strong, compliant buffalo was good training for a would-be priest. His village in northern Thailand was predominantly Catholic and, as a child, he said he wanted to be a boxer. Yet even when only eight or nine, his exposure to the Church inspired him to consider the priesthood too. His training with the Redemptorists was at the seminary in Sri Racha and he became its director just four years after his ordination. At age forty, Father Philip was elected Vice Provincial (of Confreres), a high honor for a man of his youth, and when the end of his third and last term approached, with re-election not an option, Father Ray asked the younger priest to consider taking over his own job in Pattaya.

Father Philip was twenty years Father Ray's junior and didn't know him well, although they had first met in the 1960s. Father Philip said he considered Father Ray his senior in most ways. He was told by Father Ray not to worry about stepping into shoes that were nearly twice his own size---although Father Ray didn't put it quite that way. People would know that he was the older priest's choice and Father Ray would still be around as an advisor. Father Ray also said he wanted to continue to write the newsletters and the next was mailed soon after under the heading, "Report from the World's Greatest Orphanage."

"Semi-retirement is nice," Father Ray wrote. "One of the 'perks' is I can come to the office late, leave early, and not feel guilty. The heavy burden of responsibility is on Father Philip, who is shouldering the task very well. I help him when I can. Many people have told me they are more busy after retirement than before. I would surely agree with that. But it does seem strange though, to have someone else in charge of the work.

"Being seventy years old is nice, too. Little children only two-feet tall grab my arm and lead me to the car. Sometimes I almost trip over them because they tend to walk in front of me. But I let them do it, because it is their way of showing their love. I have been a priest for forty-four years and have spent more than half my life (forty-two years) in Thailand. There is a lot to show for all those years of labor in the vineyard. Many more than a thousand impoverished youths have been given the chance to have their life drastically changed and their future ensured. They have been able to witness, first hand, Christian love…God's love and care for the poor."

He talked also of the "circulation problem" in his legs: "It is a big problem for me because of the pain, especially when I walk." He said he was trying an herbal treatment, Ginkgo Biloba in pill form. "They tell me it will take several months before I feel its effect. Please pray that it works or I find something that does."

It was March 2003, a special month, if for no other reason than it included St. Patrick's Day. "The Irish are cartooned as having a great sense of humor and imbibing a wee drop of spirits now and then," he wrote. "But the real Irish say the Irish Americans are more Irish than the Irish in Ireland. No doubt everyone has heard of shamrocks. Saint Patrick used the three leaves of the shamrock to convert Ireland to Christianity. I was told they would only grow in Ireland, nowhere else. I wish you could see my little pot of lovely shamrocks grown in Thailand!! On Saint Patrick's Day, Father Morrissy and myself toasted them (not literally, of course) with a drop or two of the Irish I had stashed away.

"The Irish are also famous for their clever use of words," he added. "One that always brings a smile to my face goes like this: 'May your home always be too small to hold all your friends and may The Good Lord take a liking to you…but not too soon'!!"

He also introduced one of the Orphanage's new secretaries. "Her boss is a very nice man," he wrote. "Her name is Pieng Rak. She was once one of my orphans. Her nice boss is ME. She works in the front office here at the office. She is learning the ropes of being a secretary under the direction of the other secretaries. She receives visitors, answers the phone, does some computer work and so forth. As an orphan, she was always near. Now her circumstances have changed. She comes to the office every day sharply dressed, as Thai women know how to do so well. She is now a career woman. It tickles my heart."

Father Ray reminisced, recalling stories about Pheung, always identified in previous newsletters as "The Holy Terror." Once again, he delighted in the accomplishments of his disabled students and then, as always, thanked his readers. "With help from people like yourself, we are truly doing something for our poor world. Minds are being opened to new horizons. Opportunity for the future is awaiting all of them. The great miracle we are doing overwhelms me when I think of it. I know that I do not have the ability to do what I have done. That is not false humility, it is the truth. People like you who help and trust us don't know it, but The Big Boss Upstairs nudges you every so often to help this dumb priest do His work. Thanks, and our prayers are for you every day."

The newsletter was signed: Father Ray Brennan (Semi retired) and Father Philip Banchong Chaiyara (Director).

Chapter 51

On Sunday, January 26, 2003, there appeared in one of Britain's weekend scandal sheets a story that said Father Ray agreed to accept a donation from a wealthy pedophile in exchange for allowing the man to take some children on an excursion. Following what was claimed to be a three-month investigation, *The People* said Father Ray was "perfectly happy to invite wealthy pedophiles to meet street children in his care...allow perverts to take them out on picnics at the beach or public park...discuss the best places in town to pick up young boys...[and] advise on how to avoid arrest and the best way to export any kiddy videos they may have filmed."

The People admitted it was a sting, said that Father Ray had been lied to and set up, and acknowledged that the paper had hired someone to spin a story to the priest. "Our investigators," *The People* said, "used the bogus identity of a wealthy lottery winner called Robert Merlin and his friend Kenneth Draper who wished to make a large donation to the Orphanage. We corresponded with Brennan for months and told him we had regularly visited Pattaya as sex tourists interested in young boys." However false the premise, the tabloid insisted that once offered the opportunity, the priest was willing to help this spurious benefactor get what he wanted.

When news of the story reached the Orphanage offices, it was greeted with a shiver and a shrug. An almost identical story had appeared nine years earlier, when another of Britain's Sunday tabloids, *News of the World*, said pedophiles visited the Orphanage grounds openly, while volunteers working without pay for

Father Ray themselves either took children to their rooms or to pedophiles outside the Orphanage gates. The earlier *News of the World* story was also by the same freelance writer who wrote the article in The People.

"Unsuspecting British charities have poured more than £1million (US$1.8million) into the orphanage in recent years," the tabloid reported. "Celebrities who have contributed include chart hero Phil Collins, Prince Albert of Monaco, several MPs and Tory Chris Patten, now Governor of Hong Kong."

Even with all those glittery names attached, the story blew away, so when in 2003 the new smear was engineered, Father Ray and his staff believed that the same would happen again. How could anyone believe it?

It did not blow away. Whereas the leading English-language daily newspaper in Thailand, the *Bangkok Post*, took no notice of the story, recognizing the source for what it was, another English daily, *The Nation*, not only splashed the charges across its front page, it never so much as called Father Ray for comment. And in Denmark, no less than what might be called holy hell tore loose. By now, Denmark was one of the Orphanage's largest donor countries and far and away the No. 1 nation supplying volunteers and adoptive parents.

In Denmark in the days that followed, there were photographs of Father Ray taken two years before in Copenhagen with the Dalai Lama, accompanied by a headline that said "Vi Gay Penge Til Bornesex-Praest." It wasn't necessary to be fluent in Danish to know what that or "Praest hjalp paedofile", another headline, meant. Two days later, Danish television journalists arrived in Pattaya and the Father Ray story became one of the biggest scandals in Denmark.

It was as if a bomb had been dropped on the Orphanage offices. As newspaper cuttings arrived from all over the world, followed by reporters from Europe and elsewhere, the staff went into shock; it was a stink and a stain that would not go away. Many worried that the loss of credibility could lead to the foundation's crash, at the very least a crisis that would affect everyone. There were more than seven hundred children and disabled young adults dependent on

Father Ray. What now? And why was there such a difference in the reaction to the 1994 story and the one that occurred in 2003?

In a way, it didn't make sense, because of the two; the earlier "exposé " was the more damning. Sources and pedophiles were named and Father Ray admitted there was no security at the gates to the Orphanage property at that time and said he didn't check backgrounds of volunteers, preferring to go on instinct. Nonetheless, the charges went away, disappearing like smoke in the wind.

That was then, as the saying goes, and this was now. By 2003, media around the world seemed almost preoccupied by stories about charges of pedophilia in the Catholic ministry, most remarkably, though not exclusively, in the United States. It was one of the biggest continuing stories of 2001 and 2002. So it was not surprising that when the Pattaya Orphanage was linked in the media to child abuse in 2003, however wrongly, many assumed, "Ahah! Another pedophile priest!"

The location, Pattaya, didn't help, either. In 2003, the beachside city was still known as an international magnet for adult males looking for juveniles.

It was as if Father Ray were damned not only by the smear, but also by the times and geography.

Ironically, in a letter written in 2002 to his friend Bill Mangelsen in Hong Kong, Father Ray had talked about the scandals. "I am sending you this little email at the same time the Pope is bawling the hell out of the American Hierarchy for treating the sex scandals in the States so stupidly. It is hard for me to imagine how an intelligent man (we are told bishops and cardinals are sharp or they would not be what they are) could take a priest known for his sexual tendencies and simply move the bastard to another parish. As you can imagine, I have to keep my eyes open all the time when volunteers come. I have kicked more than one ass out the door."

Still, what happened was as inevitable as it was unavoidable. Despite the priest's watchful eye and no matter what safeguards were put in place, no organization was impregnable, in Thailand or anywhere else. Schoolyards, church choirs, summer camps, playgrounds, Boy Scout troops, orphanages, and in recent years, shopping malls, wherever children were found in numbers, around the world…there came predators drawn sexually to youth. Many years earlier, the infamous Willie Sutton was asked why he robbed banks. He said, "That's where the money is." So, too, it was with pedophiles. They went where the children were.

Father Ray had been a likely target for decades and, in the final analysis, the only surprise was that there hadn't been more predators and trumped-up accusations.

According to his secretary, Toy, Father Ray was devastated. "Those who know you will not believe this," she told him, holding back her tears.

He replied, "I know, but it's going to mark my history and it makes me sad."

When Audrey Williams entered his office, he asked, "How could anyone think I'd hurt a child?" Audrey was from England and she knew the newspaper. She told him it was a "rag" and said no one would believe anything reported in it, said it was so sleazy that no one even admitted they read it. "Besides," she told him, turning her comment to the dark side of Father Ray's sense of humor, "they didn't accuse you of being a pedophile, they said you were a pimp. I knew it would make him laugh," Audrey said later, "and he did laugh."

Later in the day, when Pat---the stellar student who entered the Orphanage in 1990 at age 11---came to visit, Father Ray said, "Well, what does it feel like to have a pedophile for a father?"

Pat replied---automatically, instantly, defiantly, sincerely, sweetly, and almost in tears---"I don't know, I don't have one." Nor was Pat alone; many of the older boys shyly came to the office to add their disbelief.

The story appeared in the London tabloid on a Sunday, in *The Nation*, and several Thai-language newspapers and in Denmark on Monday. On Tuesday, Father Ray invited the press to Pattaya.

"I have called this press conference to safeguard the reputation of my children and clear my name," he said. "I have never been involved in, or arranged any pedophilic rendezvous during my whole life. I condemn pedophiles, totally."

The priest said the man identified as Robert Merlin claimed that he had been diagnosed with terminal cancer and wanted to donate lottery winnings of £1.8 million (U.S. $2.7 million) to the Orphanage. "Now I realize that this was a provocation and manipulation. I agreed to meet him because he asked to come here. We had a one-hour conversation, during which Mr. Merlin asked me many questions. It was at that time we discussed the pedophile situation in Pattaya. I was uncomfortable with the conversation. He took bits and pieces of the conversation and turned them to serve his purpose.

"I've worked all my life here for children and you're all welcome to go to any project---the blind school, deaf school, the Orphanage, the home for kids off the street, the vocational school for handicapped young people---and you can ask anybody you want anything you want. You'll get nothing negative about our way of doing things here.

"I've spent forty-two years here helping people and I've taken care of kids with no parents, kids with no money. I have given them an education. I have twenty kids in university. I spent my whole life working for the children, not to hurt them. I'd like to ask this man what he's done during his life.

"I'm afraid it is going to hurt my kids, first of all, because their parents read the papers. Then I'm worried about the reputation of the Orphanage, second, and finally myself. This is a thing that will stick; this is a negative point on my life for the rest of my life, whatever I do. I'm not bothered about being hurt. I'm seventy years old and probably don't have long to live, but the Orphanage does and these kids do, too."

The statement was strong, but Father Ray was not. Even *The Catholic Herald*, published in England, said in a story that "he looked old, tired and defensive at the press conference; in short, unconvincing. It was a public humiliation."

Letters of protest poured into *The Nation, Pattaya Mail* and other newspapers. Pattaya's mayor, Pairat Suttithamrongsawat, came to Father Ray's defense, as did the provincial governor, Pisith Gatephasuk, and dozens of volunteers and staff who had worked at the orphanage over a period of decades.

Another contingent of press from Denmark arrived, interrupting an English class at the vocational school where Danish volunteers were teaching, demanding comment. One of the young female volunteers told them to get the hell out. The Danish reporters also confronted Suwanna Cheownawin, for twenty years director of the adoption program, who told them the same thing. They then pushed their way into the local police station, where they were threatened with arrest.

Andrew Scadding, administrator of the Pattaya Orphanage Trust in the U.K., also flew to Thailand and spent two weeks interviewing people both on and off the Orphanage grounds and returned to London calling the allegations "malicious… a complete fiction. I'm absolutely convinced that there was no risk whatsoever to those children," he said. "Father Ray believed he was dealing with a dying man who was going to give a large donation to the Orphanage, at least in part as an act of contrition for his past misdeeds."

The Danish press wouldn't let go. The Ronde Rotary Club, regular donors to Father Ray, as well as Vagn Christensen---the one-time airline pilot who for so long supported Father Ray---issued a news release saying they would cease supporting the Orphanage unless the priest was replaced; that made headlines, too, although, in fact, the priest already had turned over control of the Orphanage to Father Philip. As did a spurious story which quoted the chief of the Pattaya Tourist Police to say that several officers had been assigned to investigate the Orphanage. When shown the article, the police chief stated he had never said that and he told the journalists that Father Ray was a good man who helped the police, and that the priest and the Orphanage were assets to Pattaya.

Oddly, it was never made public that the source of both tabloid stories was a freelance writer who engineered the charges in 1993 and again in 2002. This was a man named Roger Insall, the subject himself of a story in the conservative London *Times* that had been written by a Bangkok-based investigative journalist named Andrew Drummond. When Insall had written stories about massage parlors in the U.K., Drummond identified Insall as the operator of a "no-hands" restaurant and massage parlor in Bangkok.

Father Ray and others at the Orphanage decided not to sue the London tabloid, believing it would serve little purpose and only drain away cash and energy that was better dedicated to the kids. The effect was lasting, nonetheless, as small changes were made in Orphanage operations. "It made us paranoid and we stopped taking the kids to Foodland to buy food that they were allowed to take to their rooms," said Derek Franklin, director of volunteers. "We were afraid people would make comments and we might get more bad press."

Most important was the impact on Father Ray. "It didn't kill him," said Audrey Williams, "but it made his last months miserable."

Chapter 52

From the time of his open heart surgery in November 2000, Father Ray's health continued to sink. His secretary, Toy Chomjinda, said that the circulation in his legs---now generally blamed on half a century of nicotine---got worse and it became more and more painful when he walked. Where once he said it felt like walking on pads filled with stones, he now told a friend it was like "walking on a rope." On good days he used a cane, on bad ones a wheelchair. He also gave up driving and was taken to and from his room and office in his old Mitsubishi, usually by Father Morrissy or Brother Denis, by now two of his closest friends. He could have had a driver assigned, but didn't want to ask someone with a family to be available when he dined in the evening with sponsors and important visitors.

"I don't feel old, except for my feet, where I have a real problem," he wrote to a friend in a rare display of sorrow. "It's funny, when I ask God to help someone else, they usually get help. When I ask Him to do something for me, He is deaf."

There was another angioplasty in February 2003, but Toy said Father Ray continued to come into the office most days, often in the afternoons and only for a few hours, especially when his sleep was fitful. He called in the mornings and told her how he felt. Once he was behind his cluttered desk, she said he worked at his correspondence and maintained his open-door policy.

"We'd change appointments if necessary," Toy said. "Sometimes he'd come in when he looked terrible."

"Father came even after the transition had been made to Father Philip," Audrey Williams said. "I'd see him in the office, obviously in great pain, and when a visitor would come, he'd become the actor, not showing the pain. He kept up appearances, carrying on as he always did, thinking of others and not himself. When my dad died, he was at my office door in ten minutes with condolences. My father died in his sleep. Father said he didn't want to die that way, he wanted to talk to people first."

As his condition deteriorated, Audrey and others took most of the visitors on a tour of the grounds as it became difficult now for Father Ray to walk from his office to the car, let alone go to the baby room thirty meters farther on. He was not eating much now, either, but he continued to smoke. So when he agreed to be hospitalized, in June 2003, it was to a private clinic he was taken, rather than to a hospital, because the physician in charge permitted tobacco and alcohol. The doctor also asked him to sign a form that released the clinic from any responsibility for whatever might occur during his stay.

Alun Jones went to visit with his wife. He said the priest fell asleep while talking about deep-sea fishing, one of his favorite pastimes, although he hadn't indulged often. When Alun and Sally tried to leave, the priest woke up and halted them. Alun was a smoker, too, and Father Ray said, "No, don't go, stay for one more cigarette."

His old friend Father Joe Maier came to say goodbye. "Ray-Ray was so heavy, he couldn't even roll over by himself," Father Joe said, "and he could walk only a few feet. I told him I was going to the States and would be gone for some time. He asked me to bring back some good limburger and bleu cheese. When I asked about his chances, the doctors just shook their heads."

Not long after that Father Ray was taken to Pattaya International Hospital. When two sisters from the Orphanage visited, Audrey said, "He sat up as best he could, held their hands and told them a joke, and when they left, he collapsed again." Audrey said that Sister Supatra Nonthasuwan, in charge of the daily operations of the Orphanage, told the children that "Paw Lay" ("Father Ray" in

Thai) was very sick and the symptoms were not good, so they should pray for him every night. "I told them that Father Ray wanted them to be good, well-behaved, and to study," she recalled. "I took some of the older ones to the hospital to visit. It was always cheering to him, if he was awake, but they cried or remained silent in sadness."

Some of the younger children went as well, accompanied by their teachers. But not all could go, so those who did were asked to write about their visit and their little essays were posted on the Orphanage bulletin board. Prayers continued every night.

Tom Vincent, a close friend and loyal supporter, visited him, too, and was told by the priest that friends in Canada had urged Father Ray to collect his Orphanage newsletters into a book. Tom said he thought it was a good idea, said that, over the years, he'd probably read three-quarters of them. Father Ray told him where he had the complete file and insisted Tom read them all, then report back honestly. Tom did that, saying he still thought it was a wonderful idea. "I know Tom will do a good job of it," Father Ray said.

Bill Mangelsen flew in from Hong Kong and the priest asked him to buy some ice cream, and when Bill returned, he devoured the entire carton. Toy visited him in the mornings and afternoons and Audrey brought him home-cooked meals at noon and six. Toy's husband came every day to massage his legs, which by now looked like raw meat. Their visits continued for five weeks.

It was decided to renovate his room at the Redemptorist Center to make it easier for Father Ray when he returned. At Father Philip's request, the bathroom was enlarged and tiled and equipped with stainless steel handles on the walls. As this was being done, in late July, Father Ray was moved into a private room in the Intensive Care Unit at Bumrungrad Hospital in Bangkok, a medical facility offering care that provided care thought to be on par with the best in developed countries.

There was an argument over how to get him there. His staff wanted him to go by ambulance, but Father Ray said it would cost too much and there was no need because Brother Denis or somebody could take him up in his beloved Mitsubishi. Father Philip wanted Father Ray to take the ambulance for his comfort and in case something unexpected occurred. Father Ray finally agreed, although upon arrival in Bangkok he complained that the two nurses who sat with him chattered all the way.

Toy and Audrey took rooms at a hotel not far from the hospital, continuing their daily visits. Toy showed him the E-mails she'd been writing, including one that she'd sent to one of Father Ray's nieces revealing why he was in the hospital. "He was furious," she recalled. "He said, 'I'm a private person! No one has the right to talk about my liver, my lung, and my heart!' He calmed down and said he didn't want anyone to worry about him."

Father Charlie Cotant, who had come to Thailand in 1949 and knew Father Ray from the time of his arrival twelve years later, was retired and living in Bangkok when he visited his old friend. "He was very bad, people were helping him to eat," he said. "I stayed to help and he said, 'Damn it, Charlie, you're so busy, how can you waste your time with me here? Get back to work.'"

Two other visitors were Father Pat Morrissy and Father "Gogs" Gautreaux. Both said it was clear he knew he was dying and Father Gogs said, "He didn't seem angry. Impatient, maybe. He knew the end was coming." Father Morrissy wanted to tell Father Ray's brother and sister, Don and Sharron, who were flying in from the U.S., that there was no hope. The dying priest said, "No, tell them I'm sick, but don't tell them I'm gravely ill." A week later he told Father Morrissy not to take Father Don and Sharron to the hotel when he met them at the airport, but to bring them directly to the hospital.

"His family was coming that night, the fifteenth" Audrey remembered. "He was disoriented; he thought they'd already arrived. He said he'd been dreaming about them. I hadn't given him his sleeping pill. I washed his face and put talcum on his neck rash. I put Vitalis in his hair. It was one in the morning when they arrived. Father was very polite, asked them if they'd had a good flight."

It was clear that Father Ray was dying and Father Don asked the others present to step outside the room for a moment. Other priests had given Father Ray the Final Rites in recent days and now his big brother performed the last anointing. Father Don asked the others to return and after Audrey gave Father Ray a sleeping pill, they left.

Father Ray said many times that he had no favorites at the Orphanage, but surely Pat Wongsrikaew was one of the most cherished. In the priest's care from the time he was eleven years old, Pat had been recognized for his scholarship by King Bhumibol and now was in his fourth year of university study. He had spent a night in the hospital room with Father Ray earlier in the week and when Toy asked her boss if Pat could stay the night of the fifteenth as well, he consented. Pat later said that when Father Ray fell asleep, so did he, sitting in a chair near the bed.

Pat awakened several times, looked at the form on the bed, saw that Father Ray's stomach was rising and falling, and then he returned to sleep. About 5:30 a.m., when he awoke, Father Ray's body lay still. Pat called for a nurse and after she'd made her examination, confirming his death, Pat placed a call to Toy.

Chapter 53

On August 23rd, one week following Father Ray's death, his final newsletter went into the mail to his countless friends and supporters. It was accompanied by a note from Father Philip asking readers to "pray for him and remember the love he had for all."

August Mid-Year Report 2003

"Martial arts are very popular in Thailand," he wrote, "and the kids at the Orphanage love to watch all the kung-fu movies and then try to emulate all the movie stars. Every Sunday about forty of our orphans are taught Taekwondo. Most of them have now moved up from beginners white belt to the next level, a yellow belt. Recently, one of our younger teenagers, my little 'Holy Terror,' was chosen by the instructor as the one student who showed some extraordinary talent. After several weeks of intense training, Pheung was entered into his first ever competition, where after beating six other fighters he returned home with a gold medal. He has also been entered into an international competition, which will be held in Bangkok on August 19th, and will include fighters from Taiwan and the U.K. When it was mentioned to Pheung that thirteen-year-olds from the U.K. are bigger than most thirteen-year-old Thais, he said, 'No problem, I will beat them.' And I am sure he will. But whether or not he wins his next fight, I'm personally very proud of him.

"There are many birthdays at the Orphanage and it is impossible to celebrate everyone's birthday on the actual day. We recently had a first birthday party in the baby room, and the smaller children feasted on BBQ, fresh fruit, cookies and chips, and one of our volunteers made three chocolate cakes to go with the sponge cake that our cooks made. As you can imagine, there was more chocolate on their face, hands and legs than what was actually eaten. Even the walls were covered in chocolate, but the children enjoyed it very much.

"One of our older boys will be leaving the Orphanage to start a new life in the real world. This young man recently graduated from university with a degree in English and now is working as a teacher at a very good school north of Pattaya in Sri Racha. He arrived at the Orphanage when he was just nine days old, and now twenty-five years later, we have fed him, clothed him, educated him and made him ready to be able to take care of himself. He will always know that this is his home, and that he is always welcome to return. Like any parent, I feel a bit sad when the day comes when it is time for my kids to leave home.

"Every year the handicapped students from the Vocational School volunteer to take part in the 'Clean Pattaya Campaign.' This year, the students went to the local beach and spent a whole morning cleaning all the rubbish and generally making the beach a cleaner place. It does not matter what disability our students have, they all do their best to do whatever they can. This year, one of our female students got her wheelchair stuck in the sand. She was a little embarrassed, but made no complaints when two of her handsome male colleagues picked her up and carried her to safety.

"This year's annual Pattaya marathon took place in July, and our projects were well represented. One of our teachers from the vocational school took part in the full marathon and seven students and teachers took part in the wheelchair marathon. One of our ex-students came in third and one of our electronics teachers came in fifth. In the children's race, we had several orphans and street kids taking part, as well as four students from the Blind School who were led around the course by a teacher.

"August 12th is a very special day in Thailand. It is the birthday of Her Royal Highness Queen Sirikit, and it is also Mothers Day. Although our children are not with their birth mothers, there are many here who play the role of 'Mother.' For them, they will be honored by our children just the same as children honor their mothers all over the world.

"There is a tradition in Thailand that to pay respects to the Queen, people clean their houses and wear new clothes. All our children will wear new clothes and make sure that their rooms are clean, the classrooms will be cleaned, and last year the older boys painted the wall that surrounds the Orphanage.

"Our street kids home for girls has been open just over one year now, and we have almost doubled the number of residents. Progress on the new boys' home is going well, and I hope nothing holds up the building work and every week we are welcoming more and more kids into our home.

"In early July, a sad, but typical, street kid case came our way. We were approached by a nice young Thai couple who had shepherded in two young children, a boy of ten and his sister, aged seven. The young couple had come from Bangkok to spend the weekend in Pattaya on the beach in order to paint some of the scenery. They were approached by the two kids who were begging. Taking a look at the condition they were in, they took pity on them and escorted them to the nearby police box for help. The police recommended they take them to a local government-run Home for Boys. When they arrived, they found out that they would accept only the young boy, but there was no question of their being separated. Remembering having seen our sign on the road, they brought them to us. All they had in their possession was the clothes they were wearing and a small blanket with a smaller pillow. They couldn't even identify themselves other than by their nicknames.

"The story came out that they had run away from their home about fifty kilometers from Pattaya because of abusive parents who had forced them into begging and never sent them to school. Not having much success begging in their hometown, they came to Pattaya in the hope of being able to fare better among foreign tourists on the beaches here. Their luck was not better until the young couple met them and brought them to us.

"After several months of living at our Street Kids home, another ten-year-old boy decided he wanted to leave and return to the streets where he had lived for four years. Knowing the dangers he could face being back on the streets, our outreach workers went to Bangkok to try and find him. After searching for many hours, the young boy was eventually found with a gang of homeless kids. All the kids were high from sniffing glue, and the young boy was shocked to see the workers from his former home. After another several hours of trying to persuade the boy to return to the home in Pattaya, he agreed to travel with the workers. Another five young boys came along at the same time. Once back at the home, they were given help with their addictions, counseling and will hopefully be able to return to having a normal childhood again.

"Without your continuing help, we cannot give these kids the start in life that they deserve. Thank you and our prayers are for you every day."

The letter was signed "Father Ray Brennan (Still semi retired)" and "Father Philip Banchong Chaiyara (Director)."

The immense pride layered beneath the matter-of-fact style of this report made clear how Father Ray felt about his kids. In the hands of a novelist, or even a newspaper or television journalist, the stories likely would drip with pathos and certainly would be presented with an abundance of graphic detail.

For the seventy-year-old, semi-retired priest from Chicago, who didn't even mention his illness and who at the time he wrote the letter was in almost continuous pain, it was just another middle of the month.

Life went on, as it always did, bumpity-bumpity-bump.

Chapter 54

On August 16, 2003, a Saturday, as Father Ray's body was prepared for his funeral, Father Philip met with the heads of all the projects and key staff. Brother Denis was in Canada, but all the others were present for a brief meeting when all were given assignments. Andrew Scadding, director of the Pattaya Orphanage Trust in Britain, happened to be in town and he sat in.

"We never expected it, it was stunning," said Toy, "but there was no panic. It was so quiet at the Orphanage. But from that minute, we worked non-stop."

After dictating an announcement that was to be sent to all the Orphanage supporters, Father Philip went to Bangkok to make arrangements there for a service to be held at Holy Redeemer Church, just a few blocks from the hospital where Father Ray died. Toy remained in Pattaya to organize and start informing absent staff along with Father Ray's closest friends, both in Thailand and elsewhere, and to juggle the hundreds of E-mails, faxes and phone calls that soon began pouring in.

The older children at the Orphanage were told of the death after breakfast and they, along with Sister Supatra and Suwanna and others, informed the other children. Word spread quickly, to the schools for the deaf and blind and to the vocational school, and into the Pattaya community. A public relations firm had been hired just a week before to help offset damage caused by the pedophile stories and it was given information for a press release. On the second day, Toy sent an announcement to everyone on the mailing list.

In Bangkok, services at a wake were conducted by three bishops and many priests. Several hundred mourners attended, including many of the older children who had been bussed up from Pattaya. When the body was returned to Pattaya, the long driveway leading from the highway was lined with children in clean and neatly-pressed uniforms, and with young men and women in wheelchairs. The coffin was placed in the auditorium, above the new dining room, now newly decorated and set out with an altar and chairs, church style.

There was nothing extravagant about Father Ray's last entrance to the grounds where he had spent more than thirty years of his life. The inexpensive white coffin with gold trim was carried in the back of a station wagon and was followed by a pickup truck containing several floral displays. That was it.

The impact on the children was great. Pachanee Nanthaniran, who had come to the Orphanage when she was ten, was now a university graduate. She was working as a secretary to the finance and accounting manager of a company at Laem Chabang Port when she heard that Father Ray had died. She went directly to the Orphanage and, speaking for so many, cried aloud, "I'm an orphan again!"

It was raining when one of the students at the vocational school, located nearly a mile away, wheeled himself in his chair to the Orphanage grounds. He sat there in the rain for a while, and then wheeled himself back to his dormitory.

"Everyone lost their father that day," said one of Father Ray's friends.

Mourners filed past the coffin, many of them approaching it on their knees, carrying roses. The kids from the deaf school held sticks with a plastic hand at one end, fingers folded and extended in the sign that said, "I love you."

That night, after the body had been removed from the white coffin to a brown one bearing his name on the side in block letters---FR. RAYMOND A BRENNAN--- many of the older boys decided to sleep on the floor near the coffin. The casket remained open so the boys, in their grief, could see him and, in Sister Supatra's words, "touch him, squeeze his nose, feel his belly a final time."

This is where the coffin remained for three days and nights when services were held. By then a large, somber crowd of friends had joined children and staff, approaching the coffin singly and in small groups, many of them meeting for the first time. Everyone was fed rice and stir-fried pork. Finally, the coffin was taken to St. Nikolaus Church, where the number of mourners was expected to be so great the adjacent property had been bulldozed to accommodate more than a hundred automobiles and buses.

The service was presided over by the Most Reverend George Phimpisan, Bishop of the diocese of Udon Thani. Representatives of King Bhumibol seated in the front row of the small church, brought a "royal specimen of earth" from the palace in Bangkok for the burial ceremony, the soil symbolizing that Father Ray was laid to rest on royal ground. Eulogies were given by clergy, Orphanage staff, friends, and the children.

At the end of the funeral Mass, the coffin was carried to the small cemetery behind the church as the children sang "Unsung Hero," a song composed for Father Ray's seventieth birthday by Jimmy Scott, a Pattaya resident from Britain whose earlier compositions were recorded by Ray Charles and Bonnie Raitt:

You're an unsung hero
You're always there to help us,
Father Ray.
And you're right beside us everywhere
We go, every day.
And our lives are so much brighter
We can reach the highest star
And the world's a better place, it's true.
Thanks to unsung heroes
A ray of sunshine just like you.

You're an unsung hero
You don't want the glory or the fame.
You just keep on giving
And sharing all your love just the same.

And our hearts are so much lighter
We can dream the biggest dreams
And it's all because of what you do.
You're an unsung hero
Father Ray, we love you.
You're an unsung hero
Father Ray, we love you.

In the weeks of grieving that followed, the Orphanage staff planned a memorial service one hundred days after Father Ray's death, as was traditional in Thailand to mark the end of formal mourning. They also prepared and had printed an elaborate funeral book that told his life in text and photographs, and, most impressively, designed and commissioned a life-size bronze statue to be unveiled at the service.

On the day, November 23, a threatening rain backed off, leaving the air humid but cooler than the day had been. The priests, bishops and others leading the service were on a high stage erected on the Orphanage playing field, where more than a thousand folding chairs had been set up in rows for the children, handicapped, and guests. A children's choir that had been rehearsing all afternoon sang. There were long speeches, most delivered in Thai. Then everyone sang. In the background, from the Orphanage buildings nearby, could be heard the laughter and playful screams of the youngest children, considered too young to sit still for the ninety-minute ceremony…giving the somber nature of the tribute a joyous connection to the life that goes on after death.

As the formal occasion neared its conclusion, a hundred or so children formed in a line along a driveway behind the stage. Each carried a yellow paper lantern with a glowing candle inside. More children approached from another direction, bearing red lanterns. The lines led to the statue, hidden by a pink curtain. The curtain was drawn, revealing an appropriately larger-than-life-sized Father Ray, seated on a chair, holding twin sisters in his lap, small children who had been on the cover of the first *Thoughts from the Pattaya Orphanage* book. The twins were subsequently adopted and now teenagers living in Italy.

The blind children were led away in lines, holding hands. The disabled young students clanked and clicked and wheeled their way down the road to the vocational school. Those in the Orphanage and deaf school walked to their nearby dormitories; after all, there was school the next day.

Epilogue

In the end, Father Ray died of excess, a common way to go. One dictionary defines the word as "being more than what is necessary, usual, or specified; extra." That was Father Ray all over: extra.

As a Roman Catholic priest "married to Christ," he sacrificed many of the earthly pleasures, yet that may have been one of the reasons he gave so much of himself to others and indulged himself in the pleasures with which he was left.

He dedicated himself, devoted himself, to The Boss Upstairs, determined to do good works in his name.

He was a man who could never say no, standing---if it doesn't stretch the point---like the Statue of Liberty, past which his grandparents sailed in the nine-teenth-century in search of greater freedom and opportunity. "Give me your huddled masses," Lady Liberty proclaimed, and that same phrase could have been added to the others on Father Ray's office walls.

That was his Redemptorist pledge: to help the poorest of the poor and it wasn't enough to help a few. He wanted to help them all. At the time of his death, he was responsible for seven hundred and fifty individuals, and thousands more had come and gone on, safer, brighter, and more confident. Give me more, he said in his final days, insisting on construction of a five-story building for street kids when he had no money to pay for all of it. (The Pattaya Orphanage Trust in the U.K. pledged to build all five floors, but that left Father Ray looking for cash for the furnishings and staff and maintenance).

And so, too, he drank and smoked and ate too much. That seemed to be part of what was required. All those vows to diet and quit smoking were ultimately in vain, not that the more common meaning of the term ever applied to the man. There was nothing vain about him and his body seemed a part of his giving. That he was forty-five kilos (one hundred pounds) overweight merely gave his kids more to love.

The clouds of cigarette smoke in his office were in a partnership with the electronic toys on his desk that he surreptitiously activated with a remote control when talking with a stranger...the whiskey and beer in the evenings with friends fueled the man who chased the children across a playground in his holy robes, a photograph of which is on the cover this book (after being nominated for a Pulitzer Prize for its photographer, Val Mazzenga)...the verbal and practical jokes provided more release...along with the daily Mass he conducted in his inspired and quirky chapel, and his constant prayer to The Boss Upstairs.

Father Ray died of excess: abundance and glut. He couldn't get enough of anything. It can truly be said that he recognized no human bounds.

The months passed. New orphans arrived and others left, while more of the older ones finished their education and looked for work. Many of those still in residence could be seen standing in front of Father Ray's statue in the morning before going to school, talking to his towering bronze edifice as earnestly as if he were there in the flesh.

In the first year, Pat Wongsrikaew, who had been with Father Ray when he died, graduated from Assumption University.

The Holy Terror was reunited with his father, with the Orphanage staff holding its collective fingers crossed.

The Cambodian-born American man that Yai Deekham met and married was among the first soldiers sent to fight in Iraq but was returned home safely.

While pediatrician Dr. Sophapan Puenpatom, Brother Denis Gervais, Audrey Williams, continued on staff without salary...Supagon (Ja) Noja still cruised Pattaya's nighttime streets, offering hot meals and a safe place to sleep to the kids he met…the deaf and the blind were enrolled in new classes…the handicapped still had jobs waiting at the end of instruction.

Father Pat Morrissy died less than five months after Father Ray and was buried in the St. Nikolaus Cemetery next to his old friend. One of the last things he did was write a loving obituary of Father Ray for the Redemptorist newsletter that was distributed worldwide.

Father Frank (Gogs) Gautreaux was serving as a confessor to the boys at the minor seminary at Sri Racha and conducting an English language Mass at the nearby beach town of Bang Saen.

Father Joe Maier by now had paralegals representing one hundred kids in trouble in police stations and courts every month, operated thirty-four slum schools, an HIV/AIDS hospice and shelters for Mothers and Babies with HIV/AIDS, five street kid homes, and was still living in Bangkok's largest slum.

The two Sisters Shark, Nomchit and Chalam Aripak, were in retirement at their order's Mother House in Chanthaburi.

Sister Michelle's Fountain of Life added a day care center and school that was underwritten by the Japanese Embassy and regularly attended by one hundred and forty kids…while continuing her drop-in classes for Pattaya's sex workers, attracting about 250 women per day.

Father Don Brennan was retired and living in Texas, and described by his sister Sharron as "busier than ever with different ministries without the paperwork and responsibility of being a pastor. He plays golf at least once a week and sometimes he plays forty-five holes. He has always been the most athletic of my brothers. I live in Dallas and enjoy being grandma to five, soon to be six, granddaughters. Luckily, three of the girls live nearby and we see each other often. Babysitting is also on the list of things I do with great frequency. Like Don, my husband and I are also golfers and actually live on the golf course. I adored my brother Ray, even though most of our lives were lived on different continents. I miss him terribly, but truly believe he lived a wonderful life and was very happy. It is a privilege to have known and loved him." The first structure at the Street Kids Home is named for Sharron.

Walter Meyer, aged eighty-eight, hosted yet another open house at his Bangkok estate for the Swiss expatriate community, a fund-raiser for the Orphanage…and the church he helped finance, St. Nikolaus, which started with only a few pews' full of worshippers, most of them from the U.S. military, now had a congregation of 3,000.

Mrs. Lamom, Father Ray's housekeeper and cook when he was pastor at St. Nikolaus, and to whom he entrusted the first orphans, celebrated her ninety-third birthday and shared a house with her daughter next to the Redemptorist Center.

Corinna Davidson, Father Ray's first secretary, lived in New Zealand and Betty Roy was in Denton, Texas, where her husband Joe's work with a local university band brought them to Thailand in 2004 to play for the King. Another early secretary, Somnuk Pao-ngon, was Senior Executive Secretary at a large export company in Laem Chabang.

Johnny Pe, the Burmese refugee who worked as Father Ray's handyman during the 1970s and took Brennan as his new surname, was in the United States, working in the fiber optics cable industry, and had a son named Ray.

During the same year, it was decided to make a larger commitment to the farm and do something, finally, about improving the quality of the soil to make it more productive. It was also decided to merge the electronics repair shop in downtown Pattaya and a repair center in the Vocational School and to add a class in How to Start Your Own Business. While one of the benefactors, Tom Vincent, whose foundation underwrote the production of this book for the benefit of the endowment for the kids' higher education, started counseling the disabled students on how to succeed in a job interview.

And in the end, the impact of the pedophile scandal was less than feared. The Pattaya Orphanage Trust in Britain estimated a loss of about US$150,000, but at the close of the first year, donations and the number of sponsors were rising again. In Denmark, where the headlines were thought to be the most damaging (and the original benefactor, Vagn Christensen, declined to be interviewed for this book), a new foundation was formed to coordinate contributions, adoptions, and volunteers. And in Thailand, it appeared that hardly anyone even remembered it.

As for Pattaya itself, despite ongoing efforts and claims by the local, provincial, and national governments, the one-time quiet fishing village Father Ray called home for nearly half his life, remained a sinkhole, with new sex venues spreading like an ugly yeast and the Russian mafia becoming the most prominent of the foreign gangsters operating there. Even Pattaya's mayor, Phairat Suthithamrongsawad, confessed that Father Ray's operation was far more efficient than any government's.

"My goal is not to change the world," Father Ray once said. "I can't do that. Great people throughout the history of the world have tried that. None of them succeeded. I just want to teach the children enough to hold their heads high, to 'earn their own rice', and to have a good human life in this crazy, wonderful world of ours."

Afterword

Everything has its origin and this book is no exception. Father Ray Brennan wrote letters about the kids and young people he cared for for nearly 30 years. In these letters he included short stories about the kids, which were always done in a most extraordinary manner. One would read them and easily imagine being right there with him and seeing the events as they took place.

Sister Shark, Pat, Pachanee, Katt, Yai and her three siblings and others, all real people, became characters he wrote about and who we got to know through his letters.

There were happy stories with smiles and heart-tugging ones with tears. We learned of the projects Father Ray started and of the problems he encountered. None were easy, but he never gave up. We shared in his joy and in his frustration.

On numerous occasions it was suggested to him that the letters should be reprinted in one form or another. Always he refused, saying they weren't good enough. In fact, he apologized often in his writings because he felt they were too impersonal. He would rather have written and sent individual letters to each of his many supporters, which was impossible because of the numbers.

In the last days of his life, in late July 2003, Father Ray sent word to Bangkok, where I live, that he wanted to see me. I went to Pattaya and visited him in the hospital where he had been for a couple of weeks. First, he told me his doctors had said it was 60/40 against his getting well and leaving the hospital (alive).

He said he wanted to discuss an idea advanced in a recent letter from John and Lucinda Flemer of Canada. The Flemers met Father Ray while they were traveling on board the Queen Elizabeth 2 as it made a stopover near Pattaya a few years before. In their letter, written to him earlier in the month, it was suggested that his newsletters be put into book form, "as everyone who reads them has a good chuckle and feels not only inspired but full of admiration for all you do." He asked what I thought of their suggestion. My response was I thought it to be a good idea. He refused to accept such an offhand answer and insisted that first I read all the letters, then comment. I reminded him that because of the years of our association (more than fifteen) I had probably read two- thirds of them.

That wasn't good enough for him and, after further insisting I read them all (which he had in his room), I agreed. The conversation was very trying as Father Ray was in the bed, lying on his side, gasping to breathe and falling asleep every two or three minutes. I would ease back from the stool I was sitting on but never got but a foot or two away before his eyes fluttered and he awoke. "Sit down, I haven't finished," he would say each time. I assured him I would read all the letters and then tell him what I thought of the idea. He further said he wanted me to be critical. When I told him I knew he expected nothing less, he smiled.

I took the letters and read them all. I sent word to Father Ray through his secretary, Khun Toy and Audrey Williams, a longtime volunteer at the Orphanage, who were visiting him two or three times a day at the hospital. I asked them to tell Father Ray, "I read all the letters and still have the same opinion, only stronger. It could make a wonderful book." He responded, "Tom will do a good job, but I have the final say in the editing."

Somewhat shocked by his response, I thought now here's a tough situation. I am not a writer, nor could I ever be. In those first thoughts was also the feeling a book with only letters, entertaining as they were, would be rather boring to a more general readership. However, a biography of a man who led a fiction-like life, using his letters to tell part of the story would be a good book and would appeal to a greater number of people.

I needed an author who was experienced. One such writer, Jerry Hopkins, a friend of more than ten years and my neighbor in Bangkok, was contacted.

While Jerry had never met Father Ray, he certainly knew of him. In fact he knew quite a bit about Father Ray as one of Jerry's closest friends is Father Joe Maier, a Redemptorist priest in Bangkok, who also works with the poor and disadvantaged. I presented Jerry with a number of Father Ray's letters and explained the idea of the biography using the letters as part of the story telling. Jerry accepted the challenge for which I am most grateful.

Mr. and Mrs. Flemer were also pleased with the plan and have contributed most generously toward the book's production.

That was the beginning of this book.

Father Ray passed away within three weeks of my last visit with him. I sincerely miss the get-togethers we enjoyed over so many years. As for the 'final say in the editing', here it is, Father Ray. I gave it my best shot.

Tom Vincent
The Thomas J. Vincent Foundation
Kaneohe, Hawaii
June, 2004

Acknowledgements

The author wishes to thank the following for their time, memories, and love of Father Ray:

Family

Father Don Brennan, Sharron Brennan Purtell

Father Ray Foundation Staff (Former and Current)

Samphan Akrapongpanich, Phongsri Anusassanee, Tawee Anusassanee, Sister Chalam Aripak, Sister Nomchit Aripak, Srikanya Boonserm, Krisana Chaiwat, Father Philip Banchong Chaiyara, Suwanna Cheownawin, Radchada (Toy) Chomjinda, Corrina Davidson, Piangrak Duangjai, Derek Franklin, Brother Denis Gervais, Tim Hague, Alun Jones, Mrs. Lamom, Father Patrick Morrissy, Supagon (Ja) Noja, Sister Supatra Nonthasuwn, Somnuk Pao-ngon, Sister Pavinee Pichaisrisawadi, Dr. Meyasan Puenpatom, Dr. Sophapan Puenpatom, , Betty Roy, Tamonwan (Mon) Saiying, Sister Petcharat Setchareon, Ron Small, Aurora Lee Sribuapun, Thaworn Srisook, Amnoy Taolim, Pranom Taolim, Wantanee Tiptong, Audrey Williams, Asaraporn Yolsophon.

Graduates (some now on staff)

Sumitra (Ning) Deekham, Kattareeya (Katt), Suporntum Mongkolsawadi, Luksamapa (Luke) Monyarid, Pachanee Nanthaniran, Supaphon (Apple) Ngern-Opas, Wanna Ninrath, Phennipa (Phen) Rachakit, Sompong (Henry) Rattanasang, Wanrunee Samnaksakul, Somkid (Pat) Wongsrikaew, Duangdoaw (Nok) Yothsari.

Friends and Co-Workers

Father Charles Cotant, Father Francis (Gogs) Gautreaux, Sister Michelle Lopez, Father Joe Maier, Father Robert Martin, Canon John T. Taylor OBE.

Supporters

Ron Biho, Baron Riccardo Carini, Richard Clark, Susan J. Cunningham, Arlette Cykman, David Duesler, Bjorn Falkenbrink, John and Lucinda Flemer, Sean Godsell, Paul Knights, Patrick McGeown, Bill Mangelsen, Val Mazzenga, Walter Meyer, Paul Ross, Joe Roy, Vijendran, Sathyaraj, Andrew Scadding, Mayor Phairat Suthithamrongsawad, Tom Vincent, The Thomas J. Vincent Foundation, J. T. Warring, Kirsten Berth Windfeld.

Photo credits

Every effort was made to identify photographers of all the visuals used in the book; some go here without credit but with thanks:

Brennan Family: Pages *1*, *2*, *3*

Paul Knights: Pages *6*, *7* (bottom), *8* (top right), *23* (lower), *30* (top)

Sean Godsell: Pages *8* (bottom), *9* (bottom), *16*, *17*, *18* (top), *19*, *20*, *21* (bottom right), *22* (bottom), *23* (top)

Patrick McGeown: Page *21* (top)

Pattaya Orphanage Trust: Page *21* (bottom left)

Ron Biho: Page *22* (top)

Aung Ko Ko: Page *25* (top)